Tiling

by Josh Garskof and the Editors of Sunset Books, Menlo Park, California

contents

SUNSET BOOKS

VP, EDITORIAL DIRECTOR
Bob Doyle
ART DIRECTOR
Vasken Guiragossian

STAFF FOR THIS BOOK

MANAGING EDITOR
Bridget Biscotti Bradley
PAGE LAYOUT
Maureen Spuhler
COPY EDITOR
John Edmonds
PRINCIPAL PHOTOGRAPHER
Image Studios
CONTRIBUTING WRITER
Steve Cory
PROOFREADER
David Sweet
INDEX
IRIS Indexing
PREPRESS COORDINATOR
Eligio Hernández
PRODUCTION SPECIALISTS
Linda M. Bouchard
Janie Farn

FRONT COVER PHOTOGRAPH
Photography by Michele Lee Willson; styling by
Laura del Fava.

For additional copies of *Tiling* or any other
Sunset book, visit us at www.sunsetbooks.com.

For more exciting home and garden ideas, visit

myhomeîdeas.com

READERS' NOTE: Almost any
do-it-yourself project involves
risk of some sort. Your tools,
materials, and skills will vary, as
will conditions at your project
site. Sunset Publishing Corpora-
tion and the editors of this book
have made every effort to be
complete and accurate in the
instructions. We will, however,
assume no responsibility or
liability for injuries, damages,
or losses incurred in the course
of your home improvement or
repair projects. Always follow
the manufacturer's operating
instructions in the use of tools,
check and follow your local building codes, and observe all standard safety precautions.

1 All About Tile | 6
- 8 A Glossary of Tile
- 20 What Will It Cost?
- 22 Tile Style
- 32 Grout Style
- 34 Tools and Materials

2 The Basics of Tiling | 44
- 46 Installing Cement Backerboard
- 49 Working Out the Pattern
- 54 Mixing and Spreading Thinset
- 56 Setting Tiles
- 60 Cutting Tile
- 64 Grouting
- 67 Working with Mosaic Tiles
- 70 Sealing Tiles and Grout

3 Tiling Floors | 72
- 74 Choosing Floor Tile
- 80 Removing Obstacles
- 84 Removing Old Tile
- 87 Beefing Up the Structure
- 88 Preparing the Subfloor
- 94 Adding Heat to the Floor
- 96 Laying a Stone Tile Floor
- 99 Installing Borders, Brick-lays, and Diagonals
- 100 Tiling a Shower Floor
- 104 Laying a Resilient Tile Floor
- 108 Laying a Parquet Floor
- 112 Laying a Laminate Floor
- 116 Laying a Cork Floor
- 118 Laying Carpet Tiles
- 120 Laying River Rock Tiles
- 122 Finishing the Job

4 Tiling Walls | 126
- 128 Choosing Wall Tiles
- 134 Preparing the Wall
- 142 Tiling a Wall
- 149 Tiling a Tub Surround
- 157 Installing a Shower Niche
- 161 Tiling a Window Alcove
- 162 Tiling a Fireplace Surround
- 166 Tiling a Ceiling
- 169 Hanging Shelves and Hooks from Tile Walls

5 Countertop and Backsplashes | 170
- 172 Choosing Tiles for Countertops and Backsplashes
- 178 Preparing the Countertop Substrate
- 182 Tiling a Countertop
- 186 Tiling a Backsplash
- 190 Making a Tile Mural
- 193 Installing a Metal Backsplash

6 Tiling Outdoors | 194
- 196 Choosing Outdoor Tile
- 202 Preparing a Concrete Substrate
- 204 Tiling a Porch Floor or Patio
- 206 Laying a Flagstone Walk or Patio
- 209 Tiling Stairs
- 211 Tiling a Planter
- 212 Tiling a Birdbath
- 214 Tiling a Tabletop
- 216 Making Mosaic Pavers

7 Tile Care and Repair | 218
- 220 Cleaning Tiles
- 222 Resealing Tiles and Grout
- 223 Refurbishing Grout
- 224 Replacing Caulk
- 225 Removing Stains from Tiles
- 226 Replacing Tiles

Comparing Tiles | 234

Credits/Index | 237

INTRODUCTION

WHETHER YOU ARE PLANNING A COSMETIC UPGRADE or a gut renovation, have tiled many times before, or are making a first foray into the world of tiles and grout, the decision to use tile is practically a no-brainer. After all, tile never goes out of style, having steadily grown in popularity for the past 150 years. It's long-lasting and durable and, in many cases, it's immune to the effects of foot traffic, water, and even extreme temperatures. Plus, you can find tiles that will work beautifully in any home, no matter where you live or what style of house you have.

And doing the job yourself will save you hundreds or even thousands of dollars.

On the following pages, you'll learn how to lay tile on floors, walls, countertops, porches, outdoor furniture, and just about any other surface you'd ever want to tile. Each project includes detailed step-by-step photographs and how-to instructions, so you hold in your hands everything you'll need to make your tile project happen—everything, that is, except for the tiles, tools, and other supplies. Before you start shopping for those, check out chapter 1 for a detailed glossary of all the tools and materials you'll need for your job. Also, make sure to look at chapter 2, where you'll discover beginner lessons about the basic tiling techniques used in just about every tiling project—such as how to cut tile and how to grout it.

All of the information between these covers comes directly from a panel of professional tile setters, so using this book is the next best thing to having a seasoned expert right at your side. It will make the work easy—and make the results as good-looking and durable as if they were installed by a pro.

Acknowledgments

This book was written with the help of numerous tiling experts, most notably three top-notch tile setters:

Jane Aeon See Jane Tile, Berkeley, California, janeaeon@yahoo.com

A 20-year veteran tile setter, Jane specializes in traditional tiling methods—and has worked on numerous community art projects in the Berkeley area. She has also written how-to articles for *Fine Homebuilding* magazine.

John Bridge John Bridge Ceramic Tile, Katy, Texas, 281-550-1124, john@johnbridge.com

John has been a tile setter for 34 years. He also hosts an online forum, at *johnbridge.com/vbulletin/index.php*, where professional and amateur tile setters converse about techniques, products, and everything tile. He has written three books about tiling and has taught numerous how-to classes for tile professionals.

George Taterosian Cutting Edge Renovation and Design, Trumbull, Connecticut, 203-380-2437

A tile setter for two decades, George is also a general contractor, using his own crew of employees and subcontractors for all of the work except the tiling, which he still does himself. His specialty is bathroom renovations.

We'd also like to thank the following people for providing technical expertise:
Bart Bettiga, executive director, National Tile Contractors Association, *tile-assn.com*; **Dean Cunningham,** contractor sales, New England Tile & Marble, Fairfield, Connecticut; **Clare Donahue,** kitchen and bath designer, One to One Studio, New York City, *121studio.com*; **Lee Eiseman,** color consultant, Eiseman & Associates, Bainbridge Island, Washington, *colorexpert.com*; **Dee Dee Gundsberg,** senior designer of tile and stone, Ann Sacks, *annsacks.com*; **Jane Mathews,** architect, Mathews Architecture, Asheville, North Carolina, *mathewsarchitecture.com*; **Ted Montgomery,** architect, GroundSwell Architects, Charlotte, Vermont, *groundswellarchitects.com*; **Mark Shedrofsky,** vice president, Stone Source, New York City, *stonesource.com*; **LouAnn Torres,** general manager, Klaff's Tile & Stone, South Norwalk, Connecticut, *klaffs.com*.

all about tile

A GLOSSARY OF TILE

TO HELP YOU CHOOSE THE RIGHT TILE FOR THE JOB, here's a rundown of the four basic categories of tile—ceramic, stone, specialty, and nontraditional—with descriptions of the primary types of tile within each, as well as some pros and cons of using them. The information will help prepare you for the trip to your retailer.

Ceramic Tile

• GLAZED CERAMIC These tiles (left) may be molded by hand from wet clay or pressed out by machines that use dry clay powder. What unites them is their glass-hard glazes, which come in a great variety of colors and finishes. Many tiles from other parts of the world fall into this category, and it's often the glaze patterns and colors that give them their particular regional character. Some glazes are tough enough to use on floors or countertops and even outdoors, while others are better suited to light-duty service, such as on walls and ceilings.

• PORCELAIN Machine-pressed from white clay and fired at much higher temperatures than other ceramics, porcelain tiles (below) are some of the toughest you can find. They are durable and scratch resistant, and they are excellent for demanding locations such as floors, countertops, and outdoor surfaces.

Once available only as tiny tiles because of manufacturing limitations, porcelain is now no more costly or difficult than other ceramics to produce in any size. As a result, it has come to dominate the market for floor tile, where its toughness is particularly advantageous. Porcelain lines now feature colorful glazes and assorted trim pieces, just like standard ceramics. Manufacturers are even making faux-stone porcelain tiles using layers of glaze to replicate the multihued look of stone—with the cost and durability advantages of porcelain.

Quarry tile

- **QUARRY** They look a bit like stone—hence the name—but these tiles (left) are actually unglazed ceramic. (Some glazed quarry tiles are available, but the glazes are typically translucent.) Machines produce quarry tiles by extruding wet clay through a slot (much like on a pasta maker) and then cutting it into squares, leaving telltale ridges on the back that help adhesive lock onto the tiles. Because they're mass-produced and unglazed, these are among the least expensive tiles on the market.

- **TERRA-COTTA** Like quarry tiles, terra-cotta tiles (right) are made from pure clay, most often without coloring or glaze. Unlike quarry tiles, they are typically hand-molded. That means you'll find a lot of natural variation in size and shape, making a field of terra-cotta tiles pleasantly rustic-looking. They come in reds, browns, or yellows, as determined by the clay in the places where they are made, including Italy, France, Portugal, and Mexico. Saltillo, Mexico, for example, is the source of the popular low-fired and highly variegated saltillo tile.

Terra-cotta's durability depends on the clay and the temperature at which it's fired. Many terra-cotta tiles are soft and porous. That makes them susceptible to staining, scratching, and chipping if used on high-traffic floors or countertops—even if they are sealed, which they should be. But some terra-cotta is quite strong and scratch resistant, in which case it's a beautiful choice for the toughest applications.

Porcelain

Stone Tile

- **GRANITE** It's not just granite's crystalline character and range of colors that make it so popular. Formed from slow-cooled magma under tremendous pressure, it is one of the hardest stones available. Having withstood centuries of use as an exterior building material, it is up to any job you might have in mind. It won't be scratched by knives, scorched by cookware, or etched by household acids (unlike many stones), so it's a popular choice for stone countertops (right).

That said, some granites, especially those with a lot of surface pattern, are fairly absorbent and can stain. Test for this by dripping water on the tile. If the stone darkens, it is absorbent and will stain. (The front of the tile may have been treated, so to be sure you know what you're getting, test the back side of the tile.) Regular treatment with an impregnating sealer (see pages 70–71) can protect porous granites.

Granite commands a high price, though tiles cost far less than solid slabs. You can choose a polished finish, which offers a gleaming shine but will show smudges, or a honed finish, with a matte look that's easier to maintain. Some stores sell tiles cut from basalt, a black volcanic stone that offers granite's toughness and acid resistance but has a less formal look.

- **LIMESTONE** The result of bone and shell fragments collecting underwater and being compressed, limestone (left) is typically pale in color and has a casually elegant appearance. Often it is extremely soft, which means it is easily scratched, worn, and stained. This has given limestone a

Limestone

Granite

bad name, but it actually comes in a range of hardnesses and can be as tough as granite. Ask your seller how hard a particular tile is and what it's appropriate for.

All limestone shares one weakness: The surface begins to dissolve immediately when exposed to acids, such as citrus juice, vinegar, coffee, wine, and cola. You literally don't have time to wipe up the spill. If you choose limestone for a countertop, be prepared to seal it regularly to protect it. Small problems on matte stones sometimes can be evened out with steel wool. Limestone is a better choice for master bathrooms, where it can create a serene and relaxing atmosphere with far less risk of damage. For countertops, consider ultra-tough porcelain tiles glazed to look like limestone.

● TRAVERTINE Cut from a deeply pitted form of limestone—the result of gases mixing with the minerals as the stone forms—travertine tiles (right) are a bit like slices of Swiss cheese. But they're often factory filled with resin or marble-dust cement to give them a smooth surface. Alternatively, the holes can be filled with grout during installation. Travertine is popular for its rustic look, but when it is used on horizontal surfaces, such as floors or countertops, wear and tear can cause new holes to open up. Use travertine for vertical surfaces or plan to refill the surface from time to time as needed. Travertine is subject to breaking when it's being cut, so tile setter Jane Aeon recommends purchasing at least 20 percent more than you expect to need (instead of the standard 10 percent overage) to compensate for damaged tiles.

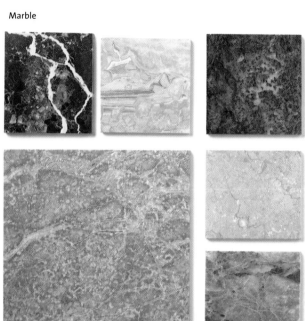

Marble

● **MARBLE** Marble (above), which is limestone crystallized by heat and pressure, has two defining qualities: a striated appearance and an ability to be polished to a glass-like shine. These features give marble a formal look, and it's also durable. Marble still survives, worn but beautiful, in structures built by the ancient Greeks and Romans.

These days, three-quarters of the stone sold as marble isn't technically marble but rather limestone with the look of marble. While many of these stones are very durable, some of them, along with some true marbles, are quite soft. A good retailer should be able to recommend the right marble for your project.

Onyx is an expensive and delicate form of marble, with intriguing folds and layers that are exposed when the tiles are cut. Keep in mind that marble does scratch, and it will require repolishing if you want to maintain a glassy finish. A honed finish will show wear less quickly and is easier to refurbish when it does. The white crystals that form along scratches will also be less apparent in light-colored marble than in dark.

Stone: The Living Finish

If you can think of a soft stone such as limestone, marble, travertine, and slate as a "living finish," meaning one that grows in beauty as it takes on small scratches and stains, then consider using it for hard-wearing locations. But if every defect will tear your heart out, stick to more durable options, such as porcelain, and use stone only for walls or backsplashes.

• SLATE Slate (left) is composed of many layers formed by underwater clay sediment metamorphosed by the earth's shifting crust. Manufacturers split blocks of the stone into sheets along their natural fault lines and then cut the sheets into tiles. The resulting cleft surface is rough and imperfect, which makes for a good nonslip walking surface but not such a good countertop. It's most commonly used for floors and backsplashes. Some slate is now honed to a smooth finish, creating a better work surface but making scratches and stains more obvious. Whether you choose cleft or honed slate, you'll want to treat it with a special slate sealer to hinder staining and chipping.

Slate

Because of varying mineral deposits in different parts of the world, slate may be black, blue, green, maroon, red, orange, or any combination of these. But those colors can wear away over time, especially on high-traffic floors. If surface coloration comes off on your hands in the store, it's probably not going to last very long in your home.

• QUARTZITE One of the hardest stones in the world, quartzite (right) is essentially sand that's been pressed into stone by the same tectonic forces that created limestone. Tiles come with a cleft face, like slate, but are less likely to chip. Quartzite also resists acids, though it is often absorbent and therefore subject to staining. Treat it with an impregnating sealer.

Stone mosaic

Specialty Tile

• Mosaics Any grid of smallish tiles that work together to create a whole is a mosaic (left). In some mosaics, the tiles function like the pixels of a digital image, creating a mural effect. Other mosaics are composed of an eye-catching pattern of colors. Even a field of like-colored squares is considered a mosaic if the tiles are 3 inches or smaller.

You'll find mosaics made of virtually any tile material, from glazed ceramic to natural stone, colored glass to metal, or combinations thereof. And the tiles of a mosaic aren't always square. They can be hexagons, rectangles, circles, random shards, or even the shapes of little fish or vege-tables. (The more irregular the shape, the thicker the grout lines likely have to be.) Tiny, opaque glass mosaics are particularly popular now, as are mixed textures—smooth glass with rough stone, for example. Another intriguing look is that of a river rock mosaic of whole round stones, an inch or two in diameter, packed tightly together and grouted (see pages 120–121).

Almost all mosaics are sold already assembled on a mesh, paper, or rubber backing, typically as 12-by-12-inch squares, making installation not much more difficult than for standard tiles. Some prefab mosaics are specially designed as borders or inlays for floors. Of course, you can also use individual tiles to create a custom mosaic in any artistic pattern you can dream up.

• Decorative Retailers use this term for highly orna-mental tiles—anything beyond the basics. A decorative tile might be brightly colored, painted with an image

Decorative tiles

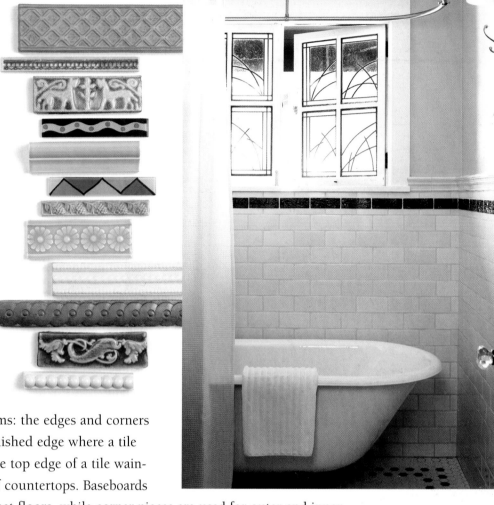

Trim tiles

or pattern, filigreed, embossed, or otherwise textured. It might even be encaustic tile, with an embossed decorative pattern filled with clays of different colors (a process invented by 12th-century Cistercian monks).

Use decorative tiles en masse to create striking focal points, or sparingly as accents to dress up a field of simpler tiles. Either method is an effective way to create something special when you're tiling on a budget.

• **TRIM PIECES** Trim tiles are the solutions to three-dimensional problems: the edges and corners of tile jobs. Bullnose tiles provide a finished edge where a tile field ends, chair rails offer a cap for the top edge of a tile wainscot, and V-caps finish off the edges of countertops. Baseboards are the finishing touch where walls meet floors, while corner pieces are used for outer and inner corners of walls, fireplaces, and other complex surfaces. You may also find crown moldings, picture frames, and any number of other useful shapes.

Some tile lines include matching trim. Others come in limited configurations, while still others are available only in field tiles. If you're using tiles that have no matching trim pieces, look for complementary trim from another line.

• **ACCESSORIES** For bathrooms, some tile lines include soap dishes, towel bars, toothbrush holders, and robe hooks, all made to match the tile. For backsplashes and walls, matching switch plates and receptacle covers may also be available.

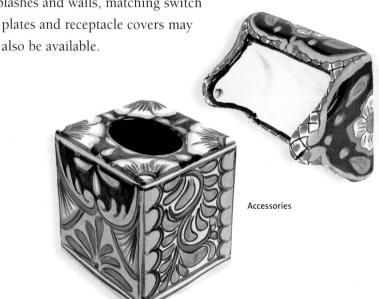

Accessories

Nontraditional Tile

- **CONCRETE** Available in a rainbow of colors, concrete tiles (left) are an economical choice. Some are hand-tinted when the concrete is wet, while others are surface-colored after curing. In either case, the variation in color combined with the uneven texture offers a pleasingly informal look. Pricier concrete tiles may have etched-in patterns, which can be filled with contrasting grout. Extremely durable, concrete is safe for just about any application, including counters, floors, and patios. It is porous, though, so it's subject to staining unless sealed regularly. And it's heavy, so to avoid cracking it must be well supported by thick subflooring (see page 88) or, in the case of countertops, by sturdy cabinets (solid wood or plywood, not fiberboard).

- **GLASS** Relatively new to the scene, glass tiles (right) are durable and practical, with a sheen that exceeds even that of the glossiest of ceramic glazes. They're also pricey. They may be clear, opaque, frosted, or tinted. Some beautiful blues and greens actually come from the recycled bottles the tiles are made from. Color can also come from a Mylar backing (which also hides the adhesive below) behind clear glass. If you use clear glass, be aware that your thinset will be visible, so it's essential that you lay an even bed and set every tile perfectly without gaps or air pockets. It's also a good idea to test some glass tiles in the space to see how their shimmering effect looks with your lighting, suggests tile setter Jane Aeon. For floors, look for textured or sanded surfaces—meaning sand was sprinkled onto the molten glass—so they won't get slippery when wet.

- **LEATHER** Tiles made from tough, thick leather (left) are a high-end product that offers visual warmth and richness. They can be had in a range of colors far beyond the usual browns and blacks of leather boots and jackets. You'll find tiles stamped with decorative patterns or as smooth as fine leather upholstery. Some leather tiles are approved for wet applications and even floors, but they're most often used on

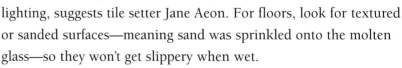

Leather

Terrazzo

the walls of a home library or office, where they also provide excellent soundproofing. Each manufacturer has its own specific installation procedures for its products, generally involving techniques similar to those used for resilient tiles (see pages 104–107).

• TERRAZZO This combination of stone chips in concrete, polished smooth, originated in 15th-century Venice. Since then, it has been popular in everything from Art Deco interiors to mid-20th-century tract housing. For instant results, you can now buy thin terrazzo tiles and adhere them to a concrete floor without any of the on-site mixing, pouring, or polishing required for custom terrazzo.

• METAL Metal tiles (right) are made of stainless steel, copper, brass, or iron and offer a very up-to-date look, especially for kitchen backsplashes. They may be smooth, cast in shapes, or stamped with patterns. Some metals react with moisture and cannot be used in wet areas, while others are too soft for use on floors or countertops. Depending on the tile and where it will be used, it may or may not require grout. Solid metal is expensive and difficult (if not impossible) to cut, so use it sparingly as an accent. But many metal tiles are actually ceramic tiles coated with metal, and they can be cut and grouted much like traditional tiles (see page 193).

Metal

• "TIN" Squares of embossed decorative steel (left), typically 18 by 18 inches, were popular ceiling treatments a century ago. They're still manufactured and offer a traditional look for tiled ceilings—instead of, say, acoustic tile in a finished basement—but you can use them in other places as well. They're ideal for backsplashes because they're perfectly sized to fit the common 18-inch spacing between countertop and upper cabinet. They get nailed into place and have interlocking joints along their edges that hide the nail heads.

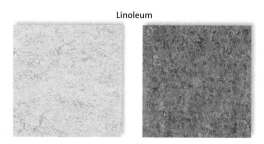

Linoleum

● **RESILIENT MATERIALS** Unlike sheet versions of the same materials, vinyl and linoleum (left) tiles are easy for do-it-yourselfers to install. They're also inexpensive. Resilient tiles are most often used for floors, but they come in a wide range of designs—including the classic 1950s diner style called "amoeba"—that make great backsplashes too. Also available are tiles inlaid with contrasting colors of the same material.

● **LAMINATE** Made to convincingly mimic wood, stone, or ceramic tile, laminate tile (right) gets its look from a photograph of the real thing sandwiched between a clear plastic covering and a fiberboard backing. The main benefits of laminate are its low price and ease of installation. It's almost always laid by do-it-yourselfers, who simply snap together the tongue-and-groove edges, usually as flooring. For faux wood or stone laminate, look for a product with at least six different photographs so that the tiles don't all look identical. Also, choose a laminate on which the edges of the photographed tiles align with the real edges of the laminate, which makes for a more authentic look.

Laminate

• **CORK** Derived from a Mediterranean oak tree that regenerates its bark every decade, cork is as environmentally friendly as it is beautiful. It's available in a range of hues from light tan to dark walnut—and even bright colors (above)—and has surface patterns that are part wood grain, part bulletin board, and part tiger stripe. Filled with millions of tiny air pockets, cork is soft underfoot and provides a great sound barrier. It's also surprisingly durable and water resistant.

Cork tile flooring was popular with mid-20th-century Modernist architects in California, and floors from that period, while sometimes showing signs of wear, still look great after half a century of use. These days, cork tiles typically come with a factory-applied protective sealer, so they're even tougher, though some require an annual waxing to ward off stains. Some are designed to snap together like laminates, making them even more do-it-yourself-friendly and usable directly over concrete. Some are made of a combination of cork and colorful rubber, tough enough even for commercial flooring.

• **CARPET** Carpet tiles (right) are a snap for homeowners to install, and any damaged sections can be replaced easily. (As with any tile, buy extras with your initial purchase to ensure color-matched replacements.) Carpet tiles are not suitable for wet areas, but consider them for a home office, music room, family room, or bedroom—anywhere you'd like the pattern possibilities of tile along with the softness, warmth, and sound dampening of carpet.

• **PARQUET** Parquet tiles (right) are essentially wood mosaics made of small strips of hardwoods arranged on a mesh backing. They are glued to the floor, require no grout, and come already finished (no need for sanding), so they're quick, easy, and suitable for do-it-yourselfers. They're also an inexpensive way to get a wood floor. Because of all the seams, parquet floors are not suitable for damp environments.

Parquet

WHAT WILL IT COST?

TILE PRICES VARY TREMENDOUSLY. A basic commercial tile may cost as little as $1.50 per square foot, specialty or handmade tiles as much as $50. Don't be discouraged, though, if your taste says elaborate while your budget says basic. Terrific options are available in every price range.

You may also want to consider some strategies for stretching your tile dollars. Porcelain tiles, for instance, can effectively mimic much costlier natural stone. You might use inexpensive tiles for large surfaces and invest a little more in a smaller area—for example, a vinyl tile on the kitchen floor and a glass or stainless-steel tile for the backsplash. Or use fancier tiles—patterned or handmade or in an exotic material—as inlays to bring a little extravagance to a field of more basic tiles. Even if you stick with entry-level ceramic tiles, a rainbow of colors, a host of finishes, and a mix of sizes provide plenty of raw material to combine in creative and beautiful ways.

Running the numbers. Here's how to translate a per-square-foot tile cost into a rough total project cost in order to get a sense of which tile you can afford.

1 **DETERMINE THE SQUARE FOOTAGE.** For a simple rectangle, all you need to do is measure length and width—rounding each dimension up to the nearest foot—and multiply the two figures. For example, a floor that measures 15 by 20 feet is 300 square feet. If you're tiling more than one surface, like the four walls of a bathroom, multiply the length and width of each wall and then add the areas together.

For an odd space such as an L-shaped hallway floor, divide the space into component rectangles so you can measure each. If there are large spaces that won't be tiled, such as a window within a wall or an island in the middle of a floor, measure those spaces, round the dimensions down, and subtract their square footage from your total. Add up all your measurements and you have a rough job size.

2 **ROUND UPWARD.** The last thing you want is to run short of tile, so it's a good idea to figure a fudge factor of at least 10 percent for a standard pattern, 15 percent for a diagonal or intricate pattern, or 20 percent if the tile is handmade or if it's on sale (meaning it's probably been discontinued and you won't be able to buy any more). That's the standard amount professional tile setters overorder, to accommodate fractional tile pieces as well as any that break or are cut incorrectly along the way. It would also provide a few extras to save for replacing broken or chipped tiles in the future. If you're new to tiling, however, you might want to add another 5 or 10 percent cushion to the total.

3 **DO THE MATH.** Whatever the size of the tile, it's sold by the square foot. So all you need to do now is multiply the square-foot cost of the tile (let's say $4) by the total square footage (let's say 300) to come up with the total cost ($1,200 in this case). If you're using tiles that have different prices, estimate by figuring what proportion of the job each tile will make up and multiplying accordingly. Figure another $2 to $5 per square foot to cover other materials, and you'll be able to ballpark the total cost of any tile job. Before ordering tile, however, ask your installer or seller for guidance about exactly how much to buy.

You'll pay extra for imperfection. Handmade tiles can easily cost twice the price of manufactured tiles, but their slight irregularity looks pleasing on the wall.

LEFT: Glass mosaic tiles create gleaming surfaces in a bathroom, and they easily wrap around undulating walls. OPPOSITE: Quartzite tiles make a stunning and economical transition between indoor and outdoor spaces.

TILE STYLE

TILE COMES IN A WIDE ARRAY OF STYLES and substances, so how do you choose? A good way to begin narrowing your design focus is to think about what suits your taste, your lifestyle, and the architecture of your home. You can play with countless different themes, but they can generally be grouped under three broader categories, according to your objective.

Evoking a place. Nearly every culture has a rich history of tile making and an assortment of distinctive tiles that you can buy today—from Moroccan mosaics to Italian majolica to Mexican saltillos. If your goal is a room that reminds you of the land of your ancestors, a favorite vacation destination, or any place that stirs your imagination, you'll want tile that's in step with that setting. A terra-cotta floor would be appropriate for a Southwestern-style kitchen, for example, whereas a Balinese bath might call for slate.

Honoring a heritage. Maybe it's an era rather than a place that you want to evoke, be it your own past or your home's architectural inheritance. It is not uncommon to choose tile from the period in which a home was built—either actual vintage tiles or replicas. Or you can look for tile that simply captures the feeling of that period.

Of course, you don't have to live in a period house to choose traditional tile. If you're creating a Shaker kitchen or a Victorian bathroom, you'll want tile reminiscent of that look regardless of the overall style of the house.

OPPOSITE: **Are those traditional Southwestern hand-woven blankets hanging from the balcony?**

ABOVE: **A closer inspection reveals that they are actually unique tile mosaics created to look the part.**

Keeping current. You needn't look to faraway places or long-ago times to find interesting choices. We're in the midst of a tile renaissance of sorts, with an explosion of new styles in the marketplace over the past few years. Whether you live in a contemporary home or just want to be on the cutting edge, choices abound.

Beyond traditional stone and ceramic, there are new options in glass, metal, concrete, and leather. Meanwhile, innovative glazing technologies have joined the unparalleled durability of porcelain with a host of faux finishes that convincingly mimic everything from classic ceramics to natural clays and stones, making those looks available for even the toughest flooring and exterior applications.

You might aim for some combination of these approaches—choosing, for example, an old-fashioned penny-round tile that's made of stainless steel. In any case, once you've zeroed in on the style you're aiming for, you can start to consider what colors, sizes, shapes, and layouts are typical of that look. And a good retailer can help you make choices in keeping with your design goals.

Some aqua-colored glass tiles take their coloration from the recycled soda bottles used to make them—a very contemporary look.

ABOVE: It looks like a quilt Grandma might have made, but this "wall hanging" is pieced together from heatproof ceramic tiles.

BELOW: Alternating square and rectangular tiles give this wall an eye-catching brick-like pattern.

Pattern, Shape, and Size

Much of the character of a tile floor or wall comes from the interplay of the individual tiles—the shapes, sizes, and patterns in which they're laid. A grid of squares is the simplest arrangement, of course, but even if you're using only square tiles in a single color, you can jazz up the pattern. You can stagger the rows, for example, turn them on a diagonal, or even position them in a spiral that radiates from the center point of the space. Combine tiles of different colors, and those uniform squares can become anything from a simple checkerboard or geometric pattern to an abstract array of colors or a pictorial mosaic.

If you're an experienced tile setter, you can create visual intrigue with an almost unlimited number of patterns. Hexagons can be laid in offset rows, while rectangles arranged in zigzags result in a herringbone pattern. More complex geometrics combine octagons and squares. By adding a second color, you can call more attention to the overall pattern or individual shapes, or create more elaborate effects such as the basket weave, in which rectangles and squares create the illusion of longer pieces woven under and over each other.

And there are dozens of other choices, whether you're working with tiles that are less than an inch across or more than 2 feet. There are triangles, circles, and abstract interlocking shapes such as paisleys and jigsaw pieces. Some tile manufacturers even sell shards of broken tile and stone that are prearranged into abstract mosaics on mesh backings. These offer an environmentally friendly choice that, with plenty of grout, turns factory waste into a beautiful surface.

No matter what type of tile you choose, just remember that the pattern you select can have a major impact on the feel of the space. A busy grid of small floor tiles may make the room seem smaller, for instance, while large tiles can make it feel open and spacious. An arrangement that has strong lines running across a narrow space—on a hallway floor or a backsplash, for instance—can make it feel wider, while if they run the length of the space, they can make it feel longer. Turning any pattern on the diagonal can bring drama to the room and make the tiles seem larger, thereby making the surface feel bigger.

Even the littlest twist on what is expected can take your project beyond the ordinary. If you're using rectangular subway tiles, which are typically staggered, try installing them vertically instead of in the expected horizontal arrangement, or lay them without the stagger. Or bring some surprise to the traditional mixture of interlocking white octagons and black squares by trading the squares for circles, stars, or shields.

Here are a few tips to keep in mind while you are planning your tile pattern:

- IF YOU'RE USING THE SAME SIZE TILES ON ADJACENT SURFACES—where floor and wall tiles meet or where countertop tiles meet backsplash tiles—you'll want to make sure the seams line up at the meeting point. (Either all of them should align or none of them should.) To avoid that concern, use different size tiles on each surface. The largest tiles might get installed on the floor, with medium-sized tiles going on walls and countertops, and the smallest tiles reserved for backsplashes and shower floors. Some companies sell kits with the same tile in multiple sizes and configurations for different surfaces.

- WHEN YOU'RE PLANNING YOUR TILE ARRANGEMENT, try to borrow a few sample tiles from your retailer so you can lay them out in the space and test your plan. You may even find prelaid sheets of tiles and trim you can borrow. If you can't get samples, simply create your own by cutting cardboard to the sizes and shapes you're considering and giving them at least a hint of the tile's color with spray paint or a felt-tip marker.

- ALSO REMEMBER THAT THE MORE COMPLEX THE TILE ARRANGEMENT, the more challenging the installation is going to be. Fancy patterns and diagonal layouts can be difficult for novice tile setters, from planning out the tile placement to doing the cutting to keeping everything properly aligned. If this is your first tile project, start simple.

Combining different shapes and sizes creates a harmonious look when you use a consistent color scheme.

By making certain elements of a pattern look like they overlap others, mosaic designers can lend a sense of three dimensions to their work.

Color and Texture

We're accustomed to thinking of color as merely a decorating tool, but color can actually affect human emotions as well. That's why many exclusive spas use chromatherapy to help relax their clients, and it's why choosing colors can feel like such a daunting challenge. Add in the numerous choices of surface texture, from glass-like glossy to sandpaper rough and everything in between, and the selection process gets even more difficult. But picking colors and textures isn't as hard as it may seem. Here's how to do it.

If you can select clothes in colors that you like and that look good on you, you can select tile in colors that will meld with your taste and your home. In fact, you might even look to your wardrobe for inspiration about colors that resonate with you. Or you might take your clues from the paint, upholstery, and furnishings in your home. Once you've found a hue or two that you're comfortable with, consider a few rules of thumb about color and texture.

● WHITE, CREAMS, TANS, AND NATURAL STONE COLORS are neutrals, which will combine well with just about any other colors that might be used in the space. That's because neutral tiles leave the decorating punch to other elements of the room—perhaps the paint, drapery, or furnishings, which are easier to change than tiles when you're ready for a new look. Neutrals also may be more appealing to potential buyers should you decide to sell your home. But neutrals aren't the only way to go. Colorful tiles can also harmonize with numerous different decorating schemes, and a unique tile job might even be the feature that sells your house someday.

● LIGHT COLORS tend to make spaces feel larger, while dark tones (and high-contrast color combinations) can make them feel smaller.

● REDS, YELLOWS, AND ORANGES—the colors of fire—are considered warm colors; they are attention-grabbing and invigorating.

● BLUES, GREENS, AND VIOLETS, on the other hand, are thought of as cool colors and have a calming, soothing effect.

● MOTHER NATURE also provides color combinations that work beautifully together and that we're accustomed to seeing, such as the deep green of foliage with the gray-brown of bark, or the aqua blue of water with the beige of sand.

● TO GET A FEEL FOR HOW YOUR TILE WILL AFFECT THE SPACE, try using paint. Select hues that approximate the tile color and paint the unfinished surfaces accordingly.

● LIGHT WILL ALSO AFFECT COLOR. Natural light can be more yellow than the artificial light of a bulb, and fluorescent, halogen, and other bulb types each put out slightly different colors of light. Always try to take tile samples home and set them in the space in order to see how they'll really look.

The Color Wheel

Based on the work of Sir Isaac Newton, the color wheel starts with the three primary colors: red, blue, and yellow. Between each pair are the secondary colors that result from mixing the adjacent colors. Blue and yellow make green, yellow and red make orange, and red and blue make purple. Between those are tertiary colors that result from mixtures of the adjacent secondary colors (yellow-orange, red-orange, red-purple, blue-purple, blue-green, and yellow-green).

You can choose colors from any part of the wheel, of course, but if you want more concrete guidance, use their spatial relationships to determine how well they harmonize and to create one of three types of schemes:

MONOCHROMATIC. This is the simplest approach, and, as the name suggests, it means using a single color. The result is a straightforward, soothing look that has long been the most popular choice for tile. It's an opportunity to use a large swath of color, whether white or turquoise, almost like paint, while letting the geometric beauty of the tiles stand out. Some monochromatic schemes include multiple sizes, shapes, and textures of tile—or even numerous shades of the same color.

ANALOGOUS. For a bit more variation, combine colors that are adjacent on the color wheel, such as blue-green, green, and yellow-green; or red, red-orange, and orange. You might want to let one color predominate and use its analogous colors more sparingly. Because the colors are close on the

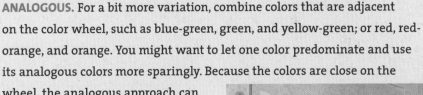

wheel, the analogous approach can soften the effect of bright, heavily saturated color choices because your eye will be comparing them with like colors.

COMPLEMENTARY. For contrasting colors that work well together, choose colors that lie directly opposite each other on the color wheel, such as blue and orange, or yellow-green and red-purple. Complementary colors can intensify the visual impact of your colors because they will be viewed next to such different colors.

Unique prefab glass mosaic tiles cover a backsplash, sink, and countertop.

Texture

Texture has a profound impact on both design and practicality. Many stone tiles have naturally textured surfaces, while others have been polished to a high shine. Meanwhile, unglazed ceramic tiles tend to have a rougher finish than glazed ones. But not all glazed tiles are glossy. Their surfaces can be quite coarse if they were given a dusting of sand or stone over the surface of the wet clay or wet glaze as the tile was being made. Texture can also come from the molds used to form the tile, which can be designed to impart roughness or intricate designs to the surface. Some textures are stamped, carved, or pressed into the wet clay. And you can find a wide array of textures in nontraditional tile, from the deep pores of cork to the embossed tread patterns of some rubbers.

As with color, the choice of texture is largely a matter of selecting a look that you like while considering a few practical factors:

- THE FINISH OF A TILE AFFECTS the way its color will be perceived. Glossy glazes, for example, can intensify colors and give the space a formal feel. Matte finishes, such as unglazed ceramics and honed stones, soften the color and feel more casual. Surface sealers leave a glossy finish on the tile, so you'll want to choose your sealer accordingly (see pages 70–71.)

- A ROUGH TEXTURE makes for a tile that's less slippery when wet, which is a major consideration for floors. Unglazed ceramics, honed stones, embossed or debossed tiles, and tiles with sand or stone pressed into their surfaces or mixed into their glazes will provide surer, safer footing for any floor that's likely to get wet, such as in a bathroom or mudroom, or on a pool surround or outdoor patio.

- TEXTURE CAN ALSO BE A DESIGN ELEMENT. You can alternate the texture of your tiles to create patterns in much the same way you might use a mix of colors. Changes of surface texture can lend intrigue to a monochromatic scheme. They can also help to distinguish like-colored tiles that are used on different surfaces, such as a countertop and floor.

The shimmering surfaces of hundreds of tiny metal subway tiles give this wall an undeniably cutting-edge look.

• KEEP IN MIND THAT ANY TEXTURE WITH DEEP CREVICES—such as a debossed ceramic tile or hole-filled travertine stone—is likely to collect dirt, especially when used on a horizontal surface. That can lead to floors that are tough to keep clean and countertops that are hard to keep sanitary. Better choices for these locations are textures that are relatively smooth, even if they have a matte finish. For shower walls, tile setter Jane Aeon recommends a glossy finish because it is less apt to collect and show a soap film than a matte finish.

Stone tiles' rough surfaces make them naturally slip resistant—and beautiful for any outdoor setting.

Borders, Trims, Accents, and Accessories

Whatever project you're undertaking, it's important to think about accessorizing as you make your plans. You may want towel bars for your bathroom, receptacle covers for your kitchen backsplash, or a range of trim details to complete your job.

Some tiles are available with a full offering of matching trim pieces and accessories, but don't count on finding what you need with every line of tile. If the tile you like doesn't have the accessories you need, you may find some from another line that will work with yours. Here are the components you may need:

Border and trim tiles lend a substantial, architectural feel to the edge of a soaking tub's surround.

Trim. These specialty tiles function much like wood trim around windows and doors. In addition to having a finished face like standard tiles, they have a finished edge or edges. They're used wherever a field of tile ends without abutting an adjacent surface, a wood molding, or a threshold. You might use trim pieces for the top edge of a wainscot, the outer rim of a countertop, or where tile wraps around the outside corner of a wall or fireplace. The simplest trim tile has a bullnose edge, which means one side is rounded and finished just like the face. Others have multiple finished edges or more intricate profiles. You can find specialty trim in the form of chair rails, door and window moldings, baseboards, fireplace mantels, windowsills, stair treads, crown moldings, picture frames, pool rims, and more.

The wall behind a range is an ideal space for decorative tiles, such as this painted tile mural.

A band of white tiles off-sets the green walls of this bathroom, helping to root the white tub to its environment.

Inlays and borders. These decorative tiles are used to dress up fields of plain tile. They may double as trim tile or simply add visual appeal, and they can be anything from complex mosaics to thin, colored swizzle sticks. They're generally longer and thinner or shorter and fatter than the standard tile, to offer syncopation for the pattern and color. Border tiles might run around the perimeter of a floor or the top edge of a wainscot, or be laid into a solid field to create a decorative stripe. Inlays may be patterned tiles, mosaics, or even murals placed at intervals within a field of other tiles.

Accessories. For bathrooms, you can often purchase towel racks, soap dishes, cup and toothbrush holders, towel hooks, and even shelves made to match the tile. For backsplashes, walls, wainscots, focal points, and other locations, you may be able to find matching receptacle and switch plates that you install with screws just like standard cover plates. And you might even find toilets, bathtubs, sinks, sconces, doorknobs, telephone nooks, HVAC vent registers, and other fixtures—all designed to match the tile.

GROUT STYLE

MUCH LIKE GEMSTONES, which need a setting of precious metal to transform them into jewelry, the vast majority of tiles need grout. Grout holds tiles in place and, even more important, seals the gaps between them to create a solid, watertight surface. Grout is required for any ceramic or stone tile and for most other tile types as well. And like a jewelry setting, grout involves its own set of design choices.

Color

In the past, grout came only in cement gray, but manufacturers now offer dozens of colors. Although gray remains by far the most common choice, your project might call for white or even a bright, colorful hue.

If you're using a field of like-colored tiles, you can select a grout to match. With matte tiles and color-matched grout, the lines almost disappear, resulting in a sleek, contemporary look. If you're using tiles of stone, concrete, or any other material that also comes in a solid-slab format, camouflaging the grout in this way can create the illusion of a one-piece countertop, floor, or wall. Color-matched grout is also more forgiving for novice tile setters, as tile and grout placement are far less evident.

Or you might opt for a contrasting grout. If your tile has an appealing shape—hexagonal, for instance—using contrasting grout will show off the tile silhouettes. Even for tiles in a single color, a grid of contrasting grout can be a vital design element.

Not all tiles need grout, as seen with the deep spaces around these glass backsplash tiles.

Old-fashioned gray grout still has its place too. Gray provides a neutral go-between if you're using a range of different-colored tiles. And if you've selected a handmade or traditional tile from another part of the world or from a time-honored manufacturer, you might want to go traditional with the grout as well.

Width

The width of your grout lines profoundly affects the appearance of the finished tile work. Traditionally, installers have left $\frac{1}{4}$ to $\frac{1}{2}$ inch between tiles, creating wide bands of grout. But with most tiles you can use a much narrower grout line—sometimes just $\frac{1}{16}$ inch—if you prefer. Minimizing grout lines results in a sleeker look, though anything smaller than $\frac{1}{8}$ inch requires unsanded grout (grout without sand in it), and that can be tougher to work with.

There's a practical reason for keeping grout to a minimum: It's the most difficult part of a tile job to maintain. Installed properly and sealed regularly, grout can last a lifetime, but it is usually more susceptible to stains, erosion, and chipping than the tile it surrounds. Keeping grout lines thin—and using large tiles to reduce the number of grout lines—will cut down on maintenance. Still, if you've chosen a traditional tile or a regional look complete with gray grout, you may want to stick to wider grout lines to keep the design authentic.

White grout contrasts colorful tiles, making their hues all the richer —and highlighting their arrangement.

Grout samples

Hardness

Not all grout is created equal. For some installations, you may want a grout that's much harder than the standard stuff made from portland cement. Epoxy grout, a resin activated with a hardener, is an extremely durable material that's less likely to erode, won't absorb stains, and never needs sealing.

Epoxy grout isn't right for every job. It costs more than standard grout, is harder to work with, and can't be used with some stone tiles. When suitable, however, it can be a good option for areas that receive hard wear or are subject to dampness, such as high-traffic floors, countertops, and even backsplashes.

Sealer

Standard grout should be sealed. If the tile is also being sealed, then the material is simply spread over the entire surface. If the tile needs no sealer, use a small paintbrush or grout applicator to carefully apply sealer only on the grout lines while quickly wiping away any that gets on the tile. That's a tedious job, but cement grout is extremely porous. This means it will absorb moisture from routine cleaning and therefore darken over time, especially where spills occur. Unless you're using an epoxy grout, plan to seal it, but wait three weeks after installation to make sure the grout has fully cured. For more on sealing tile, see pages 70–71.

TOOLS AND MATERIALS

THERE'S A LOT MORE TO TILING than tiles and grout, of course. You'll need everything from hand and power tools to underlayments and adhesives. Here's a rundown of the most important tools and materials involved in tiling jobs.

Check the specific project instructions you'll be using to see which tools you'll need and to see whether there are any other project-specific supplies required.

A homeowner doesn't need all of the specialty tools that professional tile setters use. On the other hand, using the wrong tool for the job can lead to problems. So throughout this book, you'll be informed when there are a range of different tools that can be used to do each job right.

Tools for Demolition

If you need to tear out an old surface before starting to tile, these are the implements you'll need.

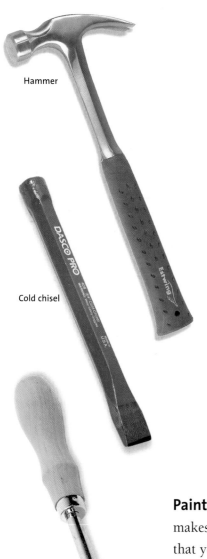

Hammer

Cold chisel

Paint scraper

Hammer. The everyday hammer you probably have in your toolbox already will take care of a host of processes in this book, from tearing out old surfaces to preparing a substrate for new tile.

Cold chisel. Compared with the sharp chisels used for cutting wood, chisels designed for cutting through masonry have fairly blunt tips and require strong blows from a hammer or a heavy mallet. Short of the jackhammers, hammer drills, and masonry saws in a professional tile setter's repertoire, the cold chisel is essential for everything from breaking out old tiles in order to replace them (see pages 226–229) to cutting fieldstones to the size you need (see page 207). Some cold chisels have rubber handles, with hand protectors to shield your hands from errant hammer blows.

Paint scraper. The sharp back-cutting blade on this tool makes quick work of cleaning up old wood moldings so that you can use them again or removing loose paint from a wall before you tile it.

Taper's knife

Taper's knife. This 4-inch-wide blade is handy for a host of jobs, including scraping up old layers of resilient flooring, stripping wallpaper, and even removing adhesive.

Pry bar

Pry bar. Unless you have a small jackhammer available, a long, heavy pry bar is the best tool for breaking up old tile floors and walls and for removing old mud jobs, those thick layers of concrete you'll likely find behind any tiles installed before World War II (see page 86).

Flat bar

Flat bar. The thin, flat profile of these pry bars makes them better choices than standard pry bars for removing materials that you want to use again later, such as wooden baseboard moldings.

Reciprocating saw. Also known as a demolition saw, this tool is ideal for cutting up old materials such as wood thresholds, plywood, and countertops.

Reciprocating saw

Wallpaper perforator

Wallpaper perforator. Wallpaper should come down before a wall gets tiled, and this is a must-have tool for the job. Roll this inexpensive gadget over old wallpaper, and it'll create thousands of tiny pierces so the wallpaper stripper can seep through the paper and dissolve the adhesive underneath.

Safety Tools

Many projects described in this book—from demolishing old tile surfaces to cutting tiles to mixing and applying thinset and grout—call for a host of safety tools: goggles to protect your eyes from flying debris; heavy-duty waterproof work gloves to protect your hands from harsh chemicals in mortars, adhesives, and grouts; and a respirator to protect your respiratory system from unhealthful airborne dust.

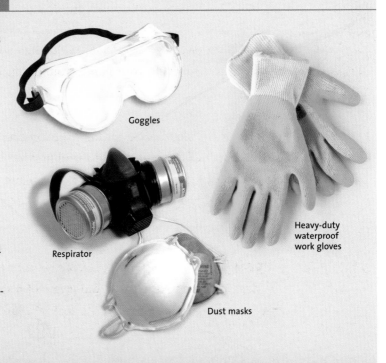

Goggles

Respirator

Dust masks

Heavy-duty waterproof work gloves

Cordless drill

Tools for Preparing Substrate

Before you lay tiles, it is often necessary to install an underlayment of cement backerboard, plywood, or fiberboard. You might also need to strengthen the structure underneath. A modest collection of carpentry tools will enable you to handle most of this work.

Drill with screwdriver bit. A $\frac{3}{8}$-inch variable-speed reversible drill is powerful enough to drive any screws you'll use for the projects in this book. A corded one will work fine, but a cordless model will be a lot more convenient to use if you have two batteries so you can always have one charged and ready when the other runs out of juice. In either case, buy a magnetic sleeve and several #2 Phillips screwdriver bits. This will enable you to drive screws more quickly than you can pound nails.

T square

T square. This T-shaped gauge makes quick work of measuring and marking straight, square cuts on cement backerboard, plywood, fiberboard, and drywall.

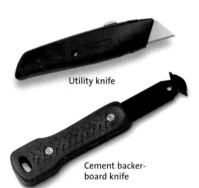
Utility knife

Cement backer-
board knife

Utility knife. A standard utility knife is the best tool for cutting drywall and fiberboard and for a host of other jobs. Make sure to pick up a sleeve of extra blades and to stash some extras in the pocket inside the tool so you can easily swap out dull blades as you work.

Cement backerboard knife. The sharp, hard carbide tip on this knife is essential for cutting through cement backerboard.

Circular saw. Although table saws and power miter boxes are sometimes more convenient to use, the circular saw is inexpensive and will handle almost any of the wood-cutting jobs outlined in this book.

Jigsaw. The thin reciprocating blade on a jigsaw makes the tool ideal for cutting tight turns and curves (that's why jigsaw puzzles take their name from it). You'll need one if you're making detailed cuts in plywood for a new subfloor or countertop.

Offset saw. This simple handsaw has an offset handle that allows you to make a cut very close to an adjacent surface. It's used for trimming up door casings so you can slide the tiles right under them instead of trying to cut the tile perfectly around the profile of the casing (see page 91).

Circular saw

Jigsaw

Offset saw

Layout Tools

A successful tile installation starts with working lines that are straight, square, and, in the case of walls, plumb and level. Accurate measuring and marking tools are essential to getting the job done right.

Level

Level. A bubble level is a must for any tile job, and depending on the project, you may need a few of them in different sizes, such as a small "torpedo level" and a 4-foot level. Before using or buying a level, check it for accuracy. Place it on a flat surface and note the position of the bubble, then flip it upside-down. If the bubble is in exactly the same place, the level is accurate. If it's not, choose another level.

Straightedge

Straightedge. Although a straight wooden 2 × 4 or plank can be used, the best straightedges are man-made, because it's the rare board that is truly straight. You can slice a strip from the side of a sheet of plywood and use its factory edge as your guide. You can also use a 6- or 8-foot level (just be careful not to get thinset on it). Or you can use an aluminum straightedge that's intended for just this purpose.

Chalk line

Chalk line. This simple tool consists of a string that winds around a spindle. Fill the case with powdered chalk and you have an easy way to mark a straight line. Pull out the string, stretch it taut between two marks, and pick it up off the surface, then let go and it'll snap a straight line of colorful chalk between the marks (see page 49).

Tape measure. You'll need a 25-foot tape measure that's 1 inch wide. That's the easiest tape to use because the blade is stiff enough not to flop around when you're trying to measure.

Tape measure

Framing square. This L-shaped carpenter's tool is essential for checking whether surfaces and reference lines are square, meaning exactly 90 degrees, which is essential for making tile patterns come out right.

Framing square

Tools for Cutting Tile

There's more than one way to cut a tile, each with its own pros and cons. For example, for straight cuts on most tiles, you can use either a wet saw or a snap cutter. Snap cutters are cheaper to buy and seem less daunting to use because they're not power tools, but you can rent a good wet saw inexpensively. For a big job, you'll also find the wet saw much faster and easier to use. Also see the safety tools described on page 35.

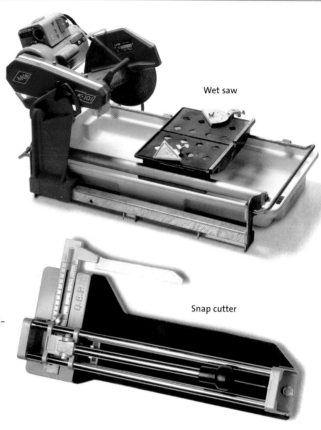

Wet saw

Snap cutter

Wet saw. A wet saw is by far the best and most versatile way to cut ceramic, stone, and porcelain tile, though typically not glass. It produces precise, clean cuts, even right next to the edge of the tile. Water sprays continually onto the blade, preventing the blade from wearing out. Adjustable guides make it possible to mass-produce cuts at 45 degrees or at other angles. Generally, rented wet saws are of a higher quality than the inexpensive homeowner-grade ones you can buy. Make sure to purchase a blade suitable for your tile type.

Snap cutter. Most ceramic, porcelain, and glass (though not stone) tiles can be cut quickly along a straight line with this inexpensive tool, which scores the surface of a tile and then snaps it in two along that line (see page 60). Check that your snap cutter is large enough for the tiles you need to cut. It should have an adjustable guide that you can set to a particular measurement (and even for a 45-degree angle) and then cut multiple tiles to that dimension. Look for a snap cutter that has a replaceable scoring wheel (the blade that cuts the tile).

Tile nippers

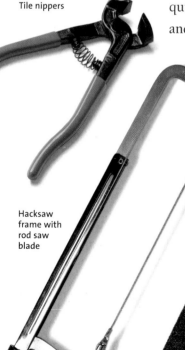

Hacksaw frame with rod saw blade

Tile stone

Tile nippers. Also called tile biters or a nibbling tool, a pair of tile nippers can break a small chunk off almost any tile. To make a cut with nippers, you break off tile gradually in tiny bites (see page 61). You must be patient and careful, as it's very possible that you will break a tile or two in the process. But if you have only a few nonstraight cuts to make—or some straight lines that have been scored on a snap cutter but are too close to the edge of the tiles to actually snap—this tool could save you the trouble of renting a wet saw.

Hacksaw frame with rod saw blade. If you're working with a soft tile (meaning most ceramic and stone wall tiles), a hacksaw equipped with a cylindrical blade can cut curves and cutouts.

Tile stone. A tile stone is a file for taking a bit off the edge of a tile. Still, you don't necessarily need one. The rough face of a cinder block works nearly as well.

Grinder

Grinder. A grinder cuts quickly through any type of ceramic or stone tile, but it kicks up lots of dust, doesn't make very precise cuts, and can easily damage the tile (or the surrounding tiles if you're repairing a finished surface). For soft tiles, you'll need an inexpensive masonry blade. For hard tiles, consider investing in a diamond blade to make quicker, easier cuts.

Hole saw. A hole saw loads into a drill bit and makes quick work of cutting round holes in tiles, plywood, and cement backerboard. Hole saws are available in a wide variety of diameters, with steel teeth designed for cutting wood, or diamond teeth for cutting tile and stone.

Hole saw

Rotary tool. The rotary tool is a relatively recent entry into the tile setter's toolkit. It's a great do-it-yourselfer's tool because it easily does the work of an angle grinder, a hole saw, tile nippers, and a rod saw. It's something like a small drill, but instead of working only when pressed down on the surface, like a drill, the rotary's bits also cut sideways. So you can press the bit into a tile and then move it along a line and cut out any profile you need. There are bits for cutting ceramic tile, stone tile, cement backerboard, and drywall, plus special bits that cut grout without harming the tile. These are terrific for tile repair jobs (see page 227).

Rotary tool

Power miter box. Whether you're cutting laminate tiles, parquet flooring, baseboard molding, thresholds, countertop edging, or any other narrow pieces of wood, a miter box is the easiest way to make the cuts. The blade is adjustable to make angled cuts, and there's a stop that allows you to mass-produce cuts in a certain size.

Table saw. This is the easiest saw to use when you're cutting big pieces of wood, such as plywood or large laminate tiles. But if you don't have one, you can do the job with a circular saw.

Power miter box

Table saw

Tools for Setting Tile

Mixing mortar requires power tools. But if you're using mastic to tile a wall that won't get wet, it doesn't have to be mixed. Either type of adhesive gets spread with special notched trowels. And you'll need beating tools to bed the tiles in the adhesive. Also see the safety tools described on page 35.

Mixing paddles. Very small amounts of thinset or grout can be mixed by hand, but for most jobs you'll thank yourself for buying a mixing paddle. Don't use mixing paddles with your $3/8$-inch drill or you're likely to wind up with poorly mixed thinset and a burned-out drill motor. For mixing thinset and grout, buy, borrow, or rent a $1/2$-inch drill.

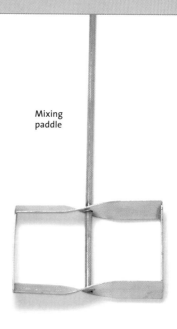

Mixing
paddle

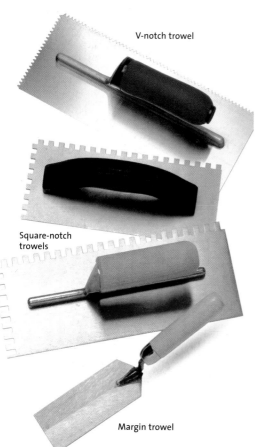

V-notch trowel

Square-notch
trowels

Margin trowel

Trowels. Choose trowels with thick, comfortable handles made of wood or rubber. Examine the blades for straightness, and see that none of the teeth on a notched trowel are bent. Buy a notched trowel to match the job—usually a V-notch trowel for wall tiles and a square-notch trowel for floor tiles. The thicker the tile, the deeper the notches must be. Consult your tile supplier to find out what size notch your project needs. A margin trowel, which looks a bit like an egg turner, is a great general-purpose tool for mixing mortar, back-buttering tiles, and scraping excess mortar and grout from surfaces.

Spacers and wedges. Use plastic spacers between all of your tiles and you'll have consistent grout lines. Spacers come in a range of sizes, so you can choose the best ones for your project. Plastic wedges aren't as precise, because the deeper you press them into the joint, the wider they will space the tiles. But they're useful for tiles that aren't uniform in shape, and they can support the weight of large wall tiles until the adhesive sets.

Spacer

Wedge

Mosaic tape. If you're installing mosaic tiles, pick up a roll of mosaic tape. It's similar to clear contact paper but with a super-strong adhesive. You can place it over a 12-by-12-inch square of prearranged mosaics to hold them steady while you make any necessary cuts using a wet saw, rotary cutter, or other tool (see page 67).

Mallet and beater board

Mallet and beater board. To ensure that your tiles get set properly in the adhesive, tap them with a beater board, also called a beating block, which you can purchase from a tile store or make yourself using a 12-inch-long 2 × 4 or plank. You can cover the wood with cloth or carpet to prevent damage to soft tiles. Tap the board lightly with a rubber mallet to bed the tiles. For large tiles, especially if they are irregularly shaped, use the mallet by itself. And make sure to purchase a white mallet, says tile setter Jane Aeon, because dark ones can leave marks on your tiles.

Finishing Tools

Grouting is the most important—and the trickiest—aspect of a tiling job. You need to fill the spaces between all tiles evenly and remove all excess grout from the tiles before it hardens. The good news is that the tools are simple to use and inexpensive.

Wiping tools

Wiping tools. Always have a bucket and a large sponge on hand to wipe the tiled surface after grouting (see page 66). A wet towel can make the job go faster on a floor. To clean away grout or mortar that has hardened, use a pot-scrubbing pad; anything harsher might scratch the tiles. Have a faucet or hose handy so you can change the water in the bucket often.

Laminated grout float. Purchase a grout float with a face that is laminated with hard rubber. You'll use the float to press grout into place, and then the rubber surface will act like a squeegee to clear away excess grout (see page 65).

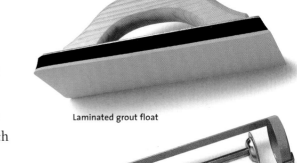

Laminated grout float

Caulk gun. Forget about those little toothpaste tubes of caulk that don't require a gun. To caulk the joints around your tile job, you'll need the real thing—a gun that dispenses standard 10-ounce tubes of caulk. Make sure to press the release button on the gun after each time you apply caulk. Otherwise, the caulk will just keep coming out and make a mess.

Grout sealer bottle. The foam wheel on this plastic bottle makes quick work of applying sealer to grout—an otherwise tedious job if you're not also sealing the tiles themselves (see page 71).

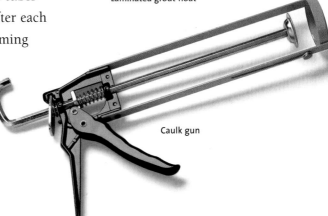

Caulk gun

Underlayment Options

If a wall or floor is solid, it may be possible to tile directly over it. However, if the existing surface is not strong enough, or if the area will get wet, install materials designed specifically to support tile and, in some cases, to withstand moisture.

Fiberglass board

Drywall

Cement backerboard

Plywood

Plywood. Plywood is the best underlayment for nonceramic flooring such as vinyl tile, cork, wood parquet, and laminate tiles. It is inexpensive and easy to cut and install, and it can form a very smooth surface—important when you're applying thin resilient tiles that show every imperfection in the subfloor. Ceramic or stone floor tile can also be installed on plywood, as long as the floor structure is firm and the tiles will not get very wet.

Cement backerboard. The best surface for tile, short of a thick slab of poured-in-place mortar, which few pros do anymore, is cement backerboard. It gets screwed into place much like drywall. It's available in thicknesses ranging from $1/4$ to $5/8$ inch. Use it under any tiles that are likely to get wet. You'll attach it with backerboard screws and then seal the seams between the boards with thinset, which is the mortar used for setting tiles (see page 48). Tile setter Jane Aeon recommends square-drive backerboard screws, which are less likely to snap than standard Phillips screws. (You'll also need matching square-drive screwdriver bits for your drill.)

Drywall. You can lay wall tile over standard drywall—also known as wallboard or sometimes by the brand name Sheetrock—as long as it's not in a wet location, such as a shower or bath surround. Greenboard and blueboard, which are special moisture-resistant types of drywall, are no longer recommended. If there's any chance of water getting on the tiles, use cement backerboard or fiberboard instead. See page 136 for information about preparing existing drywall for tile, or pages 137–139 for instructions on installing new drywall.

Fiberglass board. Until recently, special types of drywall (greenboard or blueboard) were commonly used for damp locations, but now there's a new alternative that offers much better moisture resistance. It's similar to drywall in makeup, but instead of a paper surface, it is covered in fiberglass mesh with an acrylic finish. Paper can harbor mold, even if it's chemically treated, as greenboard and blueboard are. In contrast, fiberglass provides a true moisture barrier to keep the interior of the board dry even if moisture migrates through the wall tile or grout.

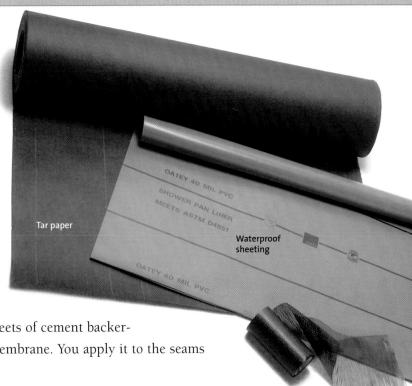

Tar paper

Waterproof
sheeting

Mesh tape

Membranes

Two situations call for the installation of a membrane: an extremely wet location (such as a shower base or surround) or a substrate that may shift or crack (such as an old, broken-up concrete floor).

Sheet membrane. Waterproof sheeting, usually vinyl, should be used under any tile floor that's subject to daily doses of standing water—in other words, under tile shower floors (see page 101).

Painted membrane. To seal the joints between sheets of cement backerboard in a shower or tub surround, use a painted membrane. You apply it to the seams with a brush (see page 159).

Isolation membrane. Rather than lock water out, some membranes keep the tiles separated from the surface below—generally because that surface is cracked and subject to movement that would damage the tile. There are a host of high-tech isolation membranes available, but all you really need is good old-fashioned tar paper. You lay the tar paper over the subfloor, then lay galvanized welded wire, and then a thick bed of mortar (see pages 100–101).

Adhesives

Consult your tile dealer to find the right adhesive for your tile and substrate. Generally, it's best to use thinset for countertops, floors, stone tiles, and shower and tub surrounds. You can use mastic for all other traditional tile jobs. For nontraditional tiles like cork, carpet, and vinyl, you'll need a specialty product for the particular material. To learn about grout, see pages 32–33.

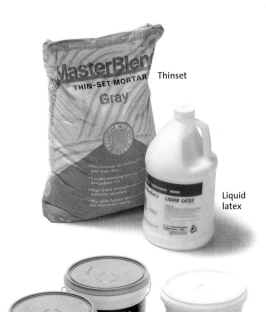

Thinset

Liquid
latex

Mastic

Thinset. Thinset is strong concrete without large stone pieces. It provides a durable, water-resistant bond between the tiles and their substrate. It comes in a premixed powder, to which you add water. Make sure to choose a latex-fortified thinset to give the tile job some much-needed flexibility and reduce the likelihood that tiles or grout will crack. Thinset might come this way, or you might have to add liquid latex instead of water. For heavy wall tiles, you'll also want a sag-free mortar, which quickly grabs the tiles and holds them so they don't slide down the wall, as they can with standard mortar.

Mastic. If the tile surface won't get wet and you're not using stone tiles, you can use mastic instead of thinset. Mastic comes premixed; it grabs the tiles immediately, with no sagging, and it's far less expensive than thinset.

the basics of tiling

INSTALLING CEMENT BACKERBOARD

SOME PROS STILL INSTALL tile the old-fashioned way, by pouring a thick slab of mortar and setting the tiles directly in it. But a mud job, as this technique is called, is a time-consuming operation that requires a practiced hand, and it increases the thickness of the floor or wall considerably. That's why most tile setters now use cement backerboard, 3-by-5-foot sheets that get screwed in place much like drywall and then topped with a thin layer of mortar to bed the tiles. This is a far easier process for the do-it-yourselfer. You should lay $\frac{1}{2}$-inch-thick backerboard over any wood subfloor before laying tile on it. Cement backerboard must also be used for wall tile installations in shower surrounds. For bathroom and kitchen walls where the tile may see occasional moisture but not direct, daily contact with running water, you can use drywall or fiberboard instead of backerboard (see pages 137–139). In completely dry locations, you can simply install tiles directly on existing or new drywall or plaster.

1 **PREP THE SURFACE AND START THE LAYOUT.** If you're tiling a wall in a wet area, remove any existing tiles and the existing drywall or plaster down to the studs (see page 134), making sure to pull loose nails or sink their heads. If you're tiling a floor, remove old flooring and other debris from subfloors (see pages 84–86). Then plan your layout. Starting in a corner, place the first sheet of cement backerboard. Use strips of $\frac{1}{4}$-inch plywood to create a gap around the perimeter of the surface, and make sure the length of the sheet crosses the joists in the floor or the studs in the wall. The tile side of the sheet (which is the rough-textured side) will be identified on the product label and should face outward. Plan the layout so that none of the backerboard joints fall directly over joints in a plywood subfloor. Stagger backerboard joints by 18 inches or more, so that there is no place where four corners meet, and keep a $\frac{1}{8}$-inch gap between backerboard sheets. For walls, you'll need to cut the sheets to end at the center of the studs so that you can fasten them, but for floors, you can fasten the ends to the subfloor wherever they wind up.

TRICKS OF THE TRADE

Floor Thickness

Your floor will very likely grow 1 inch thicker by the time you add $1/2$-inch cement backerboard, two layers of thinset, and $3/8$-inch tile. That's not too bad if you're working off the subfloor and the neighboring floors are $3/4$-inch hardwood. But if you're starting on the same level as the surrounding floors, people will have to step up onto the tiled floor, creating a tripping hazard, even with a wooden reducer threshold to bridge the transition. The maximum acceptable height difference is $3/4$ inch. So limit the height differential as much as possible by removing any old flooring before laying backerboard and, if necessary, choosing thin porcelain tiles instead of thick stone.

2 **SCORE THE CUTS.** To cut a sheet of cement backerboard, measure for the cut and subtract $1/4$ inch, since the cut end will be rough, with jagged bumps that will jut out beyond your cut line. Make your mark at both edges of the board and hold a straight 2 × 4 between them. Mark the line with a carbide-tipped cement board knife. Then, pressing hard enough to hear the blade tearing through the cement, make about 10 more passes along it to score a $1/16$-inch-deep groove. You can use a standard utility knife, but be prepared to change the blade after every cut.

3 **SNAP AND CUT AGAIN.** Slide the 2 × 4 under the sheet and align it just under the score line. While holding one side of the sheet firmly, press down on the other to snap the board along the cut. Stand the sheet on its edge and make a pass with the knife from the back to make the final cut. Use a rasp, a tile stone, or the rough finish of a cinder block to smooth any rough spots so the sheet can sit tight against its neighbor.

continued ▶▶

4 **MAKE CUTOUTS.** To make holes for pipes to go through, you'll need to use a $\frac{1}{2}$-inch drill loaded with a hole saw. For other odd cuts, you'll need to use an angle grinder, rotary cutter, or circular saw with a masonry blade. Wear a respirator when cutting the sheets with power tools, as you'll make a lot of cement dust that's unhealthful to breathe. You can also make a 1-inch hole for standard plumbing pipes by hitting the board hard at just the right spot with a hammer and then cutting away the debris with a backerboard knife.

5 **ATTACH THE SHEETS.** For a wall, attach the sheets to the studs behind them as you go, using backerboard screws spaced 6 inches apart. For a floor, continue dry-laying all the sheets until the entire floor is ready, then number them, pick them up, and sweep away all debris. Mix thinset mortar (see pages 54–55) and spread enough for one piece of backerboard on the subfloor using a $\frac{1}{4}$-inch square-notched trowel. Carefully position the first sheet in the mortar. Drive backerboard screws through the board into the subfloor every 8 inches (6 inches along the perimeter), or as recommended by the manufacturer. Tile setter Jane Aeon recommends square-drive screws, which are less likely to snap or strip than Phillips heads. Continue across the room, making sure to leave $\frac{1}{8}$-inch gaps between sheets.

6 **TAPE THE JOINTS.** Once all of the sheets are laid, stick a strip of fiberglass mesh tape over each joint. (It's sticky and can be pressed into place with a taping trowel.) Then, using the flat edge of a trowel, spread a thin layer of thinset mortar over the tape. Take care to fill only the groove and not to create any high spots. Feather the thinset on each side and smooth away any lumps or mounds. Wait 12 hours for the thinset to cure, and you're ready to tile.

WORKING OUT THE PATTERN

YOU CAN MAKE A SCALE DRAWING of the floor, wall, or whatever surface you're tiling in order to plan out the pattern. Simply use graph paper and make each segment equal to a tile plus a grout line. But unless you're plotting out a very complex pattern of different tile colors or shapes, a drawing is not necessary. You'll get a better result by planning out the fit in the real world rather than trying to do it in the abstract on paper.

Make Reference Lines

The first step is to draw two reference lines on the surface that you'll be tiling. They will form a + and must be perfectly perpendicular to each other, and as perpendicular as possible to the edges of the surface that they intersect. For a wall or other vertical surface, you can use a level to make these lines. For a floor or other horizontal surface, there are two methods you can use: You can measure each of the surface's four edges, find their midpoints,

TRICKS OF THE TRADE

Don't Use Hairspray

Some experts recommend using hairspray to protect chalk lines from getting rubbed away prematurely. But it can weaken the thinset's bond to the floor, so don't use it, says tile setter John Bridge. Instead, use a straightedge to trace chalk lines with a permanent marker, or just be prepared to resnap them as needed using your existing marks.

Diagonal Installations

For a diagonal tile pattern, start by making two reference lines as described on the previous page. Then measure 3 feet from the center point of each line and make a mark. Next measure the distance between each of those marks and make a new mark at the midpoints between them. Using those new marks, snap two new diagonal chalk lines. Then proceed with the layout process described on the next page using these new reference lines.

and then snap chalk lines between the opposing marks, and use a framing square to check that the lines are at 90 degrees to each other. Or you can pick the most visible edge (a primary wall, for example, if you're tiling a floor) and make a mark roughly halfway across the surface from one of its ends. Then measure off the other end and make another mark that's equidistant from it. Snap a line between those marks and then use a framing square to create a second line that's perpendicular to it near the center of the surface. You can use whichever technique you're comfortable with—and that the surface's layout makes convenient.

Check for Square

It's the rare house that's completely square, so it's a good idea to check all sides of the surface before laying any tile. Otherwise, you may wind up with drastic angled cuts along some edges, says tile setter Jane Aeon. Measure from each end of each reference line to the edges of the wall or floor that are parallel to it. If things are out of sync, adjust your reference lines so they're parallel to the most visible edges. This could be the counter-top if you're tiling a backsplash or, if you're tiling a floor, the wall you see when you enter the room. Hide the problem along the least visible edge, such as along the upper cabinets for that backsplash or along an out-of-the-way wall for that floor. "Exterior walls are usually straighter than interior ones," Aeon says, "so I trust them more when I'm making reference lines."

Lay Out Floor Tiles

Once you have the layout lines, you can start dry-laying the tiles. A tape measure could do the planning job instead, but you'll get the most accurate plan by actually placing tiles and spacers into position.

1 **START PLACING TILES.** On a floor or other horizontal surface, dry-lay a row of tiles along each of your two reference lines, so that you make a tile X over the floor. Use spacers that are the size of the grout lines you want (see tip below). Plan a ¼-inch gap around the perimeter of the floor, and determine how much you'll need to cut off the tiles at the edges. Pros try to avoid anything smaller than one half of a tile, because it looks unprofessional, so shift your tiles as needed to avoid that problem. You may need to make new reference lines to do so. If necessary, adjusting your spacer size slightly can also help, as long as you stay with a look you like and spacing that's approved by the tile manufacturer.

2 **MARK TILE LOCATIONS.** Once you're happy with your arrangement, dry-lay additional tiles to test the cuts around major obstructions in the middle of the space, such as an island in a kitchen floor. Tweak things again to avoid anything smaller than half-tiles around them as well, if possible. Check the tiles to ensure that they're all arranged on the reference lines and spaced properly. Then use them to make reference marks on the floor. Mark the location of each side of each tile on each reference line.

TRICKS OF THE TRADE

Getting the Spaces Right

A few decades ago, the standard grout line was ½ inch wide, but the trend now is toward much narrower spacing. "The largest grout lines I ever do these days are ¼ inch," says tile setter Jane Aeon. Often they're only ⅛ inch. Somewhere between ⅛ and ¼ inch is ideal for a floor, as smaller grout lines require unsanded grout, which is harder to work with than grout containing sand. Always check with the seller to see what's recommended for your tile.

Lay Out Wall Tiles

A batten board made of a piece of straight 1 × 2 stock will hold the tiles up on the wall while you dry-lay the first row. If your tiles won't stay on the batten, use a thicker board. Later, you'll use a second board to plan the vertical layout.

1 PLAN THE FIRST ROW. Use a level to find the low point of the floor, countertop, tub, or other surface that acts as the bottom of the wall. Set a spacer there and then a tile (or the base trim tile) above it and mark the top of the tile. Use a level to draw a horizontal line across the wall at that mark.

2 INSTALL THE BATTEN BOARD. From left to right, measure the wall or area that you're tiling and mark the exact center. Use a level and a pencil to draw a vertical line on the center mark, then use drywall screws to temporarily attach the batten board to studs in the wall. Make sure its top edge is up against the horizontal line that you drew in step 1.

3 DRY-LAY THE TILES. Measure and mark the midpoint of a tile and set it on the batten board so that it is centered over the vertical line. Then dry-lay a row of tiles to the left and right of the first tile on the batten board and put spacers between them. If you're using self-spacing tiles (as shown here), they'll have lugs on their edges to create the spacing for you. Once you've filled the whole batten area, check the cuts you'll need for the tiles at each end. If they're going to create less than half a tile, re-lay the row starting with a grout line, instead of a tile, over the center point. If that doesn't do the trick, you can also adjust the spacer size to make grout lines a bit thinner or thicker—as long as you stay with a look you like and spacing that's approved by the tile manufacturer (see tip, page 51).

4 **MARK HORIZONTAL LAYOUT LINES.** Use a pencil to mark the vertical reference line and the tile locations on the batten board. Remove the tiles and transfer the marks to the wall. Then remove the board and attach it near the top of the wall, keeping it level and placing the proper mark on the vertical reference line. Transfer the tile location marks there as well.

5 **MARK VERTICAL LAYOUT LINES.** Cut a second batten board to the height of the tile job, position it against the vertical reference line, and temporarily fasten it in place with drywall screws. Mark on it the location of the horizontal first-tile line, as well as any points on the wall where you plan to install trim or specialty tiles. Then move the board to the floor, lay tiles, spacers, and specialty tiles along it, working off that first-tile reference line, and mark their locations in pencil on the batten board. Temporarily tack the vertical batten board, also called a story pole, in place near the left side of the wall, aligned with the first-tile line, and transfer the marks to the wall. Do the same on the right side. You can use the story pole again for adjacent walls.

6 **SNAP GUIDELINES.** Snap chalk lines between your marks every 2 feet or so, as that's a good amount of tile to work with at one time. Choose the appropriate marks on the surface given the size of tile you're working with. For example, for 12-inch tiles, you'd create a guideline for every other tile; for 8-inch tiles, every third. There's no need to snap lines for the spaces between tiles. Just be consistent about always marking the same side of the tiles.

TRICKS OF THE TRADE

Making a Mark

When you're making a mark on tile, cement backerboard, greenboard, or anywhere, put the pencil or marker tip against the exact spot on the tape measure and draw a roughly 1/2-inch line away from it. Then put your writing implement back at the measurement and draw a second line at about 90 degrees to the first, so you wind up with a V. You'll be able to spot that easily and will know that the intersection is the exact point you measured.

MIXING AND SPREADING THINSET

THINSET, ALSO CALLED MORTAR, is a special concrete that's designed for setting tiles. It comes in a powder that you mix with water. Check with the tile seller to see what type you need. For most applications, you'll need a thinset that contains latex, which adds some flexibility and prevents cracking. Standard thinset is gray, but there are also white thinsets for use behind marble, glass, and other translucent tiles, as well as behind light-colored grouts, and epoxy thinsets for countertops. Wear rubber gauntlet gloves and a respirator when mixing and using thinset. And if the manufacturer's instructions differ from ours, follow them. For light-duty wall applications, there's an alternative to thinset, called mastic, which is discussed beginning on page 142.

1 **MIX A SMALL BATCH.** Thinset begins to cure about 30 minutes after it's mixed, so make small batches that you can use up in that much time. Start with about 2 inches of room-temperature water in a clean 5-gallon bucket and begin adding thinset to it a little at a time. Mix the powder into the water using a mixing paddle loaded into a rented drill that can

TRICKS OF THE TRADE

Add Thinset to the Water

Many tile books suggest pouring the thinset powder to your bucket first and then mixing in the water, but you'll create a lot less airborne dust if you do it the other way around, says tile setter John Bridge.

handle a $\frac{1}{2}$-inch bit. Place your feet against the bucket to keep it from spinning, and don't rev the paddle too fast, so you don't cause splashing or beat air into the mix.

2 **TEST THE THICKNESS.** The consistency of the mortar is critical. You want it soft and flexible but still stiff enough that when you pull a trowel through the mix, the mortar retains its shape without settling or falling in on itself. You also want it to stick to the trowel for a couple of seconds before dropping into the bucket. Add water or powder, and mix until you achieve that consistency. Keep mixing until all the lumps are gone. Then let the thinset stand for 10 minutes before mixing it again and using it. The waiting period allows the powder to fully hydrate and is a crucial step that too many first-timers unwittingly skip.

3 **SPREAD THE MORTAR.** Use a trowel to move a glob of mortar onto the tiling surface and to spread it inside one of your chalk-lined sections (see page 50). Take care to bring the thinset right to the lines without crossing them. You want to spread the mortar in one section at a time, then lay the tiles for that section before moving on to an adjacent one. For a floor, make sure to work toward the exit so you can get to every spot and so you can get out of the room without having to walk over the freshly laid tiles.

4 **COMB WITH A NOTCHED TROWEL.** To get the thickness of the mortar right, use a notched trowel. A $\frac{3}{8}$-inch notch is a good all-around choice, although some large tiles require a $\frac{1}{2}$-inch notch and some smaller ones require a $\frac{1}{4}$-inch notch. Check with your tile supplier to see what size your tile needs. Hold the trowel at a 45-degree angle and comb over the mortar, allowing the trowel's teeth to scrape the substrate gently. Use long, sweeping strokes wherever possible and keep the trowel angle consistent. Remove any globs or debris. Once the unused mortar starts to harden, don't try adding more liquid. Instead, throw out the mortar and wash the bucket. Finish laying that section of tile before mixing a new batch of mortar.

SETTING TILES

NOW IT'S TIME TO LAY THE TILES and see your creation take shape before your eyes. It's one of the most crucial steps of the job, because you need to lay the tiles in straight lines with consistent spacing and without any high or low tiles. You also have only about 10 minutes before the thinset begins to set up, after which adjusting tiles may weaken the thinset bond. To help you ensure that the tiles are placed properly, you'll want plastic spacers in the appropriate dimension for the grout lines you're planning (see tip on page 51). And you will want a straightedge. The best straightedges are aluminum, which also have helpful ruler markings on them. If you don't have a metal straightedge, you can use a framing square, a level, or the factory edge on a strip of plywood.

Following are general directions for laying tile. See chapters 3 through 6 for details on specific applications.

1 **BACK-BUTTER THE TILES.** Once you have the thinset spread out (see pages 54–55), you're ready to start laying tiles. As you place each one, use a margin trowel to apply a thin layer of thinset to its back. This will ensure good adhesion between thinset and tile and will level out low spots in the substrate. It's also more forgiving if the thinset was mixed too dry or has begun to cure.

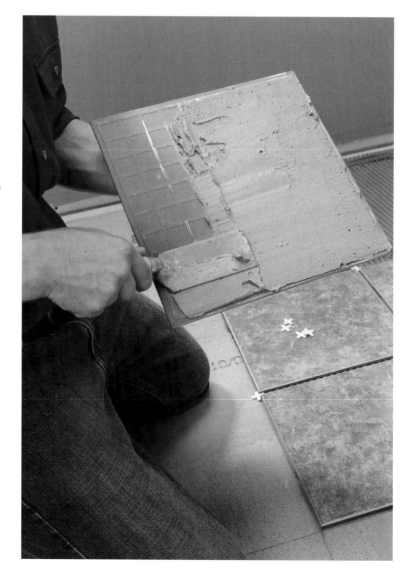

TRICKS OF THE TRADE

Laying Nonuniform Tile

Spacers are all well and good when the tiles are perfectly uniform, but they won't work if you're dealing with tumbled or rough-cut stone or handmade ceramic tiles. In that case, try wedge-shaped spacers, which are adjustable, and rely on your guidelines and a straightedge to keep the tiles aligned.

2 **SET THE TILES ON GUIDELINES.** Set each tile fairly precisely so you don't have to slide it more than an inch or so. Align the first tile with two guidelines, then set additional tiles against it, inserting spacers at every corner. Don't press down on any tile.

Make Your Own Beater Board

You can easily buy a beater board, which is just a piece of wood with a rubber surface to cushion it against the tiles. But many tile setters prefer to make their own from scraps of 2 × 4 lumber wrapped in carpet remnants. They're easy to make in whatever size works for your job—it should be about as long as two tiles (or two sheets of mosaic tiles)—and you can use a staple gun to fasten the carpet in place.

3 **TAP WITH A BEATER BOARD.** After you've set a few tiles, place a beater board (see above) over them and tap it with a rubber mallet. This helps ensure that the tiles' backs are set firmly in the mortar and that their top surfaces are flush with those of their neighbors. But don't beat limestone or other fragile tiles.

continued ▶▶

TRICKS OF THE TRADE

Using a Batten Board

To ensure that your tiles are positioned perfectly against your grid-line, temporarily screw a 1 × 2 board to the floor so that its edge rides along the grid line. Then butt the tiles against it as you lay them.

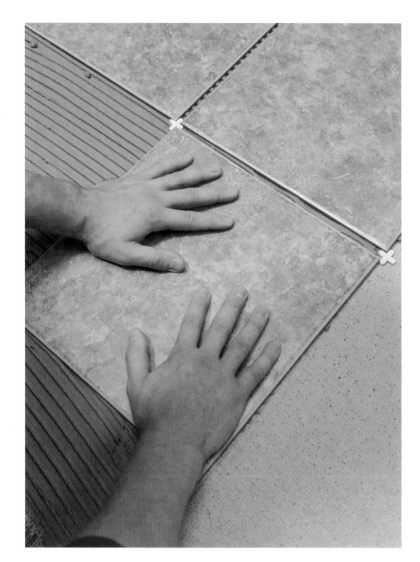

4 **FINE-TUNE AS YOU GO.** To adjust a tile slightly, place your hand on top, fingers splayed out. Press gently as you slide the tile. You should be able to make a small adjustment, but if you feel resistance followed by a sudden movement, the mortar has probably begun to set. In this case, pick up the tile and attempt to recomb the mortar below. If the mortar has started to harden, scrape the tile and the surface below it clean of mortar and start over with fresh thinset. Place a straightedge over the tile surface to test whether the tiles form a flat plane. If a tile is too high, try pressing down on all four corners. If a tile is too low, remove it, apply additional mortar, and reset it.

5 **CHECK ADHESION.**
About every 10 minutes,
pick up a tile that you've just
set and look at the back. Mortar
should be stuck on the entire
surface. It probably is if the tile
strongly resists being picked up,
in which case everything is fine.
If you find only partial adhesion,
either you don't have a thick
enough bed of mortar or the
mortar is beginning to set up and
you need to scrape it off and mix
up a fresh batch.

6 **REMOVE EXCESS MORTAR.**
Clean out any excess mortar that
squeezes up between the tiles as you go.
It will be much trickier to remove when
it hardens, especially on a floor, since
you can't walk on the tiles for 12 hours.
A carpenter's pencil works well for
removing mortar between tiles, as do
spacers. If necessary, you can even use
a flathead screwdriver to scrape out
excess mortar the next day.

CUTTING TILE

YOU'LL LIKELY NEED TO CUT ALL OF THE TILES around the perimeter of the floor or wall to make them fit, and you will need to notch around objects like doorjambs and make holes for pipes and other penetrations. Many first-time tile setters worry more about cutting than anything else, but it's actually a fairly easy job. There are many different tools you can use, and none of them—even the power tools—are difficult to operate. Just make sure you always wear eye protection when cutting tile using any of these methods. Wear respiratory protection when doing any power cutting.

Using a Snap Cutter

A snap cutter is inexpensive and it isn't a power tool, so it's a good choice for beginners. However, it can make only straight cuts and it doesn't work on stone, porcelain, or some other extremely hard tiles, including many quarry tiles. It's also difficult to use a snap cutter for cuts near the edge of a tile.

Mark a cut line on the tile with a wax pencil. Position the tile firmly against the snap cutter's front guide so the cut will be square. Lift up the handle and push or pull it to score a line across the tile. It's best to score a single, continuous line, but if you score an incomplete line, go over it again. Allow the wings of the cutter to rest on both sides of the scored line. Push down on the handle (as shown above), and the tile will snap in two. If the cut is within an inch or so of the edge of the tile, use a tile nibbler (shown at left) to break away the excess material little by little. Brush away all debris from the base of the snap cutter before making the next cut.

TRICKS OF THE TRADE

Cutting Stone

Because of the natural fault lines running through stone, it can't be cut with a snap cutter or nipper. Straight cuts should be made with a wet saw fitted with a diamond blade. Curved cuts should be made with a carbide-tipped rod saw on a hacksaw handle.

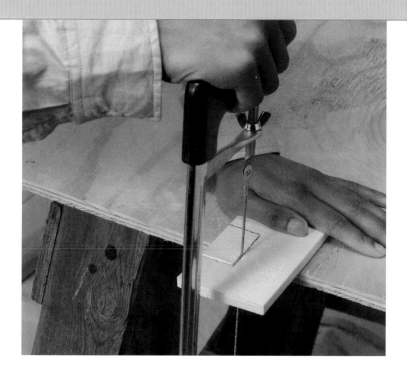

Using a Rod Saw

If your cut isn't straight and you're working with a soft ceramic tile, you can make the cut freehand using a hack saw loaded with a rod saw blade. Mark the tile with the cut you need and then hold the tile firmly in place on a work surface so that the area to be cut is overhanging the edge. Saw with steady, gentle strokes (shown above).

Using a Nibbling Tool

It may seem unlikely that this simple tool can cut curves and notches in hard ceramic tiles. It can, as long as you're not working with stone or porcelain tiles. It just takes practice and patience. Your nibbled cuts won't be as crisp and precise as those made with other tools, so they're best made where they'll be covered by moldings or plumbing hardware later. The key is to nibble slowly, taking lots of tiny bites. You can also use a nibbling tool to make a cut that runs in two directions by first scoring the lines with a snap cutter, then taking small bites out of the cut-out area (shown at left). If you take a big bite, you might shatter the tile. Work your way slowly toward the corner of the cut. When you reach the scored lines, you can nibble more accurately.

continued ▶▶

Using a Wet Saw

This is what the pros use, and it's also the best do-it-yourself choice—for both straight cuts and notches—because it produces the cleanest, most accurate cuts and does so very quickly. You can purchase inexpensive wet saws at home centers, but you'll get a higher-quality machine by renting one from a tile shop or tool rental store. If the saw is equipped with a splash guard, you can use it indoors as long as you don't mind some scattered spray, but working outside will guarantee a dry room. Set the saw on a worktable or two stable sawhorses. For a saw with a pump, fill the pan with water, set the pump in the water, and test to make sure there is a continuous stream directed at the blade while it is on. For other saws, just make sure to keep the water supply filled.

To make a straight cut, slide the tray all the way toward you and position the tile, pressing it firmly against the guide. Turn on the saw and slide the tile forward (top left). Hold the tile firmly in place on the tray at all times, pressing gently against the blade as you cut through the tile. For an angled cut, adjust the cutting fence accordingly (left). Use a clean towel, a heat gun, or plenty of sunshine to dry the tiles before laying them, as a wet tile won't adhere well to thinset or mastic.

Cutting Notches with a Wet Saw

To cut out a notch, first use a snap cutter to score the cut line that's parallel to the tile's edge—along the notch only. Then use the wet saw to make cuts that are perpendicular to the edge, both along the cut lines and throughout the material that will be removed (right). Hold the tile at a steep angle, so that the saw blade will cut deeper on the back side, and make a series of cuts about 1/4 inch apart. Finish by using a nibbling tool to remove the remaining strips (bottom right) and to clean up the edges of the notch.

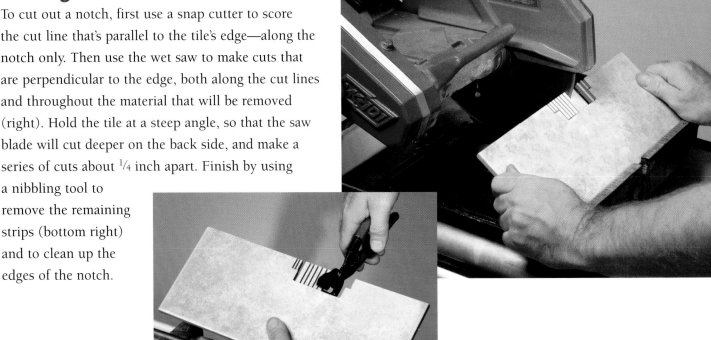

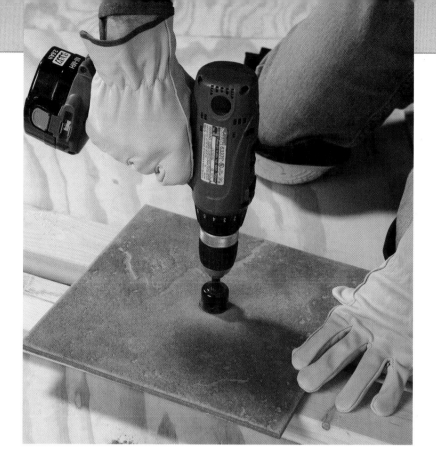

Using a Hole Saw

To cut a circle through the middle of a tile to accommodate a plumbing pipe, radiator pipe, or other round object, you'll want to use a hole saw, which is a saw with a circular blade that you load into a drill. You'll need a tile-cutting hole saw, which has a diamond-tipped blade. If you're cutting a hole for a hot-water pipe, choose a saw that's about $1/8$ inch larger than the pipe so the pipe has room to expand when it heats up. Mark the center point of the hole on the tile and place the hole saw's bit on the mark. While holding the drill perpendicular to the tile, drill out your hole (above).

Using a Rotary Cutter

A rotary cutter is something like a miniature drill, except its bits are designed for more than just punching holes. You can cut in any direction you want, making easy work of notches, circles, and just about any other freehand cut you'd ever want to make in a tile (right).

GROUTING

ONCE ALL OF THE TILES ARE IN PLACE, allow the mortar to set for at least 12 hours before walking on the floor. If the weather is humid, if you're using a dense tile such as porcelain or slate, or if any of the exposed mortar is not completely dry, wait another day. The mortar will become lighter in color as it dries.

Use needle-nose pliers to pull the spacers out, taking care not to nick the tile as you work. The mortar in the spaces should be $\frac{1}{4}$ inch below the surface of the tiles, so if there are spots that are higher, dig them out with a flathead screwdriver. With a wet rag, wipe away any dried mortar on the surface of the tile. For particularly stubborn areas on nonglazed tiles, you can also try a pot-scrubbing pad, but test in an inconspicuous spot first to make sure you won't scratch the tiles.

If the spaces between the tiles are $\frac{1}{8}$ inch or smaller, use unsanded grout. For larger spaces, you'll need sanded grout, which contains a bit of construction-grade sand to strengthen the mix. You'll also want a grout containing latex, which makes it more flexible and less prone to cracking, though it's always a good idea to check with the tile supplier to find out the best grout to use with your particular tile. Wear rubber gauntlet gloves and a respirator when mixing grout. And if the manufacturer's instructions differ from ours, follow them.

TRICKS OF THE TRADE

Colored Grout

Grout need not be gray. You can match it to the color of your tile and make the granite tiles on your countertop look like a solid slab. You can contrast the grout color with that of the tile, or even use a brightly colored grout against white glass mosaics to bring an element of surprise or whimsy to a backsplash. Manufacturers sell dozens of premixed colors, or you can create your own with grout colorants.

1 **MIX THE GROUT.** You'll need to mix many small batches and use up each one before it dries out. Fill a clean 5-gallon bucket with about 2 inches of room-temperature water and gradually add grout powder to it, mixing with a trowel as you go, until the grout is about the thickness of toothpaste and free of lumps. Wait 10 minutes, then mix again. Add a little more liquid if necessary.

2 **PUSH THE GROUT INTO PLACE.** Using a rubber grout float, scoop some grout onto the surface. Holding the float nearly flat, push the grout into the grout lines with sweeping back-and-forth strokes. Be sure to push in two or more directions. Stop after you've grouted no more than a 10-by-10-foot area, so you're sure to have enough time to wipe away the excess grout before it sets.

3 **WIPE AWAY THE EXCESS.** Tip the float up and use it like a squeegee to clear away most of the grout from the surface of the tiles. Move the float across the tiles diagonally so its edge does not dig into any grout lines. Aim to remove at least three-quarters of the surface grout, but don't worry if you miss a few spots.

4 **WIPE WITH A SPONGE.** When the surface of the tiles begins to haze over with drying grout, it's time to start wiping away the excess. Depending on various factors, including the temperature in the room and how dry the grout mix was, this can start happening in 20 minutes or an hour. Pay close attention, because the longer you wait, the harder it will be to get the grout off. Dip a large sponge in clean water and squeeze some of the water out so the sponge is wet but not dripping. Run the sponge across the tile surface gently to wipe grout from the tile surfaces, but do not dig into the grout lines. Rinse the sponge frequently with clean water. *continued* ▶▶

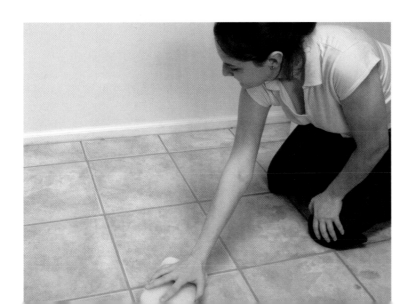

TRICKS OF THE TRADE

Removing Hardened Grout

If you find some surface grout still remaining on your tiles a day or so after the job is done, you can remove it with a delicate pot-scrubbing pad or cheesecloth. Slightly dampen a clean pad or cloth and use elbow grease to scrub away the material, says tile setter Jane Aeon. If you don't take care of this in the first 24 to 48 hours, you'll need to use a chemical grout remover to get it off.

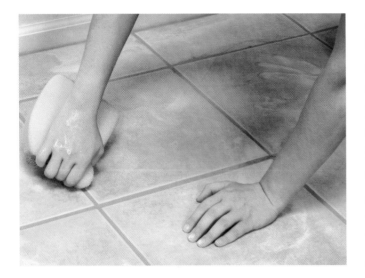

Joint the Grout

Once the grout is firmly embedded and most of the excess is wiped away, it's time to remove the rest of the surface grout and to make consistent grout lines, a process called jointing. Don't take this process lightly, as it's more than just cleaning up. A tile job that has been wiped carelessly will look unprofessional. Grout should be just slightly below the tile surface; deeper grout will be hard to keep clean. Moisten a sponge with clean water and wring it out so it is just damp. Run it along each grout line, working first in one direction, then in the other. You may find it easier to work if you ball up a corner of the sponge. Have a bucket of clean water on hand so you can continually rinse the sponge. Once the water starts to get murky, change it. As you work, take care not to step or kneel in the grout lines.

Buff Away the Haze

Allow the grout to dry until it is lighter in color. Using a dry, lint-free rag, buff the surface of the tiles until they shine. If any holes appear in the grout lines, fill them with fresh grout and smooth the area out with a sponge.

Caulking Joints

Ceramic and stone tiles expand and contract with changes in temperature. This movement is slight, but it can cause tiles to crack if you don't provide for a little movement. Where tiles on different surfaces meet—such as between a backsplash and a countertop, a floor and a wall, or two adjacent walls—don't grout the space. Instead, fill it with silicone caulk in a color that matches the grout (available at tile stores). You can do it either before or after grouting as long as you allow whichever comes first to cure fully before applying the other. The caulked line will be flexible so that tiles can move without cracking.

WORKING WITH MOSAIC TILES

ALTHOUGH THEY ARE composed of hundreds of tiny tiles arranged in sometimes intricate patterns of colors and shapes, almost every mosaic tile is sold in 12-inch-square sheets of preassembled tiles on a mesh or paper backing or stuck together with rubber spacers. So whether you're installing a retro black-and-white hex tile, translucent green glass, or colorful Moroccan ceramics, installing mosaics isn't much more difficult than installing full 12-by-12-inch tiles.

Prepare the Surface

Because mosaic tiles are often quite small, having a perfectly flat and clean substrate is all the more crucial. Otherwise, a tile may sink into a depression and rest below its neighbors. Use self-leveling compound (see pages 92–93) or cement backerboard on floors (see pages 46–48) and repair and patch walls or refinish them with drywall or fiberboard on walls (see pages 134–139) to create a smooth working surface for the tile.

Work Out the Pattern

Follow the instructions starting on page 49 for working out the pattern, dry-laying the sheets of mosaics along your reference lines.

Cut the Sheets

For some cuts, you can simply remove unneeded tiles from the sheet. Do that by peeling the tiles from their backing (right) and then cutting away the excess backing with a sharp utility knife.

Sometimes, though, you'll need to cut some of the tiles in the prefab grid. Start by laying the sheet on a flat, clean work surface so that all of the tiles are in their proper position. Then cover the sheet with mosaic tape (available at tile shops), which is like a heavy-duty contact paper. This will hold the tiles in position while you mark and then cut them using a wet saw (left).

continued ▶▶

1 **SPREAD THE THINSET.** You'll need to spread an even layer of thinset on the surface, because you can't back-butter sheets of mosaic tiles. If the layer is too thin, the thinset may not reach the tiles past the paper or plastic netting. If it's too thick, the thinset will squeeze up between the thin tiles. Test the adhesion by setting a sample sheet of mosaics, tapping it with a beater board, and removing the sheet to see whether all of the tiles are completely coated with thinset. If they are, you're ready to lay the tiles. If they're not, switch to a trowel with a larger notch and run your test again.

2 **SET THE SHEETS.** If the sheets don't have built-in spacers along their edges to assist with alignment against the next sheet, use plastic spacers (though for some mosaics with uneven edges, like circles or hexagons, you'll have to space the sheets visually). Be extra vigilant about getting the spacing right. If it's off, the 12-by-12-inch outlines of your mosaic sheets may be apparent in the finished job. If you need to set any individual tiles, do so after the neighboring sheets are placed, and back-butter them thoroughly with extra-thick thinset—the consistency of peanut butter, says tile setter Jane Aeon. Set a beater board over two or more sheets of tiles and tap it with a rubber mallet to ensure that the sheets are set

firmly in the mortar (above). Repeat so that every individual tile gets driven gently into the thinset. Use a utility knife to remove any excess mortar that squeezes up between the tiles as you go, as it will be much trickier to remove after it hardens.

3 **GROUT THE JOB.** If the spaces between the tiles are $\frac{1}{8}$ inch or smaller, use unsanded grout. For larger spaces, you'll need sanded grout, which contains a bit of construction-grade sand to strengthen the mix. You'll also want a grout containing latex, which makes it more flexible and less prone to cracking. Check with the tile supplier to find out the best grout to use with your particular tile. Follow the instructions on pages 64–66 for grouting.

SEALING TILES AND GROUT

MANY TYPES OF TILES—especially unglazed ceramics and natural stones—as well as almost all grouts are extremely porous. So unless you seal them, they're going to become stained. And not just in kitchens, in which colorful liquids like red wine and coffee can spill, but in any area where the tiles will get wet. Repeated moisture near a tub, sink, or exterior door will darken unsealed tile, stone, and grout in that area. You can test a tile yourself by simply dripping a little water onto it. If the tile darkens, it's porous and needs sealing. If water beads up on the surface, no sealer is needed. Unless you use a high-tech epoxy grout, the grout should always be sealed too, whether or not you are sealing the tiles.

The toughest sealers are topical sealers, which form a protective film over the tile and grout, but they create a glossy sheen and darken the finish. Other sealers, called impregnators, soak into and fill the pores of the tile and grout, which is slightly less effective but won't alter their appearance as much. There are also sealers that contain adhesives to help prevent fragile tiles such as slate from crumbling. A knowledgeable retailer or installer can tell you whether you need to seal your tile, and which product to use. You also need to wait 3 weeks for the grout to fully cure. And follow the specific application instructions for that material.

Clean the Surface

Before applying any sealer to the floor, wall, or countertop, make sure that the surface is absolutely clean. Remove any excess grout with a damp sponge (right), a piece of cheesecloth, or a gentle pot-scrubbing pad. Vacuum up all debris and clean the tile with a product sold for the purpose.

Sealing Tiles and Grout

If both the grout and the tiles are getting sealed, you can simply mop the sealant onto the surface. A new, clean sponge mop works well for floors (left), while a tiling sponge works well for other surfaces. Be sure to wear rubber gloves. Apply a generous amount of sealant and mop it over the surface. Remove excess material by repeatedly wringing out the sponge or mop. If the sealant soaks into the tile or grout quickly, wait for it to dry and then apply another coat.

Sealing Just the Grout

Porcelain tiles, glazed ceramics, and other types that don't need to be sealed actually make the sealing job a bit more complicated, as you still need to seal the grout while keeping the sealant off the tiles. You can apply the sealant with a small art paintbrush—or use a grout-sealing bottle, which has a wheeled applicator at the end (right) that makes quick work of the job. In either case, keep a supply of clean white terry-cloth towels on hand to quickly wipe away any sealant that gets onto a tile.

tiling
floors

CHOOSING FLOOR TILE

NOT EVERY TILE IS CUT OUT FOR FLOOR DUTY. When used underfoot—especially in areas like kitchens, entryways, mudrooms, and halls, where those feet are often wearing shoes—only the hardest, most scratch-resistant tiles will provide years of service without showing wear.

RIGHT: Smooth river rock provides an excellent nonslip surface for a bathroom floor, and it's comfortable underfoot. See pages 120–121 for installation instructions.

BELOW: A sun-drenched hallway floor provides the perfect canvas for a high-contrast collage of colorfully glazed tiles.

Tile toughness is gauged in many ways. Some manufacturers use the Mohs scale, which ranks tiles from 1 to 10 based on scratch tests using 10 different minerals. Vinyl would get a 1 rating, for example, because it can be damaged by talc. Glazed wall tiles generally rank about a 5 or 6. For a floor tile, you want at least a 7, which means it can be scratched by quartz. You might also come across the Porcelain Enamel Institute's rating system, which categorizes tile into five groups. On one end of the scale are Group 1 tiles, which are suitable for walls only. On the other end are Group 5 tiles, which can be used for commercial applications. Around the house, Group 3 tiles are acceptable for low-traffic floors, such as a master bathroom, where shoes rarely tread. Group 4 and 5 tiles are safe for any household floor. Your tile supplier can help you choose wisely.

If you select an unglazed ceramic tile, you'll need to consider an additional measure of toughness: porosity. A tile that absorbs a lot of water is going to stain, and it's also likely soft enough to scratch. So look for impervious tile, which will absorb barely any moisture and so is the least likely to discolor. Vitreous tile is also highly nonabsorbent and stain resistant, and it's durable enough for household floors. The other types, nonvitreous and semivitreous, are porous, will require regular sealing, and are likely to suffer from staining and scratching when used on floors.

Beyond aesthetics and durability, here are a few other things to consider as you plan your tile floor.

Choosing the correct size. Large tiles—12 by 12, 16 by 16, even 20 by 20 inches—are all the rage these days. They give the floor a clean look and minimize

These large-format porcelain tiles mimic the look of stone but actually resist cracks and stains better than the real thing.

the number of grout lines. And because grout is the part of a tiled floor that's most prone to breaking, staining, or eroding, the less of it you use, the less trouble you're likely to have down the road. Also, big tiles make a room feel bigger, because the floor will be less busy than if it's a grid of small tiles. This is much the same way that light, solid wall colors make a space feel larger than do dark, complex wall-papers. Just be aware that extremely large tiles are more challenging to install. You'll need a wet saw that can accommodate their size, plus an extremely flat subfloor and a helper or two to assist you with the heavy tiles.

Gaining traction. Some tiles get slick when they're wet. For bathrooms, kitchens, and outdoor patios, choose unglazed tiles, tiles with matte finishes, glazes with sand in them, or tiles with textures or embossed detailing on their surfaces. All of these surfaces provide a better grip than shiny glazes. So does using smaller tile, as it means more grout lines to improve traction.

ABOVE LEFT: Slate tiles have a non-slip texture that is ideal in a bathroom.

ABOVE RIGHT: Parquet floor-ing comes in prefabricated mosaic squares that are easy to install with adhesive and require very little sawing.

OPPOSITE: Using tiles allows you to create interesting pat-terns, such as these playful white and yellow stripes of linoleum in a nursery.

BELOW LEFT: **This unusual installation features wood floor planks surrounding 12-inch stone tiles set on a diagonal.**

BELOW RIGHT: **For an easy-to-clean mudroom, nothing beats glazed ceramic tiles.**

OPPOSITE: **Green glazed floor tiles interrupted by diamond-shaped accents coordinate with the decorative strip of wall tiles above.**

Warm them up. Do you dread stepping onto a tile floor with bare feet? Clay and stone are so dense that they tend to stay cool all the time. In a master bathroom or anywhere that you typically walk shoeless, that can be a shock to the sole. There's an easy fix: Lay a heating element under the tile. Once connected to an electrical circuit by an electrician, this system heats the floor. See pages 94–95 for installation instructions.

Hide the mess. Whether on a car, a tailored suit, or a tile, white and light colors are a lot trickier to keep clean than dark colors, as dirt stands out against their pale surfaces. For tiles, multihued glazes and textured finishes help hide grime. Also, glossy surfaces tend to show dust a lot faster than matte ones.

REMOVING OBSTACLES

AS IS TRUE in so many home-improvement projects, the quality of your results depends just as much on good preparation as on the installation itself. To begin, remove any obstacles that are in your way.

Removing Baseboard

Pulling the baseboard off the wall might seem like an extra and avoidable first step, but you'll be very glad you did it. By removing the baseboard and shoe molding now and reinstalling it over the finished tile floor later, you're actually giving yourself a 1- to $1\frac{1}{2}$-inch buffer around the perimeter of the room. If any of your cuts on those outer tiles come up short, awkward, or crooked, baseboards and shoe moldings will hide the flaws. (Each of the moldings ranges from $\frac{1}{2}$ to $\frac{3}{4}$ inch thick.) If you remove the moldings carefully now, you can reinstall the same ones later with no measuring or cutting.

1 **CUT THE PAINT AND CAULK.** Use a sharp utility knife to cut through paint and caulk as necessary, such as along seams where the baseboard meets the wall, the shoe molding, and adjoining baseboards.

2 **PRY OFF THE SHOE MOLDING.** Put on heavy-duty work gloves and safety goggles. Starting at one end of the shoe molding, press a sharp flat bar between it and the baseboard and pry the molding loose. Place a wood shim behind the bar so it doesn't dent the baseboard. Then move a couple of feet down the molding and repeat until the entire shoe molding is loose enough that you can pull it off the wall. Use a pencil to note the original location of each piece on its back side so you'll know which pieces go where when you're ready to reinstall them.

3 **PRY OFF THE BASEBOARD.** Work the bar behind the baseboard and pry the board away from the wall. Keep moving the bar to different locations and wiggling the board loose. Use a shim or taping knife to protect the wall from damage, and don't put a lot of pressure on the bar unless you feel the telltale stiffness of a wall stud behind it. Move down the baseboard and repeat until it comes free. Then note the location of each piece on its back side as you did with the shoe molding.

4 **REMOVE THE NAILS.** Most if not all of the nails will come away with the moldings. One at a time, lay the pieces of molding nails-up on a work surface, then use a pair of carpenter's nippers to pry out the nails from the back. They're finish nails, so they'll come right out. Their tiny heads have been covered with putty and paint on the front of the boards, which will be unaffected by the removal process. Set the molding aside in a safe place until the tiling is done. Check the wall for any nails that stayed put and remove them with a claw hammer or the nipper, using a shim to prevent the tool from marring the wall.

Removing Thresholds

Thresholds are those little transitions that cover the seams between dissimilar flooring materials. They can be made of stone, wood, or metal, and they're usually located across doorways. You will need to remove them to get up any old flooring, and doing so will also give you a good entry point for starting the removal process. It's not worth trying to reuse thresholds later, as it's hard to remove them without breaking them and you'll likely need a different threshold to accommodate the height of your new floor anyway. To take out a marble threshold, insert a demolition bar between it and the tile and pry it upward (as shown below). It will crack down the middle, allowing you to pull it out from under the doorstops. For a wooden threshold, cut across it with a handsaw or demolition saw and it will quickly come free with help from the bar.

Heat Registers

If you have heating or air-conditioning vents in the floor, you can simply remove them until the job is done and then place them over the top of the new tile. No adjustments are necessary. Registers are usually held in place by nothing more than gravity. You can also take the opportunity to replace them with something clean and new.

Removing a Toilet

The toilet has to come out before you remove old flooring or install new tile in a bathroom. Don't worry, you can pull it out yourself, and putting it back is a fairly simple procedure (see page 124).

1 **SHUT OFF THE WATER.** Turn the shutoff valve clockwise to stop the flow of water to the toilet. Then flush the toilet, holding the lever down to drain the tank and bowl. Make sure the tank doesn't start refilling because of a faulty shutoff valve. If you hear water flowing into the tank, try tightening the valve a bit more, and if that doesn't work, call a plumber. Once you get the valve shut, use an adjustable wrench to remove the water line from the shutoff valve, catching as much of the spillage as possible in a bucket and mopping up the rest with old towels. Sop up the remaining water in the bottom of the toilet bowl with a sponge until it's all gone.

2 **REMOVE THE TOILET.** Take off the caps on the two Johnny bolts holding the toilet to the floor and then use a ratchet set or an adjustable wrench to back off the bolts. If necessary, spray WD-40 on the bolts and let the solution stand for a couple of minutes to help loosen them up. If the bolts are still unmovable, cut them with a hacksaw, being careful not to nick the porcelain. If you're sure you got all the water out of the tank and bowl in step 1, you're ready to lift the toilet off the bolts. Have a rag handy in case any remaining water drips out. Carefully carry the toilet out of the way and set it on a tarp.

TRICKS OF THE TRADE

Take Off Doors

To get doors out of your way for the project, insert a nail into the bottom of each hinge and tap it with a hammer to release the pins. If there are no holes where you can insert a nail, try placing the blade of a flathead screwdriver under the top of each hinge pin and, while holding the screwdriver at about a 45-degree angle to the hinge, tap the base of the screwdriver with a hammer until the hinge pin comes out. As a last resort, remove the screws holding the hinges in the doorjamb.

3 **PLUG THE DRAIN.** Use a putty knife to remove the old wax ring from the drain in the floor. Then stuff the opening with a rag to prevent sewer fumes from escaping into the room. Also, remove the Johnny bolts from the toilet flange and discard them. As you prepare the subfloor, you'll need to make sure that the flange will not sit above the level of the finished tile, so that the toilet can rest properly on the floor.

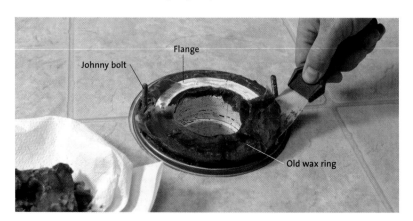

Flange

Johnny bolt

Old wax ring

Removing a Vanity

If you're tiling over existing flooring, there's no need to remove the vanity. Simply tile up against it. Cut your tiles extra carefully where they will meet it, as there will be no baseboard molding to hide problems. If you're removing old tile or resilient flooring, and certainly if you're removing old subflooring, you'll need to pull the vanity first.

1 **DISCONNECT THE PLUMBING.** Turn the hot and cold shutoff valves all the way clockwise and then try turning on the faucet to ensure that neither the hot nor cold shutoff is allowing water through. (If either valve is leaking, and tightening it a bit more doesn't solve the problem, you may need a plumber to install new valves before you move forward.) Then, with a bucket placed underneath to catch water escaping from the pipes, and with old towels handy for mopping up spills, use an adjustable wrench to disconnect the water lines from the valves. Use your hands to unscrew the P-trap from the sink. You don't need to remove the countertop or sink from the vanity.

2 **REMOVE THE VANITY.** Most vanities are screwed into the wall, and some are also screwed to the floor. Look inside the cabinet and use a cordless drill-driver to remove any screws. Then carefully lift the vanity, working it around the plumbing lines. Stuff a rag into the end of the drain line coming out of the wall to block sewer gases.

Dealing with Cabinets and Islands

Removing a vanity is one thing, but removing a bank of kitchen cabinets or an island is something else entirely. "Unless you're gutting the kitchen anyway, removing the cabinets just isn't feasible," says tile setter George Taterosian. Instead, you'll need to work around them. Generally, the tiles don't go under the cabinets anyway, but the subfloor does, and so if you're replacing the subfloor, the trickiest part of the job will be cutting out the old subfloor along the cabinet.

First remove the kick plate from the front of the cabinets by prying it off with a sharp flat bar. For any locations where there is no kick plate, such as along the side and back panels of cabinets, peninsulas, and islands, protect the finished woodwork with masking tape or by taping cardboard to them. Then use a demolition saw to cut through the subfloor along the cabinets, being extremely careful not to mar their surfaces. Alternatively, if the old flooring is sound, consider simply tiling over the existing subfloor—or even the existing finished floor.

REMOVING OLD TILE

IF AN OLD TILE FLOOR IS SOUND, you can tile right over it. But this will likely create a finished floor that's much higher than its neighbors. Also, the lower course of old wall tile, if there is any, will be reduced in appearance, so the makeshift solution will be obvious to anyone who looks closely. What's more, for durability, it's always best to remove the old materials so you can address unseen issues, such as rotted boards around a bathtub, and so a future problem that may arise with the aging tile underneath won't damage your new tile floor.

Tape plastic over the doorways to keep tile dust from spreading throughout the house. Wearing heavy work gloves, safety goggles, and a respirator, start at the tile edge you exposed by removing the threshold (see page 81). Work a demolition bar under the edge of the tile and begin prying it up from the subfloor (shown at left). You may have to hit the end of the demolition bar with a hammer (or a sledgehammer) to wedge it between the old tile and the subfloor. How easily it comes up will determine your next steps.

Removing Tile in Thinset

If the tile pops off the subfloor relatively easily, it was installed with thinset over plywood or backerboard, the same basic process you'll be using soon. That makes it pretty easy to pop the tiles off. Unfortunately, the old thinset stuck on the subfloor is nearly impossible to remove, so you'll also need to take out and replace the old backerboard or plywood underlayment to give yourself a flat and smooth surface to tile over later. You could leave the tiles in place and remove everything at once, but the added weight of thick ceramic or stone tiles can make the subfloor pieces too heavy to remove.

While wearing safety goggles, set the blade depth on a circular saw to the exact depth of the subflooring, cut it into roughly 1-foot-wide strips, then pry each strip up using a demolition bar. If it's plywood (shown at right), use an old wood-cutting blade. If it's backerboard, use a masonry-cutting blade.

Removing Other Types of Flooring

Carpeting and laminate flooring must be removed before you tile. Technically, you can tile over a single layer of sound vinyl or linoleum, but it's far better to remove the old flooring to ensure a good base for your new tile. Plus it gives you a chance to check and, if necessary, upgrade the subfloor to provide better tile adhesion. For any of these flooring types, wear heavy-duty gloves, safety goggles, and a respirator during demolition.

CARPETING. Grab the carpet in one corner and pull up on it. If it doesn't come up easily, try grabbing and pulling it with pliers. Continue pulling, rolling up the carpet as you remove it. Then, while wearing heavy-duty work gloves and safety goggles, use a flat bar and a hammer to remove the strips from the perimeter of the room.

VINYL AND LINOLEUM. Some of these materials may contain unhealthful materials, possibly including asbestos, so it's a good idea to have the old flooring tested before ripping it up. If it does contain asbestos, you might choose to tile over it, hire an abatement contractor to remove it, or remove it yourself following exacting safety procedures. These include wetting the floor to reduce the release of dust, sealing the area off from the rest of the house with plastic, wearing a respirator, and cleaning up the job site thoroughly with a high-filtration vacuum when you are done. (Some states regulate asbestos removal. Ask your local health department about laws and safety procedures.) If the flooring doesn't contain asbestos, remove it with the subfloor by slicing both surfaces into roughly 1-foot-wide strips with a circular saw set to the depth of the flooring and subfloor combined. Then pry the strips off the joists (see opposite page). If there are two layers of subflooring and you can't separate them, it may be easier to pull them both up at once and start from scratch.

LAMINATE. Laminate flooring (such as Pergo) has interlocking joints that easily pull apart in one direction but not in the other. Start at the side of the floor where the planks were ripped down to fit. These boards were the last ones to go down and should be the first to come up. Just lift up on the edge that was covered by the baseboard, and the whole row will come up. Separate the planks as needed and then lift up on the exposed edge of the next row. Continue across the room in this manner.

Removing Mud Jobs

If the tile won't budge as you pry at it, you're dealing with a mud job—a thick layer of concrete topped with tiles, the standard installation method before World War II. Mud jobs are a bear to remove. The trick is to use a long, heavy demolition bar and work it not under the tile but under the entire mud job. Pry it away from the subfloor below, and it'll break up in heavy chunks. You'll see metal lath buried in the mud job. If it was installed with staples, it will pull out easily, but if it was nailed to the subfloor, you may need to pry out the nails individually.

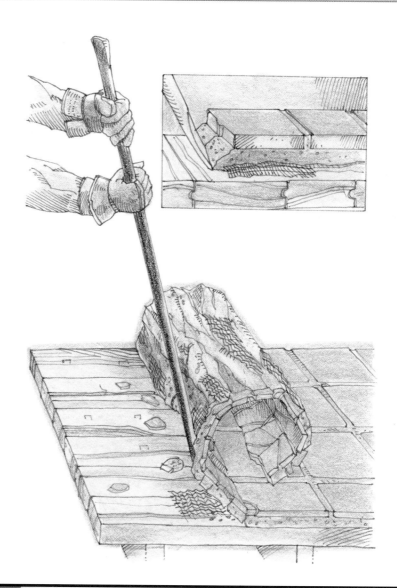

Concrete Subfloors

If your old tiles were installed with thinset over a concrete subfloor, once you get them removed, you'll need to scrape the thinset off the concrete using a metal floor scraper and a lot of elbow grease. You can then tile right over a concrete subfloor, as long as it's not severely cracked. If it's slanted or uneven, use self-leveling compound to prepare it for tile (see pages 92–93). If you're concerned about the subfloor's condition, see pages 202–203, where repairs to concrete slabs are discussed.

BEEFING UP THE STRUCTURE

IF THE FLOOR SAGS IN THE MIDDLE or bounces when you walk on it, you may need to strengthen it before tiling, because adding the weight of backerboard, thinset, and tile could worsen the problem.

1 **MEASURE THE JOISTS.** You will need to obtain access to the joists, either by removing the subfloor or by getting to them from an unfinished ceiling below. Then measure them. They should be at least 2 × 8s (which are actually 1 1/2 by 7 1/4) and spread no farther apart than 16 inches on center. If they don't meet those requirements, call a contractor or engineer to check the problem and prescribe a solution, which might include adding joists, beams, or support posts.

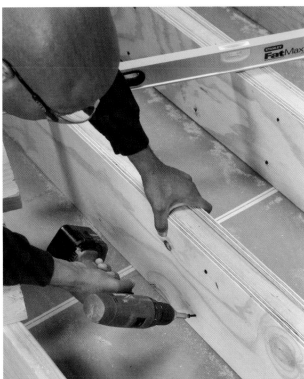

2 **STRENGTHEN WEAK JOISTS.** If the joists are big enough, aren't rotted or otherwise damaged but are still bouncy or bowed, you can strengthen them by cutting strips of 3/4-inch plywood to match their width (for example, 9 1/4 inches for most so-called 2 × 10s, and 7 1/4 for 2 × 8s) and fastening the strips to each side of each joist using construction adhesive and 2-inch drywall screws. If you're working from above, use the largest level that fits in the space as a guide to ensure that the plywood's top edges create a flat, level starting point for your subfloor.

TRICKS OF THE TRADE

Tiling over Hardwood

Hardwood floors make lousy bases for tile because there's too much movement among the boards and because the glossy polyurethane finish doesn't offer much for the thinset to grab onto. But you don't necessarily need to remove the hardwood, says tile setter John Bridge. You can just cover over it with 1/4-inch plywood or backerboard.

PREPARING THE SUBFLOOR

DEPENDING ON WHAT YOU FIND under the old flooring, you'll likely need to bulk it up with an additional layer of subflooring.

• IF YOU'RE USING BACKERBOARD, the total thickness of the subfloor should be at least $1\frac{1}{4}$ inches, so if there's $\frac{3}{4}$-inch plywood down already, add $\frac{1}{2}$-inch backerboard. If there's $\frac{1}{2}$-inch plywood on the floor, add another layer of $\frac{1}{2}$-inch plywood and then a layer of $\frac{1}{4}$-inch backerboard.

• IF YOU'RE NOT USING BACKERBOARD, $1\frac{1}{4}$ inches of total material is still acceptable, but $1\frac{1}{2}$ inches would be better. So if there's $\frac{3}{4}$-inch plywood existing, add $\frac{1}{2}$- or $\frac{3}{4}$-inch on top of it. If there's $\frac{1}{2}$-inch plywood, add at least a $\frac{3}{4}$-inch sheet, or you could add two layers of $\frac{1}{2}$-inch.

Plywood or Backerboard?

Some pros use backerboard under every floor because they feel that it provides the closest approximation to the strength and waterproofing of an old-fashioned mud job (a slab of concrete a couple of inches thick). But there are some instances in which you can tile directly over plywood, as long as you have a $1\frac{1}{4}$- to $1\frac{1}{2}$-inch-thick subfloor. Plywood is far easier to cut and install than backerboard, it comes in bigger sheets (which means fewer joints in the subfloor), and it's actually more rigid than backerboard, leading to a stiffer base for your tile. It's safe to tile directly over plywood only in rooms where there is no risk of moisture damage. If you're tiling a bathroom, laundry room, or basement floor with ceramic, porcelain, or stone tiles, you will need to use backerboard over the plywood. A good tile

---

TRICKS OF THE TRADE

How Thick Is That Old Subfloor?

Most old plywood subflooring is only $\frac{1}{2}$ inch thick. Most strip-wood subflooring is $\frac{3}{4}$ inch. But how can you be sure without ripping up a board? You may be able to measure the thickness at a penetra-

tion, such as where a heating duct or plumbing pipe passes through the material, says tile setter John Bridge. If you can't fit a tape measure into the hole, unwind a paperclip so that it's relatively straight, with a small hook at the end. Slide it into an opening, hook it under the bottom of the subfloor, and mark it at the top surface with a felt pen. Then remove the clip and measure from the hook to the mark. "If there's no place to insert the clip, you can drill a hole," Bridge says.

---

seller can advise you about which choice is best, given your subfloor and tile, and whether there are any local codes or standard practices on the matter.

Installing a plywood subfloor is described below. For instructions on how to install backerboard, see pages 46–48.

Backerboard

Plywood

Adding Plywood

A plywood subfloor should be at least $1\frac{1}{4}$ inches thick, though $1\frac{1}{2}$ inches is better. That means installing two layers over the joists (either both $\frac{3}{4}$ inch thick or one $\frac{3}{4}$ and one $\frac{1}{2}$ inch) or, if there's some subflooring there already, adding enough plywood to reach the desired thickness (see opposite page). Use CDX plywood, which has a rough, unfinished texture that's an ideal surface for thinset to bond with.

1 **DRY-LAY THE FIRST SHEET.** Use shims to create a $\frac{1}{4}$-inch gap around the perimeter of the floor. Starting in a corner, lay the first sheet of plywood so that its long edges cross the joists. If the end of the board winds up falling right down the middle of a joist, you don't need to cut it. Otherwise, you'll need to cut it back to the center of the nearest joist. If there's already a first layer of plywood subflooring, you'll also need to make sure that your new joints don't fall directly over the joints in the previous layer. Offset the top-layer joints from those in the lower layer by 1 to 4 feet (the farther, the better). Mark the location of your cut on the surface of the board and circle that mark, then mark the locations of all the underlying joists.

2 **CUT THE SHEETS.** Using a T-square lined up with your marks, draw lines across the plywood. Then set the depth on a circular-saw blade to just a hair beyond the thickness of the plywood. Set the plywood on two sawhorses, or four 8-foot 2 × 4s spread evenly under it, and cut the sheet at the line where the marks were circled. Make sure the blade rides along the side of the line that will be the scrap piece. Repeat this process, adding boards to the floor one at a time. Where you need to make holes for plumbing pipes, heating vents, or other penetrations, transfer the locations to the board using a tape measure and then use a hole saw loaded into a drill, or a jigsaw, to cut them out.

3 **FASTEN DOWN THE BOARDS.** Once all of the boards are dry-laid to form a nice, tight surface, pick the first one up, apply construction adhesive to the plywood or joists below, lay the sheet back down, and fasten it with screws. Along the joists, use fasteners that are long enough to penetrate the plywood, plus any existing subflooring, and extend $\frac{3}{4}$ inch into the joists. Space them every 6 inches or so along every joist. If there's another layer of subflooring underneath the new plywood, use screws the length of the total thickness of the subfloor to fasten the plywood every 6 inches between joists.

Setting the Floor Height

In addition to making sure that your subfloor is thick enough to support the new tile, you need to plan out the overall height of your floor at this point. There are a few issues to consider.

Subfloor strength. You should have $1\frac{1}{4}$ or $1\frac{1}{2}$ inches of subflooring to support the tile (not including self-leveling compound, if you use it, because it does not add any strength to the floor).

Next-floor height. You'll want to keep the finished tile floor as close to flush with neighboring floors as possible, but you can accommodate up to a $\frac{3}{4}$-inch step with a reducing threshold. Keep in mind that your thinset and tile will add $\frac{3}{8}$ to $\frac{1}{2}$ inch of height over the subfloor. That's about $\frac{1}{8}$ inch of thinset, plus $\frac{1}{4}$ inch for small-format tiles to $\frac{3}{8}$ inch for large-format tiles, which tend to be proportionally thicker the larger they are. If you're using a heat mat, figure another $\frac{3}{8}$ to $\frac{1}{2}$ inch. Self-leveling compound, if you need it (see pages 92–93), will add even more thickness.

Consider the toilet flange. This is a big issue that many beginners overlook. The height of the toilet flange will determine the height of the toilet. A plumber can change the flange to whatever height you need, but if you want to avoid that step, you'll need to plan your subfloor height to accommodate it. The flange can sit directly on one of the subfloor layers, or it can match the height of the finished tile, but it cannot stand higher than the tile. Otherwise, your toilet will have to be shimmed up above the floor height. That means it would need a grout line around its base, and it means that the toilet would eventually start to rock, and quite possibly leak, around the flange.

The tile floor in this master bathroom is flush with the wood floor in the bedroom, so no threshold was needed— and no toes are ever stubbed.

Trimming Up the Casing

Because it's nearly impossible to cut tile to wrap neatly around the profile of door casings (the moldings around doorways) and because there's no baseboard in front of the casing to cover any gaps, you need to trim the casing up to allow the tile to go underneath it. Pros have a special power tool that makes easy work of the job, but it's pretty simple to do with a handsaw as well. Tile setter George Taterosian recommends cutting away the door casing in two steps.

First, when the old floor is removed, lay a scrap piece of whatever subflooring material you are adding on the floor next to the casing. Then use an undercut saw, which has an offset handle to allow you to cut flush against the floor, to trim up the casing so you'll be able to slide the plywood and/or backerboard underneath it. Repeat this process after the subfloor and any self-leveling compound have been installed. This time, rest the undercut saw on a tile plus a $\frac{1}{8}$-inch piece of cardboard (to account for the thinset).

Dealing with Radiators

BASEBOARD RADIATORS. Ideally, you can tile underneath baseboard radiators. For electric radiators, an electrician can remove them before you begin and then reinstall them over the finished floor. For hot-water radiators, you could bring in a heating contractor, but you may not have to. To investigate the possibility, pull up on the copper pipe running inside the aluminum cover and see if you can easily lift it $\frac{1}{2}$ inch or so. If you can, then you can probably remove the entire baseboard cover and reinstall it on top of the new tile. If you can't, you'll need to either hire a heating contractor or tile around the baseboard cover. In either case, start by removing all of the end caps and faceplates from the baseboard radiator. If the pipe has some give to it, unscrew the baseboard from the wall and set it aside so you can reattach it over the finished job later. If the plumbing is too tight to lift $\frac{1}{2}$ inch, just bring the tile as far under it as you can and then reinstall the faceplate and the end caps after the job is done. You may need to cut the end caps shorter using a pair of tin snips.

CAST-IRON RADIATORS. Temporarily removing big old-fashioned radiators for a tiling job makes the work easier and the finished result neater. But it generally requires bringing in a plumber to disconnect the radiators and then to reconnect them later (and you may have to live without heat for the duration of the job). Alternatively, you can tile around them—making meticulous cuts around the pipe penetrations and the radiator feet. Then think about adding a radiator cover to hide the evidence.

Leveling the Floor

Before you start tiling, check to see whether the subfloor is level. You can tile over a slightly canted floor, but if it has numerous hills and valleys or is steeply sloped, you won't be able to make up for it with thinset alone. If you're installing resilient tile, it's particularly important that the subfloor be smooth and level. Luckily, there are self-leveling compounds that settle into a flat and level surface before hardening. Be sure to buy self-leveling material instead of a patching compound, which will require extensive troweling and is much harder for a do-it-yourselfer to work with. And be aware that self-leveling compound doesn't count toward the overall $1^1/_4$ to $1^1/_2$ inches of subfloor you will need under the tile. "It doesn't add any strength to the floor," says tile setter George Taterosian. "But it does add more weight, so it actually increases the importance of having a strong structure underneath."

1 **GAUGE THE SLOPE.** Place a level on the floor. If it shows that the floor isn't level, lift the low end of the level until its bubble is centered. Then measure the space between the level and the floor. For a 2-foot level, a gap of more than $1/_4$ inch needs leveling; for a 4-foot level, the distance is $1/_2$ inch; and for an 8-foot level, it's anything more than 1 inch. Repeat this process all around the floor and with the level going in different directions. Wherever the slope is too steep, you'll need to apply self-leveling compound to the top of the subflooring.

2 **SEAL THE EXITS AND GAPS.** Cut 2 × 4s to the width of doorways and other places where the floor you're tiling opens onto other floors. Tack the 2 × 4s in place with drywall screws driven into the floor and/or doorjamb. Then, with masking tape, duct tape, or blue painter's tape, cover the seam where each 2 × 4 meets the subfloor. Use additional tape to seal any gaps in the subfloor. Otherwise, the compound will pour through the holes.

3 **PRIME THE FLOOR.** Most self-leveling compounds require a latex primer on the subfloor to ensure good adhesion. Following the package instructions, apply it using a roller and brush and allow it to dry for a couple of hours before you mix the compound.

4 **POUR THE COMPOUND.** Follow the package instructions for how much water to add to the bag of self-leveling compound. Combine the ingredients in a 5-gallon bucket using a mixing paddle loaded into a drill with a $1/2$-inch shank. Then gently pour some compound onto the low spot on the floor. "Don't take the self-leveling name too literally," says tile setter George Taterosian. "Use a flat trowel to push and pull it around the floor." Keep adding more compound as you back out of the room, and then leave it alone. The compound will level out and harden into a flat plane and be ready for tile in about 12 hours. Don't pour a thicker layer than the instructions recommend (usually 1 inch is the maximum). If you need a thicker pour, do a second one the next day.

Adding Heat to the Floor

IMAGINE STEPPING OUT OF THE SHOWER or coming down into the kitchen for that first coffee of the day and feeling your bare feet touch warm tile. You can enjoy that luxury if you install an electric heat mat under the finished floor. Electric heat mats are safe to use under ceramic floor tiles and most stone tiles. Check with your tile supplier or the mat manufacturer to make sure the products you're using are compatible.

Ordering the Mat

If your room is a square or rectangle of a standard size, you may be able to use stock mats, such as a 4-by-5-foot rectangle. (It doesn't have to fill the entire floor, since the heat reaches about a foot beyond its edges and since people seldom walk near the walls anyway.) Otherwise, you'll have to draw a scale plan of the floor and have a mat custom-made to fit it. "Leave a 4-inch buffer zone around the perimeter of the floor as a fudge factor," suggests tile setter George Taterosian, "and keep it 12 inches from the toilet flange so it won't melt the wax ring that seals the drain pipe to the toilet."

There are also products that consist of a wire that you weave across the floor yourself, so you can fit it to any floor. Installation is a lot more involved, however, and follows different steps than described here.

TRICKS OF THE TRADE

Heat-Mat Alarm

"The heat mat is one continuous strand of wire, and if it gets dinged while you're installing it, the system won't run at all," says tile setter George Taterosian. So manufacturers sell alarms that will warn you of trouble before you lay a tile floor over damaged heat mats. Powered by a battery, the alarm clips to a mat's lead wires and sounds if the path of the current is broken. "Hook up the alarm first and leave it hooked up for the entire installation, so that if it tings, you'll know the problem occurred wherever you're currently working, or stepping, rather than having to track down where the problem is."

---

1 **DRY-LAY THE MAT.** Whatever heat mat you select, it needs to be installed over the top layer of sub-flooring, whether it's plywood, backer-board, self-leveling compound, or a concrete slab. Lay it out on the floor, positioning it exactly where you want it. Make sure the lead wires for the electrical connections are near the exit so you can reach them after laying the mat.

2 **MORTAR IT IN.** Carefully fold the mat back on itself, exposing the half of the floor farther from the door. Mix up a batch of thinset and trowel it onto the exposed portion of the floor using a ¼-inch V-notch trowel. Then, being very careful not to trample roughly on the mat, fold it back down on the thinset. Use the grout float to press the mat into the thinset until the thinset oozes slightly into the mat's grid of wires. Repeat the process for the other side of the mat.

3 **PREPARE THE ELECTRICAL CONNECTIONS.** You'll need an electrician to connect the mat to the house's wiring and to set up the wall thermostat, but for now just make sure to position the lead wires appropriately. If the walls are unfinished, you can simply coil the wires in a stud bay. If the walls are finished, you may need to puncture one hole to insert the wires into the wall, plus another hole where the thermostat will be, so you can snake the wires up and out. You'll also need to position the heat sensor that communicates with the thermostat. Follow the manufacturer's instructions for all the wiring procedures, as they vary from product to product.

4 **TOP OFF THE MAT.** Once the thinset has cured overnight, you could trowel on another layer of thinset, but there's an easier way, says tile setter George Taterosian. Mix up a batch of self-leveling compound and, being very careful while walking on the surface of the mat, start in the far corner of the room and pour the mix over the top of it. Use a grout float to help push it over the mat. Pour on only enough to cover the top of the mat, giving you a flat surface to tile on—and to mark your tile reference lines on.

LAYING A STONE TILE FLOOR

ONCE YOUR SUBFLOOR IS PREPARED (see pages 80–93) and your electric heat mat, if you're using one, is installed (see pages 94–95), you're ready to lay out the floor tiles and start tiling. Before starting this project, see pages 49–55 and 60–63 for detailed instructions on laying out a pattern, working with thinset, and cutting tiles. For instructions on laying a ceramic tile floor, see pages 56–59.

TRICKS OF THE TRADE

Sealing Stone

Be sure stone tiles are factory sealed before setting them. If they aren't, you'll first need to apply sealant recommended for the type of stone you are using. Otherwise, the mortar may stain the stone. Also, to ensure good adhesion, make sure to dust stone tiles thoroughly before setting them.

1 **PREPARE FOR THE THRESHOLD.** If you'll be installing a stone threshold, you'll lay it at the end of the tiling process, but make sure it fits before you mix the thinset. Choose a threshold that's the right length for the doorway. It will also need to sit between the outer edge of the door when it's closed and the inner edge of the jamb, or you may need a wider one to cover exposed subflooring if the previous threshold was larger. Then use an offset saw to trim up the doorstops so the threshold can slide underneath and sit flush against the jamb (see page 91). For a wooden threshold, just tile up to the inside edge of the closed door. Applied later, the threshold will sit directly under the door.

2 **MIX AND SPREAD THE THINSET.** See pages 54–55 for detailed instructions on mixing and using thinset. For this project, we're using white thinset (see tip on opposite page). Use a trowel to move a glob of thinset onto the grid within the reference lines that are in a corner opposite the exit you'll be using. If you're using white thinset, you can bring the thinset past your reference lines. If you're using darker thinset, make sure you don't cover the reference lines. Then hold a notched trowel of the size recommended by your tile setter at a 45-degree angle, allowing its teeth to scrape the subfloor gently and combing over the mortar with long, sweeping strokes wherever possible and keeping the trowel angle consistent.

3 **BACK-BUTTER THE TILES.** You're ready to start laying tiles. As you place each one, use a margin trowel to apply a thin layer of thinset to its back. This will ensure good adhesion between thinset and tile and level out low spots in the subfloor. It's also more forgiving in case the thinset was mixed too dry or has begun to cure.

TRICKS OF THE TRADE

Use White Thinset

Tile setter George Taterosian uses white thinset for all of his jobs because he can trowel it over his reference lines and still see them. "That way I don't have to try and trowel right up to the line or trowel next to already laid tiles, which always leads to getting thinset on the tiles," he says.

4 **SET THE TILES WITH SPACERS.** Set each tile fairly precisely, so you don't have to slide it more than an inch or so. Align the first tile with two guidelines, then set additional tiles against it, inserting spacers at every corner.

5 **TAP WITH A BEATER BOARD.** After you've set a few tiles, place a beater board over them and tap it with a rubber mallet. This helps ensure that the tiles' backs are set firmly in the mortar and that their top surfaces are flush with those of their neighbors. We're using marble, but if you are using limestone or other fragile tiles, don't beat them.

continued ▶▶

6 **FINE-TUNE AS YOU GO.** To adjust a tile slightly, place your hand on top, fingers splayed out. Press gently as you slide the tile. With luck, you can make a small adjustment, but if you feel resistance followed by a sudden movement, the mortar has probably begun to set. In this case, pick up the tile and attempt to recomb the mortar below. If the mortar has started to harden, scrape the tile and the surface below it clean of mortar and start over with fresh thinset. Place a straightedge over the tiles to test whether they form a flat plane. If a tile is too high, try pressing down on all four corners. If a tile is too low, remove it, apply additional mortar, and reset it.

7 **REMOVE EXCESS THINSET.** Clean out any excess thinset that squeezes up between the tiles as you go. It is much trickier to remove if it hardens—especially on a floor, since you can't walk on the tiles for 12 hours. A carpenter's pencil works well for removing thinset between tiles, as do unused spacers. If necessary, you can use a flathead screwdriver to scrape out excess thinset the next day.

8 **SET THE THRESHOLD.** When setting the last row of tiles, spread the thinset into the doorway, stopping along the outer edge of the doorstop. Then set the threshold before placing the last row of tiles. If tile cuts are needed, the threshold will dictate them. Also, you can tweak the position of the tiles or threshold ever so slightly as needed to align them.

Grouting. Once the thinset has hardened, you're ready to finish the job with grout. See pages 64–66 for detailed information on grouting.

INSTALLING BORDERS, BRICK-LAYS, AND DIAGONALS

DON'T FEEL LIMITED to a basic grid of square tiles. Here's how to lay some other popular patterns.

Checkerboard. Whether you're alternating two colors or two textures of tile, as long as they're equal squares, the installation is no different from what's described in the previous projects. You simply need to remember to alternate the tiles. It may help to lay out each grid of tiles near where they're being installed before applying the thinset, so you can just grab the next tile without having to remind yourself each time to alternate.

Staggered brick pattern. Extremely popular for subway tile backsplashes and wainscots, this is also often used for rectangular floor tiles (as shown below). In fact, it's actually easier to lay than a rigid grid of squares, because the offset lines help to hide unevenness in the surfaces and any installation mistakes. To arrange a staggered pattern, lay the tiles row by row. Lay the first row on the reference grid and then, when starting the next row, cut the first tile in half and proceed down the row. Align the third row back on the grid lines and proceed across the floor in this manner.

Diagonal. Start by making your two reference lines as described on pages 49–50. Then measure 3 feet from the center point along each line and make a mark. Next, measure the distance between each of those marks and make a new mark at the midpoints between them. Using those new marks, snap two new diagonal chalk lines and base your plans on them, as outlined on page 50.

Border. If you're installing a border around the perimeter of the room (as shown at left), start by measuring the midpoint of each of the four walls, then snap chalk lines between the opposing marks. Use a framing square to check them for square. Starting with a tile or sheet of mosaic tiles that's centered over the midpoint, dry-lay the entire floor. If the border will be inset off the wall, you'll need to decide whether to cut the standard tile that's outside the border or the one that's inside the border, purely a matter of choice.

TILING A SHOWER FLOOR

BECAUSE OF THE INTENSE FLOOD OF WATER it faces daily, a shower pan is the most challenging of all tile floors to install. Any mistakes, and water will leak through into the structure below. This is probably not something to tackle as a first tiling job, but if you're well practiced with mortar, tiles, and grout, here's how to do it.

1 **FRAME THE SHOWER.** The shower framing consists of a subfloor and framed walls. The subfloor should include at least 1½ inches of plywood, and the walls should be framed with 2 × 4s or 2 × 6s that are 16 inches on center. Cut 2 × 10s to the right length and use nails or screws to install them on edge at the bottom of the bays between each stud. This will provide support for the shower pan later. Build a sill at the entrance to the shower by installing three 2 × 4s across the opening. Remove the loose upper portion of the drain assembly and stuff a rag into the opening to prevent debris from falling down the pipe. Next, lay 15-pound tar paper over the floor, stapling it down and trimming it around the drain. Then use tin snips to cut wire mesh to fit over the floor, stapling it in place, again with a cutout for the drain.

2 **MARK OUT THE FIRST MORTAR BED.** Next you need to lay a thick layer of mortar, and it has to be pitched inward to the center so that the water will run toward the drain. The slope should be ¼ inch per foot, but a little steeper is fine. Measure the distance from the drain to the wall that's farthest from it (or to any wall if it's centered in a square shower base) and figure out how high the mortar should be at that wall. (For example, for a wall that's 4 feet from the drain, you'd want the mortar at the wall to be 1 inch higher than the top of the drain.) Make a mark at that spot and then use a 2-foot level (or larger if it will fit) to transfer the marks into a level line all the way around the shower.

3 **MUD THE FLOOR.** Use a mixing paddle loaded into a $1/2$-inch-shank drill to make a batch of thick-bed mortar mix in a 5-gallon bucket, following the instructions on the bag. It should be a very dry mix, with just enough water to darken the powder. Dump some mortar onto the shower floor, beat it with a scrap of 2 × 4 or a grout float to press it against the subfloor, and then use a flat trowel to spread it over the pan and to slope it from the line around the edge of the walls down to the height of the drain assembly. To get the pitch right, without any dips where water could collect, cut a 2 × 4 to fit between the drain and the wall. Scrape the board over the mortar, keeping one end at the level of the drain and the other at the mark on the wall.

4 **LAY THE VINYL.** Once the mortar has cured overnight, use a utility knife to cut a sheet of vinyl shower-base membrane to cover the floor and extend 6 inches up each wall. Press the membrane down into the corners where the floor meets the wall, and then staple it to the 2 × 10 blocking. Staple only the upper 1 inch of the membrane. At the corners, fold the excess membrane into a tight fit and glue the pieces together using membrane solvent sold for the purpose.

continued ▶▶

TRICKS OF THE TRADE

Pitch Sticks

To make the mud job easier, purchase a quick-pitch kit from a tile supplier or an online retailer. The kit consists of a ring that sits over the drain, plus six sticks that you align like spokes from the center. They fit standard shower sizes and are pitched perfectly for the mud job. You simply pour the mortar over them and use a 2 × 4 to scrape it flush against their surfaces. The mud pushes into holes in the ring and the sticks, which become permanent parts of the mud job.

5 **ATTACH THE DRAIN.** Use your fingers to locate the four nuts holding the drain in place. Slice around each one with a utility knife to expose them, and then use a socket or adjustable wrench to unscrew them. Attach the upper drain plate, rotate it to lock it, and then replace the bolts, tightening them with the wrench. Cut the vinyl membrane inside the drain using a long-handled knife or a utility knife.

6 **PREPARE THE WALLS.** Insulate the shower walls with fiberglass batts and coat the interior surfaces of the walls with 4-mil plastic sheeting. Lap it over the vinyl membrane by 4 inches and tack it in place with a few staples along each stud. Make sure to tack the bottom edge through only the upper 1 inch of vinyl—no lower. Then install backerboard over the walls, using shims to create a ½-inch gap under the backerboard and taking care not to insert any screws lower than the top 1 inch of vinyl membrane. See pages 46–48 for instructions on installing backerboard.

7 **ADD THE STRAINER.** Cover the strainer with masking tape, trimming the tape around the upper circumference with a utility knife. This will protect its surface during the project. Then wrap the strainer's threads with plumber's tape and screw it into the drain assembly.

8 **MARK THE WALL FOR THE SECOND MUD BED.** Now you need to lay a second layer of mortar over the vinyl, and, again, it has to be pitched inward ¼ inch per foot so water will run toward the drain. Make a mark at the appropriate amount higher than the edge of the strainer on the farthest wall of the shower. Then use a level to transfer those marks into a level line all the way around the shower.

9 **MUD THE FLOOR.** Make another very dry batch of thick-bed mortar mix in a 5-gallon bucket. Dump some mortar onto the vinyl floor, beat it with a scrap of 2 × 4 or a grout float to press it against the subfloor, and then use a flat trowel to spread it over the pan and to slope it from the line around the edge of the walls down to the height of the drain assembly. Use a 2 × 4 to get the pitch right, by keeping one end at the level of the drain and the other at the mark on the wall.

10 **TILE THE FLOOR.** Once the mud job has cured for a night or two, it's ready for tile. Mosaic tiles are best because they will conform to the pitched surface. Don't use anything larger than 3 inches square. Install the tile using latex-fortified thinset, following the instructions on pages 67–69.

11 **INSTALL THE THRESHOLD.** Cut a solid piece of stone to fit over the sill. It should slightly overhang the wall material. Then use a ¼-inch square-notch trowel to apply thinset over the surface of the 2 × 4 sill and set the threshold. Place a level across one end of the threshold and tap the inner edge of the stone with the handle of a hammer until the bubble in the level just barely touches the line at the outside of the shower. That pitch (about 4 degrees) will make water drain inward, says tile setter George Taterosian. Repeat at the opposite end of the threshold.

Prefab Pan

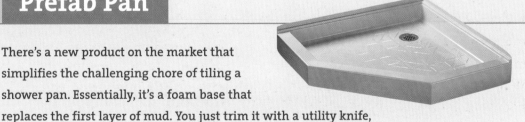

There's a new product on the market that simplifies the challenging chore of tiling a shower pan. Essentially, it's a foam base that replaces the first layer of mud. You just trim it with a utility knife, lay it in the shower (on top of a little silicone caulk to keep it in place), and then install the vinyl membrane over the top of it. "The only drawback is that you can only get them in certain stock sizes, and they're very expensive," says tile setter George Taterosian. "But they really do make the job much easier, especially for a do-it-yourselfer."

LAYING A RESILIENT TILE FLOOR

THE TERM "resilient flooring" refers to vinyl, linoleum, and rubber flooring, all of which are waterproof, durable materials. Yet unlike ceramic and stone, they have a little give to them. Sheet versions of resilient flooring offer the advantage of having few or no seams where moisture can penetrate the surface, but resilient tiles are far easier to lay and, installed properly, will yield very water-resistant floors. Allow the tiles to sit in the room for at least a day so they can adjust to the ambient temperature and humidity. Ask your tile seller which kind of adhesive you will need.

1 **PREPARE THE SUBFLOOR.** It's best to have 1½ inches of subflooring under your resilient tile. Add enough plywood to the existing subfloor to build it up to that thickness. Follow the instructions on page 89, but use AC plywood, which has a smooth-finished top. This is important because you'd see any irregularity in the plywood surface through a resilient floor. Once you've completed those steps, mix a batch of latex-reinforced floor-patching compound to the consistency of toothpaste. (Ask your supplier for a product that's compatible with the floor adhesive you'll be using.) Use a flat trowel or a taping knife to fill all fastener holes and seams between the plywood sheets. Then smooth the blade across the surface to press the material into the gap and scrape it flush with the plywood surface. Once the compound has dried overnight, use a sanding pad loaded with medium-grit sandpaper to smooth the patches. Also remember to trim up door casings as described on page 91, using a resilient tile to set the height of your undercut saw.

2 **DRAW REFERENCE LINES.** Measure each wall of the room (including doorways and other openings as part of the wall) and find their center points. If the room is L-shaped or has another nonrectangular shape, find the midpoints of the largest rectangular area of the floor. Then snap lines between the opposing marks and use a framing square to check them for square. If they don't form a perfect 90-degree angle, measure from each end of each line to the walls that are parallel to it. Pick the reference line that's farthest out of sync with its parallel walls and resnap it so that it's square to the other line.

③ SPREAD THE ADHESIVE. Check the label on the adhesive to see what size trowel notch you need—it's usually $5/32$ by $1/16$. Then tilt the bucket and pour a line a few feet down the center of one of the quadrants of your layout lines. Use the flat side of the trowel to spread the adhesive between the chalk lines from the center point outward. Aim for even coverage with no blobs and remove any excess adhesive immediately. Next, holding the trowel notch-side down at about a 45-degree angle to the floor, comb the

TRICKS OF THE TRADE

Watch the Grain

Many resilient tiles have a subtle grain running through them, usually noted on the back with arrows. You won't like the way your floor looks if you install the tiles without paying attention to the grain. You'll do better either aligning all of the grain in the same direction or, possibly, alternating it like a checkerboard. To decide, dry-lay a quadrant each way and see how it looks.

adhesive. Use long, sweeping strokes that overlap by an inch or so. It's fine to cover the chalk lines slightly with adhesive. You'll see them again when the adhesive gets tacky.

④ LAY A QUADRANT. Once the adhesive has cured for about 10 minutes and is tacky to the touch, position the first tile with a tip at the center point of the chalk lines and two sides riding the lines. Then lay a second tile so that one side is flush against the first tile and the other against a chalk line. Don't slide the tile into position, or you'll push adhesive between the tiles, which should be touching. Place the tile where you want it. Add another tile against the other chalk line and continue laying tiles out over the quadrant.

continued ▶▶

Installing Self-Stick Tiles

Some tiles require no adhesive because they already have glue on their backs. Just peel off the protective paper and stick them in place. That makes installation much easier, although some of these products call for priming the subfloor before you install the floor. Then you lay the self-stick tiles in the same way you'd lay the kind that need troweled-on adhesive, one quadrant at a time, starting at the center point.

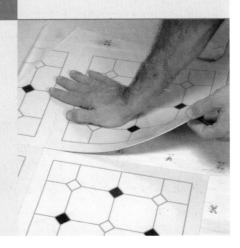

5 **CLEAN AWAY EXCESS ADHESIVE.** Occasionally, adhesive will squeeze up between two tiles. Immediately use a rag soaked with adhesive remover, paint thinner, soap and water, or whatever is recommended by the manufacturer to wipe the excess away.

6 **ROLL IT OR WALK ON IT.** Once a quadrant is done, go over all of the tiles with a flooring roller. Walking over the surface can work too, if you press straight down with your foot to firmly embed each tile in the adhesive.

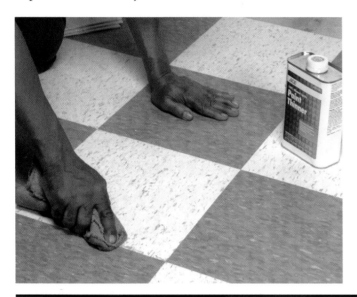

Cut the Tiles

When you reach obstacles or the walls at the end of the quadrant, you'll need to cut the tiles to fit. Don't apply adhesive until you've cut the tiles.

To measure for a straight cut, place a scrap strip of tile against the wall so that you can lay the tile you're cutting over it. Also use a shim to create a 1/4-inch gap against the wall. Place the tile into position. Using the neighboring tile as a gauge, mark the tile on the front and back where it needs to be cut (right, top). Make sure to keep the tile from touching the adhesive while you are measuring.

On a worktable or a piece of plywood, hold a straightedge between the two marks on the tile. (A full tile makes a convenient straightedge, but it will get dinged up. Mark it with an X so you will not install it on the floor by mistake.) With a utility knife, score a single line along the straightedge (right, bottom).

Then pick the tile up, hold both sides firmly, and bend until it snaps (left).

Making Specialty Cuts

To notch a tile, use a tape measure to determine the size of the notch, then mark that area on the tile with a pencil. Score the cut lines using a utility knife. Repeatedly score one of the lines

until you cut all the way through. Bend the tile along the other line until it snaps off (above). To make a curved or profiled cut, just make repeated passes with the utility knife.

When cutting around a pipe, aim to have a $\frac{1}{8}$-inch gap between the pipe and the tile. If you can't pass the tile over the end of the pipe (because there is no accessible end nearby), you'll have to cut the tile in two so that the seam falls across the pipe. Notch each cut edge and lay one piece on each side of the pipe. After installation, caulk the joint and cover it with a pipe flange.

1 **MEASURE FOR THE NOTCH CUT.** If only a partial tile is needed, cut the tile to size first. Hold the tile face up and pressed against the pipe, then mark the tile at either side of the pipe. Measure the distance that the tile must travel toward the wall and add $\frac{1}{8}$ inch. This is the depth the cut should be.

2 **MARK FOR THE CUT.** Keeping in mind that you want a gap of about $\frac{1}{8}$ inch or so around the pipe, draw the outline of the front edge of the pipe.

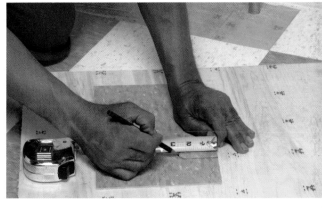

3 **CUT THE NOTCH.** Carefully score along all the marked lines using a utility knife. Then apply more pressure as you repeat the cuts until your blade passes all the way through the tile. Remove and save the cut-out piece. Check the tile for fit, as you may need to enlarge the cut slightly.

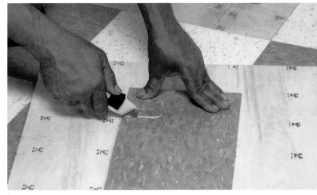

4 **CUT THE NOTCH PIECE.** Install the tile. Hold the cut-out piece next to the gap behind the pipe, mark it, and cut it to fit the space. Caulk around the pipe where it meets the tile. Install a pipe flange to cover the caulking.

LAYING A PARQUET FLOOR

PARQUET IS A REAL WOOD FLOOR that installs with the ease of tile. You can purchase parquet tiles in oak, maple, birch, or "hardwood," which usually means ash or poplar. Look for parquet flooring that has tongue-and-groove edges, so they'll interlock when you press them together, making for tight joints between the tiles. Allow the tiles to sit in the room for at least two days before installing them, so they can adjust to the ambient temperature and humidity.

Preparing and Laying Out

The substrate for a parquet floor does not need to be very firm or very smooth. You can install parquet tiles directly over an old wood or vinyl tile floor, as long as it is free of major defects, and a ¾-inch-thick subfloor is a sturdy enough support. See pages 80–93 for instructions on removing trim and moldings and preparing the subfloor. On pages 49–51, review the process of snapping center lines as reference points. Trim up door casings as described on page 91, using a parquet tile to set the height of your undercut saw.

Setting the Tiles

Vacuum the subfloor. If any debris gets into your adhesive, it can interfere with the proper installation of the floor. After test-fitting a group of tiles, have them stacked and ready to install, because the adhesive sets up quickly. Parquet adhesive is particularly sticky and hard to clean, so keep your hands and knees away from it. Clean up wayward blobs immediately, using a rag soaked with soapy water (for latex-based adhesive) or paint thinner (for oil-based adhesive).

TRICKS OF THE TRADE

Testing the Tiles for Fit

As you open boxes of parquet tiles, lay them out on the floor in an out-of-the-way spot and slide them together. Check that the edges and corners fit tightly. If two tiles do not fit snugly together, perhaps one has a tongue or groove that is slightly splintered. Cut off the offending portion with a knife. If a groove is clogged with debris, clean it out with a small screwdriver. Discard tiles that cannot be made to fit.

---

1 **SPREAD THE ADHESIVE.** Purchase the adhesive that your parquet supplier recommends. Pour some onto the floor or scoop it out with a notched trowel. Working within one quadrant of your chalk lines, spread enough adhesive to glue down about 8 rows of tile. Avoid covering your chalk lines. Use long, sweeping strokes, and work systematically so you leave no blobs. Do it right the first time and avoid trying to recomb it after a few minutes, because the adhesive starts to harden quickly.

2 **LAY THE FIRST TILE.** Set the first tile onto the adhesive at the intersection of the working lines. Push down on it gently and twist it into perfect alignment. The finished edge of the tile is what matters when you are aligning the tile with the chalk lines, so you can ignore unfinished tongues.

3 **LAY MORE TILES.** Set the next tile so it interlocks with the first and aligns with one chalk line, and then set another tile that interlocks with the first and aligns with the other chalk line. Continue laying more courses of tiles within the first quadrant. You'll be able to slide the tiles around for about half an hour. Sometimes they'll also move when you don't want them to, so every few minutes, check and adjust them as necessary. Continue spreading adhesive as you go, but don't spread it where you'll need to cut the tile. Wait to do that until the tile has been cut and test-fitted.

4 **TAP FOR A TIGHT FIT.** If the adhesive is starting to set up and some of the seams between tiles are not tight, use a scrap of tile, interlock it with the groove or the tongue of the tile that needs to move, and tap the partial tile with a hammer. As long as the adhesive is wet to the touch, the tiles will bond to the floor. But once the adhesive starts to skin over (so it feels tacky rather than gooey when you touch it lightly), adhesion will be impaired.

5 **TAP THE TILES.** To ensure a firm bond, tap each tile with a rubber mallet. After tapping, check the alignment of the tiles and adjust any that need it. To test for firm adhesion, attempt to pry up a tile using a margin trowel. If the tile won't come up with moderate pressure, it is well stuck.

continued ▶▶

Cutting Parquet Tiles

Install the full tiles first. Do not apply adhesive to the floor where the cut tiles will go until a few minutes before you will install them. Cutting parquet tiles is easy if you use a table saw, a radial-arm saw, or a power miter box. Cutting them with a circular saw or saber saw is trickier, though not overly so. If necessary, clamp the tile to the worktable to keep your hands away from the blade. Whichever tool you use, wear safety goggles.

Notching Tiles

When you need to notch a tile around a molding, corner, or any other obstruction, measuring out and marking the exact cut you need can be tricky, so here are two alternatives:

• For intricate shapes, use a profile gauge, a simple tool that you press against a molding or other complicated profile. The gauge retains the shape so you can trace it onto the tile.

• For large notches, cut a sheet of kraft paper to the size of a tile, then press it into position (allowing for grout lines, if needed) and use a razor knife to trim it to size. Trace the template onto your tile and you're ready to cut.

Mark for a cut. To measure for a straight cut, place a ¼-inch spacer on the wall. Turn the tile to be cut upside down with the tongue or groove that you're keeping lined up against the spacer, and the other end overhanging the tile it will interlock with. Use that underlying tile as a gauge to mark your cut at both edges of the tile to be cut (above). Use a straightedge to connect the marks.

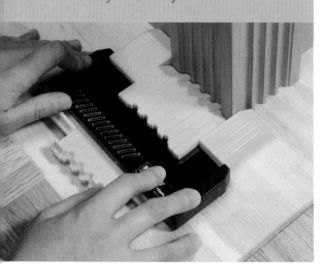

Break apart a tile. If you need a half or a quarter tile, you may be able to reduce the tile without any sawing. Simply bend the parquet along the corresponding seam between its component pieces and they will come apart (right).

Make straight cuts with a circular saw. Wearing safety goggles and holding an upside-down tile firmly in place against the work surface (using your hand or, better, a clamp), cut along the line with a circular saw. Keep the blade to the side of the line that will be scrap (right). Because you're cutting from the back, the finished side is far less likely to chip or splinter.

Make cutouts with a jigsaw. A notch is best made with a jigsaw. As long as you use a fine-toothed blade, you can cut the tile right side up if you first apply masking tape to the bottom of the saw's base plate to protect the tile from scratches. Hold or clamp the tile firmly in place. Blow away loose sawdust as you cut, so that you can see the blade and keep it on the line (left).

Sealing Parquet

Most parquet tiles come with a tough protective coating. As long as the tiles fit together tightly, the wood will be pressed together, protecting the seams. However, tiles do not always align perfectly, and the factory finish will not last forever. So, once the floor is done, you can add a coat of clear, water-based polyurethane. Using a handheld sanding block, lightly sand the floor with 180-grit sandpaper. Then vacuum up all dust and sandpaper grit so the floor is perfectly clean. Apply the polyurethane using a paintbrush or a foam applicator. If you want to add another coat, sand the first coat lightly and vacuum before doing so.

LAYING A LAMINATE FLOOR

LAMINATE FLOORING IS A MAN-MADE PRODUCT that looks almost identical to wood, stone, or ceramic tile once it's installed. But it's actually a photograph of the material it's imitating, sandwiched between a clear plastic wear layer and a fiberboard backing. There's no adhesive necessary to install laminate flooring. The tiles simply lock together with their own various versions of tongue-and-groove joints. If the substrate is smooth and you install laminate tiles correctly, the seams will seal tight and the entire floor will be highly resistant to water. You can install it over virtually any existing surface, including a concrete basement floor, as long as it is flat and solid.

Tile-setting techniques vary slightly by manufacturer, but the steps shown on these pages apply to most products.

TRICKS OF THE TRADE

Inspect the Tiles

A small percentage of the laminate tiles you buy will have defects, such as a divot taken out of the surface, or a dented corner. The time to find those problems is before you lay the tiles, because if you spot one after a tile is laid, the only way to remove that tile from the floor will be to pull up all of the tiles you laid after it. So inspect each bundle of tiles carefully when you open it, and discard the damaged ones—or mark the flaw with a marker and use the good portions for cut tiles.

Preparing the Subfloor

The floor does not have to be particularly firm or smooth, although it must be clean and free of dust and debris. You can install laminate tiles over just about any existing surface, including ceramic tile, vinyl, and concrete. Remove any obstructions (see pages 80–86). Trim up door casings as described on page 91, using a laminate tile over a scrap of underlayment to set the height of your undercut saw.

Preparing the Tiles

Store the tiles, still in their boxes, in the room where they will be used, and wait at least two days before installing them. This allows the tiles to adjust to the room temperature and humidity. Otherwise, they could expand or contract after installation, creating gaps between tiles or causing the tiles to buckle.

Installing a Laminate Floor

Instead of snapping working lines and beginning in the middle of a floor, as you would for most other floors in this book, you lay laminate flooring by starting at one wall and moving across the room to the other side.

1 **INSTALL THE UNDERLAYMENT.** A foam underlayment is an essential first step. It will prevent moisture from rising into the floor (especially if you are tiling over concrete or below grade), cushion the floor underfoot, and soften the sound of footfalls on the laminate. Choose the best underlayment that your laminate supplier recommends for the flooring you're using. Roll it out on the floor, overlapping and taping the rows as the manufacturer recommends.

2 **PREPARE FOR THE FIRST ROW.** Begin along a highly visible wall, preferably an exterior one, which is less likely to be out of square than an interior one. Measure off the wall at each end by the width of the laminate tiles, not including the tongue, plus ¼ inch. Then snap a chalk line between those marks. Using a table saw or circular saw, cut the tongues off enough tiles to complete the first row.

3 **LAY THE FIRST TILE.** Lay the first tile at one end of the starter wall, with the tongue side against the wall. Place two ¼-inch spacers between the tile and the main wall, and one between the tile and the sidewall (you can buy plastic spacers where you bought the laminate or cut your own from ¼-inch-thick wood). Check that the outer edge of the tile rides the chalk line. If it doesn't, you may need to trim the wall edge of the tile slightly to clear a bump or other protrusion on the wall surface (see step 5 for cutting instructions). *continued* ▶▶

Scribing for a Cut

To mark a tile for an intricate cut, such as around a post, a radiator leg, or a detailed corner molding on a kitchen island, hold the tile against the object and then trace around it with the pointed end of a compass, letting the pencil at the other side trace out the profile on the tile.

4 **COMPLETE THE FIRST ROW.** Lay a second tile against the end of the first, making sure to interlock the end joints tightly together. Some products simply overlap. For others, you need to insert the new tile at a 45-degree angle and press down to knit the joint. And for some, you use a tapping block that you hit with a hammer to press the boards together. Use two spacers to keep the tiles 1/4 inch off the wall, and trim the board as needed to keep it on the chalk line. Continue adding tiles until you reach the end wall. To mark the cut for the last tile, rotate it so that the mating end is against a spacer on the wall, then use the previous tile as a gauge to place a mark on the last tile. This way, when you turn the tile back around, the cut will be against the wall. Use a straightedge to draw the cut line.

5 **CUT THE TILES.** You can make straight cuts in laminate tiles using a table saw or a circular saw or a power miter saw, as long as the tiles aren't too big for its reach. Follow the same procedures as if you were cutting wood, and keep the blade on the scrap side of the cut line. To cut notches, use a jigsaw.

6 **START THE SECOND COURSE.** With the first row complete, head back to the corner where you started the first row and begin the second. Cut the first tile in half (or by whatever offset the manufacturer requires), arranging it so the cut side will fall against the end wall, and then set it into position. Use a ¼-inch spacer against the end wall and interlock the joint with the first row.

7 **COMPLETE THE FLOOR.** Continue laying the tile, row by row, alternating the first tile of each row as a full or half tile (or by whatever stagger the product packaging recommends) and placing ¼-inch spacers wherever tile meets wall. For the last row, you'll need to rip the tiles to fit the remaining width of the floor, minus the ¼-inch spacers you'll place along the wall. You'll need a table saw or circular saw to rip down the tiles if the miter cannot handle the full length. To tighten the last row of tiles, you won't be able to use a tapping block, so tap against a pull bar wrapped around the edge of the tiles.

8 **INSTALL THRESHOLDS.** Although you could install wooden thresholds (as described on page 123), most laminate manufacturers sell matching thresholds in an array of profiles that will accommodate almost any scenario you might face, such as joining the laminate to a floor of a different height or covering uneven laminate end cuts. The thresholds generally have a metal track that is screwed to the subfloor, and a tongue on the underside of the threshold slips into the channel of the metal track.

LAYING A CORK FLOOR

ALTHOUGH CORK IS BETTER KNOWN for bulletin boards and wine-bottle stoppers, the material also serves as a phenomenal flooring. Made from the bark of a tree that grows in the Mediterranean, cork is soft, warm, quiet, beautiful, durable, and eco-friendly. And it comes in tiles that are easy to install. You can get cork tiles in a rainbow of colors, or in natural hues, and with or without a clear plastic protective finish. You can even get cork in a snap-down version, which installs like laminate tiles, as seen on pages 112–115. Allow the tiles to sit in the room for four days so the porous material can adjust to the ambient temperature and humidity.

1 **PREPARE THE SUBFLOOR.** You can install cork over virtually any other flooring, over a concrete subfloor, or over a wood subfloor that's $1^{1}/_{4}$ to $1^{1}/_{2}$ inches thick. If necessary, add enough plywood to the existing subfloor to build the floor up to that thickness. Follow the instructions on page 89, but use AC plywood, which has a smoothly finished top. To finish preparing a plywood subfloor, mix a batch of latex-reinforced floor-patching compound to the consistency of toothpaste. (Check with the seller to make sure you get a product that's compatible with the cork adhesive you'll be using, unless you choose snap-down tiles, which don't use adhesive.) Use a flat trowel or a taping knife to fill all fastener holes and seams between the plywood sheets. Then smooth the blade across the surface to press the material into the gaps between the plywood sheets and scrape it flush with the surface. Once the compound has dried overnight, use a sanding pad loaded with medium-grit sandpaper to sand the patches and plywood smooth. Some cork adhesives also call for a latex primer to be applied to the subfloor (check the package instructions). Trim up door casings as described on page 91, using a cork tile to set the height of your undercut saw.

2 **DRAW REFERENCE LINES.** Measure each wall of the room, including doorways and other openings, and find their center points. If the room is L-shaped or has another nonrectangular shape, find the midpoints of the largest rectangular area of the floor. Then snap lines between the opposing marks and use a framing square to check them for square. If they're not perfectly square, measure from each end of each line to the walls that are parallel to it. Pick the reference line that's farthest out of sync with its parallel walls and resnap it so that it's perfectly square to the other line.

3 **CUT THE TILES.** Dry-lay the tiles to determine what cuts you need, as once the adhesive goes down you won't be able to make layout changes. To cut cork tiles, mark the cut you need on the surface of the tile and then score the line with a sharp utility knife. Score it repeatedly, until the blade passes completely through.

4 **SPREAD THE ADHESIVE.** Most cork products use a contact cement that will adhere to another layer of contact cement that's factory applied to the backs of the tiles (or that you apply on site). Pour some adhesive into a paint tray and use a roller to apply it to one entire quadrant of the floor, starting against the walls and working toward the middle of the room. It's fine if you cross the chalk lines, because the adhesive will dry clear before you lay the tiles.

5 **LAY A QUADRANT.** Let the adhesive sit for about 45 minutes, until it becomes tacky, and then it's ready for tiles. Position the first tile with one of its tips at the center point of the chalk lines and two sides directly over them. You can adjust it slightly as needed, then press it firmly against the subfloor to engage the two layers of contact cement. The tile will lock into place. (To move it in case of a mistake, you'd need to pry it up with a putty knife, destroying the tile in the process.) Then lay a second tile so that one side is flush against the first tile and the other against a chalk line. Add another tile against the first tile and the other chalk line and continue laying tiles across the quadrant, spreading additional adhesive and giving it time to set up as needed.

6 **TAP THE TILES INTO PLACE.** Hit the tiles with a rubber mallet or go over them with a flooring roller to press the two layers of contact cement against each other, bonding the tiles to the floor.

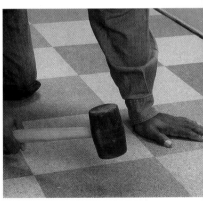

7 **APPLY SEALANT.** Even if your cork tiles came with a protective sealant, it's best to apply an additional coat once they are installed, so that moisture and dirt can't get between the tiles. Talk to your cork supplier about what type of sealant to use.

LAYING CARPET TILES

CARPET TILES COME IN A WIDE ARRAY of styles, make installing wall-to-wall carpeting a breeze, and allow you to create all sorts of interesting tile-like designs, from checkerboards to stripes to staggered brick-lay patterns. Prepare the subfloor and lay out center lines as you would for resilient flooring (see page 104). Trim up door casings as described on page 91, using a carpet tile to set the height of your undercut saw. Some carpet tiles get installed with mastic (much like resilient tile), while others are self-sticking (just peel off the backing). The process we're following here, however, is an increasingly common carpet-tile installation method that utilizes sticky dots you apply to the floor as you lay the tiles.

1 **DRY-LAY TEST ROWS.** Using your reference lines as guides, dry-lay a + of tiles through the space. If any of the edge tiles will need to be cut smaller than half a tile, try to resolve the problem by shifting the row of tiles to one side or the other. Once you're happy with the arrangement, make sure that the tiles are tight together and use an aluminum straightedge or a level to ensure that they're aligned perfectly. Then, starting in the center of the room, apply the sticky dots. Peel the backing off a floor dot, lift an edge of a tile, and place the dot halfway under the tile. The sticky top surface will hold the tiles together, and its rubbery bottom surface will keep the interconnected layer of tiles from moving around on the floor.

TRICKS OF THE TRADE

Orienting the Lay

Carpet has a grain (or lay) that you won't necessarily notice as you're installing the tile (if it's a solid color) but that will affect the appearance of the completed job. Luckily, the lay is marked on the back of the carpet. Dry-lay some tiles to decide whether you want to arrange all of them with the lay in the same direction (generally the best option) or in alternate directions like a checkerboard. Just don't let their orientation be random.

2 **MARK FOR CUTS.** With the two center lines laid down, cut the end tiles for each row. To do so, flip a tile upside down and slide it under the neighboring tile and against the wall. Then use a marker to trace the cut line on the back of the tile.

3 **CUT THE TILE.** Hold a scrap of straight wood or a level against the cut line on the back of the tile. Then trace it with a sharp utility knife. It's better to make a few light passes than one or two hard ones. Once you've cut through the backing, the carpeting will pull apart easily.

4 **COMPLETE THE FLOOR.** Once the two reference lines are laid, fill in the rest of the carpet tiles. Work one quadrant at a time, starting in the center of the room and working to the walls. As you proceed, dry-lay about four tiles, then apply the sticky dots, and move on.

LAYING RIVER ROCK TILES

RIVER ROCK TILES make an excellent nonslip surface, bring a beautiful palette of natural colors to the room, and feel good underfoot too. The smooth river stones are prelaid on a mesh backing, much like ceramic or glass mosaics. Look for factory-sealed stones so that mortar and grout won't stick to them as readily—or you can seal them yourself before installing them.

Remove the baseboards and prepare the subfloor as you would for any tile job (see pages 80–86). Trim up door casings as described on page 91, using a sheet of river rocks to set the height of your undercut saw. Then, because the odd-shaped sheets don't interlock like normal mosaics and because the rocks need not be aligned square, you can simply begin tiling on one side of the room and work your way to the other.

TRICKS OF THE TRADE

No Cuts Needed

After removing baseboards, slice through the drywall by making repeated passes with a sharp utility knife about 1 inch above the sub-floor. That way, you can slide the edges of the river rock mosaics right up to the wall framing. This provides enough of a fudge factor so that you'll almost never have to cut a stone, because you can simply remove excess stones and cut the mesh backing with a sharp utility knife. And you have at least 1 inch (½ inch of drywall plus ½ inch of baseboard) to cover up any gaps that are created. Once the mosaics are set, reinstall the baseboard to hide the irregular stone edges.

1 TROWEL OUT SOME THINSET. Mix up a batch of thinset following the instructions on page 54. Then, starting in a corner of the room, put a dollop on the floor and spread it in a strip across one wall so that you can lay a row of tiles. Use a ¼-inch square-notch trowel to comb it.

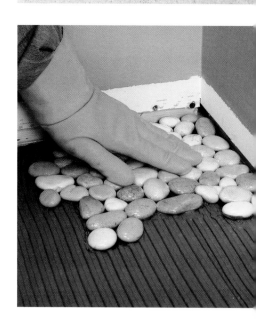

2 LAY THE FIRST SHEET. River rock goes down much easier than standard mosaic tiles. After all, the rocks are slightly different heights, so they don't have to be perfectly level. They're also rounded, so they don't have to be square to any surface. Place the first sheet against a corner of the room, then press on each stone in the mesh to ensure that it beds into the mortar. Otherwise, the mesh may prevent it from bonding and it will be loose.

3 **FILL GAPS.** Lay the next sheet against the wall and the first sheet. The edges of river rock sheets don't all interlock equally well, because the rock sizes are random, so make sure to align two well-matched pieces. Also, if a rock juts out too far from one sheet, just remove it by pulling it off the mesh backing (see page 67). Fill in the gap left behind—or any other gaps—with rocks of the right size pulled from another sheet. "I go through a couple of extra sheets of river rock tiles just grabbing the stones I need to fill between the sheets as I'm working," says tile setter George Taterosian.

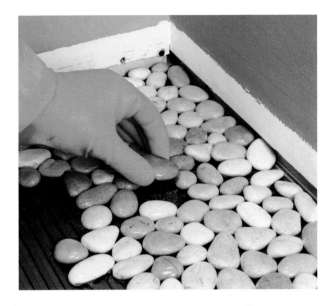

4 **WORK AROUND OBSTACLES.** When you need to shorten a sheet at a wall or to make a hole for a plumbing pipe to pass through, just remove the unwanted rocks and trim the backing with a utility knife. If necessary, patch in a smaller stone from your scrap sheets to fill in any gaps. You probably won't need to make any actual cuts to the stones, but if you do, use a nibbling tool.

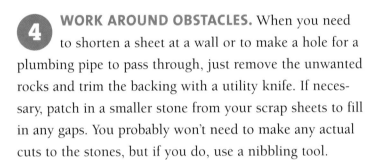

5 **GROUT THE ROCKS.** Few tiles are as easy to lay as river rock, but few are as hard to grout. The joints are large, and there are tons of them. Plus the stones are oddly shaped and contoured. Make sure the river rock tiles have been sealed—either by the manufacturer or by you—before grouting. Otherwise, the grout will stick to and stain the stones. Then grout the floor just as you would grout any tile (see pages 64–66), by pushing the grout into the joints, smoothing its surface, and wiping excess grout off the tiles.

FINISHING THE JOB

WAIT FOR THE GROUT TO CURE for the period recommended on the bag, which often depends on the ambient temperature. Then it's time to put back all of the moldings and fixtures you removed at the beginning of the job.

Replacing a Vanity

To set a vanity back in place, simply do the removal job in reverse. Place the vanity into position. If the floor height has changed, the pipes may no longer fit into the holes in the back of the vanity. If you need to, use a jigsaw to enlarge the holes, or drill new ones. Use shims and a level to get the vanity's position right (as shown at left), and then fasten the vanity to wall studs using screws. (If necessary, find the studs first with a stud finder.) Then reconnect the plumbing, wrapping all threads with plumber's tape before reconnecting the lines.

Reinstalling Radiators

If you removed the entire metal baseboard, reinstall it now, lifting gently on the copper pipe to position it, if necessary. If you didn't, reinstall the faceplates and use tin snips to trim the end caps so they close flush with the new floor. For cast-iron radiators, a plumber should reinstall them.

Reinstalling Baseboards and Shoe Moldings

If you can see the old holes in the wall where the baseboard nails were, mark their locations a few inches higher on the wall with a pencil so you can see them after each baseboard is put back in place. Then, at those marks, sink a 12d finish nail through the baseboard and into each wall stud. Use a small-tipped nail set to sink the heads below the surface of the wood. Reattach the shoe moldings using 6d finish nails (as shown at right).

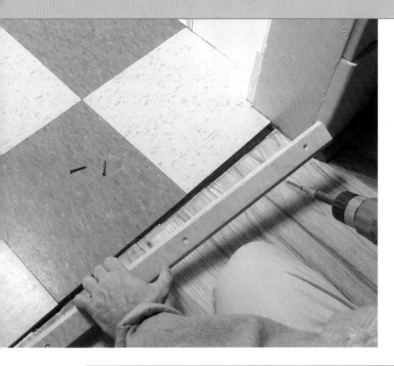

Installing Wooden Thresholds

As described on pages 96–98, stone thresholds get mortared and grouted along with the tile floor. But wooden thresholds get added after the grout or adhesive has hardened. Use an undercut saw to trim up the doorstops so the threshold can ride under them (see page 91). Then cut the threshold to length using an electric or hand miter box or a circular saw. Stain and polyurethane the threshold to match the adjacent wood flooring, predrill nail holes, and then fasten the threshold with finish nails or screws. Fill fastener holes with color-matched putty and the gap along the tiles with a caulk that matches the grout color.

Threshold Types

To transition from your new tile floor to the adjacent flooring, you'll need a threshold. You can find these in wood, as well as in materials that match specific laminate, parquet, and resilient flooring styles. All of them are available in a variety of sizes.

REDUCER. If you're working with a neat tile edge that's higher than the neighboring floor, align this strip next to the edge of the last row of tiles.

Reducer

Threshold reducer

THRESHOLD REDUCER. If the tile edge isn't neat enough to display, or if the threshold crosses an exterior doorway, use a threshold reducer. Some are beveled at the bottom to accommodate a variety of flooring heights.

T-MOLDING. Available with two level sides or with the two sides set at different heights for different levels of flooring, these thresholds can bridge two relatively even floors.

Cap

CAP. If the two floors are flush, use this strip of wood (or stone) to cover the seam.

T-molding

Reinstalling a Toilet

To reinstall a toilet, attach two new Johnny bolts to the flange and remove the rag from the drain. Turn the new bowl upside down on a cushioned surface. Place a new wax gasket over the horn on the bottom of the bowl, facing the tapered side away from the bowl, as shown above. If the wax gasket has a plastic collar, install it so the collar is away from the bowl, first checking that the collar will fit into the floor flange. Apply a thin bead of caulk around the toilet base.

Gently lower the bowl into place over the flange, using the bolts as guides. Press down firmly while gently twisting and rocking. Using a level, check that the bowl is straight. Hand-tighten the washers and nuts onto the bolts. Then alternately tighten them with a wrench until the toilet is seated firmly on the floor, as shown below. Do not overtighten the nuts, as that could crack the porcelain.

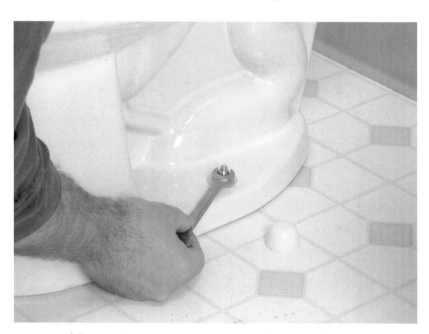

Reconnect the water-supply hose to the shutoff valve and turn the handle counterclockwise to open the valve. Once the tank has filled, flush it and look for leaks. If you see any, shut off the water, tighten the supply line and the Johnny-bolt nuts, and try again. If the leak persists, shut the valve and call a plumber.

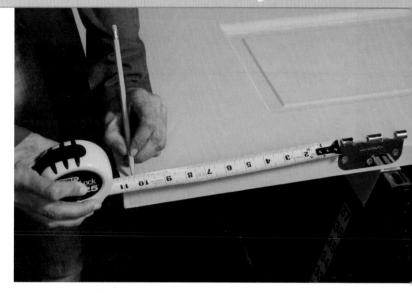

Trimming Up a Door

If your new tile floor is higher than the previous floor, any door that opens into the space
will likely need trimming.

1 **MEASURE FOR THE CUT.** If you can install
the door by swinging it out over an adjacent
floor, hang it and close it as far as possible against
the new tile and then make a pencil mark on the
door about ¼ inch above the tile. If you can't install the door until it's trimmed,
measure from the bottom of the hinge plate in the jamb to the top of the threshold and subtract ¼ inch. Then set the door across two sawhorses. Place the tip
of the tape measure at the bottom of the lower hinge plate on the door and make
a mark at the first measurement. Use a square to make a line across the door at
that mark. Hold a straightedge against the line and score it with a utility knife.

2 **CUT ALONG A STRAIGHTEDGE.** With your circular saw unplugged,
measure from the left side of the saw's base plate to the edge of the blade.
Make a mark that much higher up on the door and use a T or framing square to
draw a line across the door at that height. Fasten a straight 1 × 4 along the line.
With the left side of the saw riding the 1 × 4 brace, cut the door. Smooth the cut
edge with a file, a plane, and/or a sanding block.

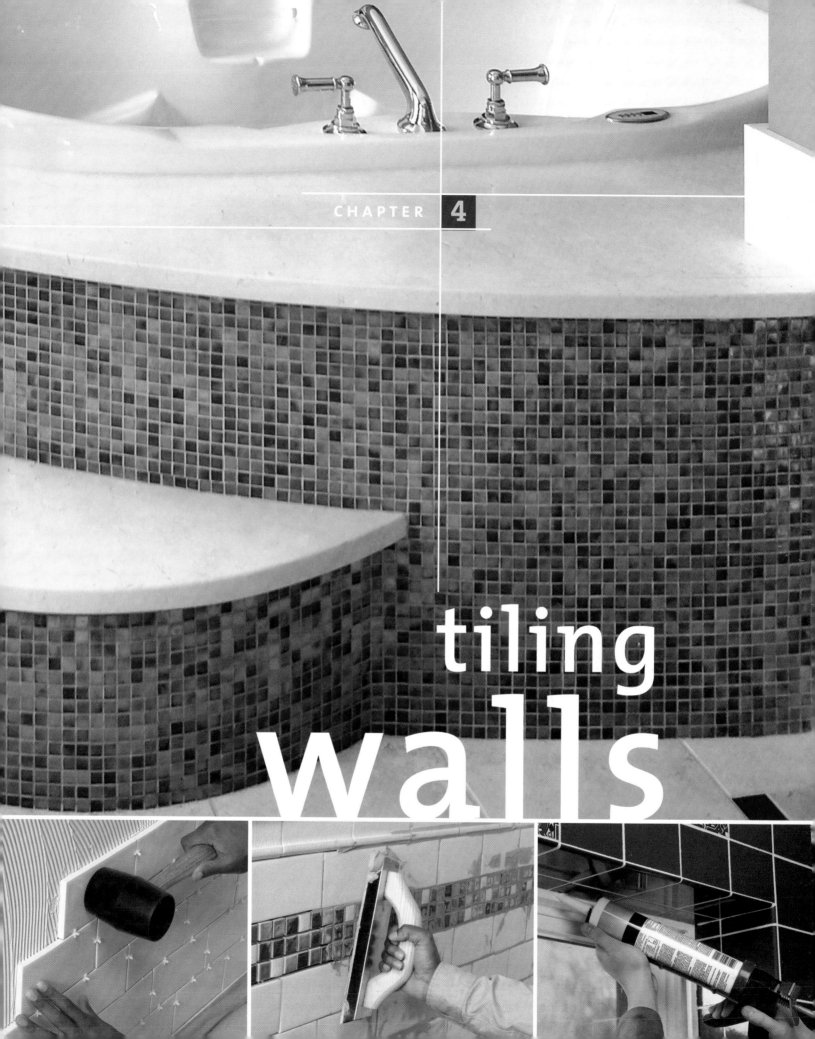

tiling
walls

CHOOSING WALL TILES

BECAUSE WALL TILES DON'T GET WALKED ON, cooked on, or left outside in the elements, they needn't meet any hardness or scratch-resistance threshold, but durability may still be a concern. For any wall that's likely to get wet or that will get dirty enough to require frequent cleaning, you'll want a tile that's waterproof, stain resistant, and easy to clean. A good solution is a tile that's glazed. Like the coatings on ceramic dinnerware, glazes create a tough shield that keeps water out and makes it possible to scrub away nearly any dirt (just think of the baked-on cheese of a casserole dish). Or you can choose an impervious or vitreous unglazed tile (see pages 8–15) and seal it regularly.

Another option is to use porcelain floor tiles, either glazed or unglazed. They're tough enough to use on floors, so you know they'll

OPPOSITE PAGE: A surface need not be flat to be tiled. Use pre-assembled sheets of small mosaics and you can easily tile around curves and undulations.

ABOVE: A stripe of decorative tiles brings a splash of color to a white bathtub surround.

LEFT: Storage niches such as the three in this tub surround are fairly easy to make if you're stripping the walls down to the studs.

resist water and stains. Some manufacturers sell kits with large floor tiles (perhaps
20 by 20 inches), wall tiles (perhaps 10 by
13 inches), and shower floor tiles (perhaps
3-by-3-inch mosaics), all identical in color
and material.

Where water isn't a factor—such as on
the walls of hallways, staircases, and any

OPPOSITE: The decorative pattern on this
kitchen island wall can be appreciated
both above and below the bar counter.

ABOVE: Because tile is spark-proof and
decorative, it is an ideal way to beautify
a fireplace.

RIGHT: Tiling stairs and risers can yield
dramatic results and eliminate those hard-
to-clean scuff marks you get on wood and
carpeting.

other areas without plumbing—you can choose practically any tile. Because we tend to get more up close and personal with wall tiles than with floor tiles, given that they're often at or near eye level, even tiny mosaics, intricate embossments, and detailed decorative images will get noticed. So although bold tiles will make the strongest statement on a wall, even understated ones will be appreciated for all of their subtle beauty.

OPPOSITE: Muted mosaics lend serenity to a spa-style bathroom.

ABOVE: The deep relief of this chic wainscot comes from the molds that were used to form the porcelain. The tiles were then coated in a metallic finish.

LEFT: These handmade ceramic tiles have a light glaze that varies in coverage from piece to piece, resulting in a watery effect.

PREPARING THE WALL

TILES AND THEIR ADHESIVES ARE VERY FORGIVING and will adhere to many different surfaces. Still, there are some wall coverings that must be removed before you can tile—and some that you'll need to prepare for tile—to ensure a good-looking and long-lasting tile job.

Removing Old Wall Coverings

If you have any of the following materials already on the walls, remove them before installing the tile.

Old tile. If the existing tile was installed fairly recently, it may have been attached to the drywall with mastic, in which case there's a chance you can pry off the tiles using a putty knife, as shown at right. Then use the knife to scrape off the residue and patch the drywall or plaster surface with spackle.

If the tiles won't come off the wall this way, remove the tiles and drywall all at once and start over from the studs. First make sure the wall doesn't contain plumbing pipes, and also turn off electrical power. Then, while wearing safety goggles, a respirator, and heavy-duty work gloves, use a sledgehammer to break a hole through the wall. Or, starting at an edge of the tile, such as at the top of a wainscot or in a corner where two walls meet, hit a flat bar or crowbar with a hammer to work it under the tile and drywall. Then pry the drywall away from the studs with a prybar (as shown at left) or your gloved hands, pulling the drywall nails or popping the drywall off its screws.

If the tiles were installed with a mud job (a thick layer of mortar containing metal lath nailed to the studs), removal will be far more difficult than with tile-over-drywall installations. Still, it requires essentially the same technique of using a pry bar to pull the lath from the studs. Around plumbing penetrations, you may also have to smash tiles with a sledgehammer to break them apart.

Wood paneling. Whether it's knotty pine, beadboard, or any other style, wood paneling isn't stiff enough to make a good substrate for wall tiles. So use a pry bar to pull it off the studs, working from stud to stud across the wall. If there's drywall or plaster behind the paneling, follow the instructions on pages 136–137 to repair the surface where the removal of nails, screws, or adhesive causes damage. But if there's no plaster or drywall, or if it's in serious disrepair, follow the instructions on pages 137–139 to install new drywall, either on the studs or right over the old drywall or plaster.

Loose paint. You can tile over a painted wall as long as the paint is in good condition and it's not dirty, oily, or glossy. Otherwise, you'll need to clean it with painter's detergent, or cover it with a coat of primer. If it's peeling, flaking, chipping, or bubbling, however, use a sharp paint scraper to remove any loose material. If you skip this step and attach your tiles to a failing substrate, they won't stay put for long. If your house was built before 1978, the paint almost surely contains lead. Lead is toxic, especially to children, who can suffer brain damage if they ingest dust or chips. You can purchase lead-test kits at paint stores and home centers. If the result turns up positive, that doesn't mean you should leave the peeling paint alone. Removing the loose paint and tiling over the area will make it safer, if it's done properly. For more information, see the Environmental Protection Agency brochure "Protect Your Family from Lead in Your Home," at *epa.gov/lead/pubs/leadpdfe.pdf*.

Wallpaper. If the wallpaper is relatively new, it may be made of vinyl, which means it will peel off the wall almost as easily as a giant self-stick stamp from its backing. If it's made of paper, especially old paper, it will be far trickier to remove. Some wallpapers are so well adhered to the plaster or drywall that you might be tempted to install new drywall just to avoid removing it. But it'll come off with a little effort.

1 **PERFORATE THE PAPER.** Protect the floor with a drop cloth. Use a scoring tool to perforate the paper, making sure that it gets pierced every inch or two across the entire surface.

2 **APPLY REMOVER.** Wearing safety goggles, a respirator, and heavy-duty rubber gloves, spray a generous amount of wallpaper remover onto the paper and let it soak for 20 minutes or so to work through the holes and break down the adhesive. Better yet, use an enzyme-based gel, which makes less of a mess and which you can apply with a paint roller.

3 **SCRAPE THE WALL.** Once the chemical has had time to work, use a 4-inch taping knife, a paint scraper, and a lot of elbow grease to scrape the paper off the wall.

Repairing Walls

Whether or not you had to remove an old wall covering, you'll probably need to give the walls some TLC to get them ready for tiles.

Damaged plaster. You can fill holes with vinyl spackling compound. Cover cracks with fiberglass mesh tape and joint compound as shown at right, just as if you were taping a joint between sheets of drywall. If the plaster is severely pitted, if it's crumbling, or if it's severely cracked, you could remove it by beating against it with the side of a hammer to free it from the wood lath and then prying the lath off the studs with a crowbar. But that's a backbreaking, dusty job that requires hanging plastic over door openings, wearing a respirator, and shoveling out hundreds of pounds of debris. Another solution is to simply install ¼-inch drywall right over the top of the old plaster, making sure to use screws that are long enough to pass through the drywall, plaster, and lath and sink 1¼ inches into the studs. See pages 137–139 for drywall installation instructions.

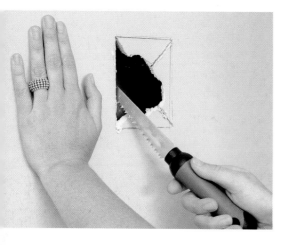

Damaged drywall. To patch dings and dents that don't fully penetrate the drywall, use vinyl spackling compound. For holes up to about the size of a quarter that pass all the way through the drywall, use fiberglass mesh tape and joint compound. To patch larger holes, follow the steps below.

1 **REMOVE DAMAGED DRYWALL.** Use a pencil and a framing square to draw a rectangle around the damage. Then cut along three sides of the rectangle using a drywall saw. For the fourth side, score the face with a sharp utility knife, snap the drywall, and cut the back side.

2 **INSTALL NAILERS.** Insert a small scrap of wood into the hole. Lay it along one side of the rectangle so that it crosses the hole and use drywall screws and a cordless drill loaded with a Phillips bit to fasten it to the old drywall on each side. Countersink the screws (see page 139). Repeat for the opposite side of the opening.

3 **INSTALL THE PATCH.** Cut a replacement piece from new drywall to fit your rectangle, reducing each dimension by ⅛ inch to ensure that it will fit. Test-fit the patch in the hole and shave the edges as necessary with a drywall rasp. Once the patch fits nicely, use

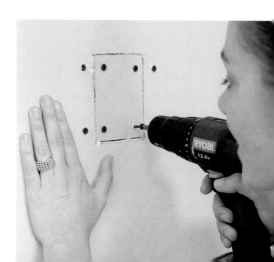

drywall screws to fasten it to the wooden nailers. Don't use joint compound to tape over the joints, as the moisture in tile adhesives will dissolve the compound and cause bonding problems. If the drywall joints are tight, there's no need to fill them. If there are gaps, apply fiberglass mesh tape and then apply one thin coat of whatever adhesive you're using.

Unpainted walls. If you're tiling over freshly installed drywall that's been taped but not painted—or over repairs made with joint compound or spackle—apply a coat of latex primer over the surface. (Only the joint compound or spackle must be coated, although it's sometimes just as easy to paint the whole wall.) This will prevent moisture in the mastic or thinset you'll be using from dissolving the water-soluble compound used on the drywall, and ensure that the new adhesive will bond properly. If you're installing new drywall, skip the joint compound and cover the joints with fiberglass mesh tape and a thin coat of thinset.

Installing New Drywall

If you stripped the walls down to the studs, if you're covering over an unsalvageable plaster surface, or if you're building new walls for your tile, you'll need to hang drywall. Make sure the studs are free of old nails, screws, staples, or other obstacles before proceeding. And for walls in wet areas, rather than using standard drywall or even moisture-resistant greenboard, upgrade to a fiberglass-coated board, which installs just like drywall but has no paper backing and contains an acrylic moisture barrier. For shower and tub surrounds, you'll need an even more water-resistant wall covering, cement backerboard (see pages 46–48.)

1 TEST-FIT THE FIRST BOARD. Position the first sheet with one edge against the ceiling and one against an adjacent wall. In the case of drywall and greenboard, which come in 4-by-8-foot sheets, an 8-foot edge should ride against the ceiling and a 4-foot edge against the wall. Fiberglass-coated boards come in a variety of sizes and can be oriented in any direction. For drywall, the white or green paper faces away from the studs. For fiberglass-coated boards, the gray surface faces away from the studs. If the end of the board that is not butting against the adjacent wall happens to fall down the center of a stud, you're ready to fasten it. If it doesn't, have a helper hold the board in place while you use a pencil to mark the location of the center of the stud nearest the end of the board. You can use a tape measure instead of holding the sheet in place, of course, but you may wind up with less accurate results, especially on complex cuts.

continued ▶▶

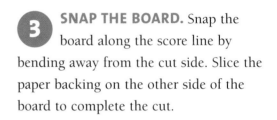

2 SCORE THE BOARD.

With the board leaning against a wall, align a T-square against the mark and use a sharp utility knife to score the face of the board.

3 SNAP THE BOARD.

Snap the board along the score line by bending away from the cut side. Slice the paper backing on the other side of the board to complete the cut.

Making Notches

To notch around electrical receptacles or windows, orient the board the same way that it will be installed and place it as close to its future home as possible. Use a tape measure and a pencil to mark the cuts you'll need.

Then use a drywall saw to make the initial cuts, leaving the last line to be

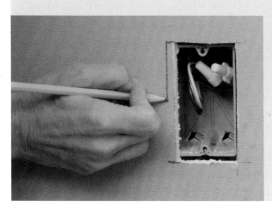

scored with a utility knife, snapped, and then cut again. Put the board into position and check the fit. If you need to widen the hole, mark the added opening you need on the board while it's in place. If the hole is too wide in one area, you can fill it later.

4 **FASTEN THE BOARD.** Reposition the sheet on the wall and, using screws approved for the type of board you're using, fasten it in place by inserting a screw every 6 inches or so along every stud. Repeat this process by butting another sheet against the end of the first, and continue moving across the wall. Then run another row of boards under the first, making sure to keep them tight against the boards above and offsetting their joints by at least one stud. It's also a good idea to shim the bottom row up off the floor by about ¼ inch to make fitting the sheet easier and to prevent moisture from wicking up into the material. Place the cut edge along the floor and the factory edge against the boards above.

5 **SKIP THE JOINT COMPOUND.** There's no need to go through all of the usual steps of taping the drywall seams that you'd do if you were painting the wall. In fact, standard

joint compound is water soluble, so the moisture in mortars and mastics can dissolve it slightly, leading to bonding problems. Most tile setters leave the joints untaped and simply fill them with mastic or thinset as they lay the tiles. But if there are gaps or uneven spots between sheets, you could fill them with tile adhesive: Cover the seam with fiberglass mesh tape and then use a flat trowel to apply one thin coat of the thinset or mastic you're using to set the tiles. Smooth the material flush with the surface so you don't create any high spots.

TRICKS OF THE TRADE

Setting Drywall Screws

There's a subtle art to setting drywall screws. If you don't go deep enough, they'll stick out from the surface, making it tough to align your tiles in a flat plane. But set the screws too deep and the head will punch through the paper facing on the drywall, which it needs to grab in order to fasten the drywall in place. "You want to set the screw head just below the surface without tearing it through the paper," says tile setter and general contractor George Taterosian. The easiest way to ensure that you set every screw perfectly is to use a drywall screw setter (shown below), an inexpensive drill bit that automatically sets the screws to the proper depth.

Remove Window Aprons

Usually, the trim underneath the windowsill—called the apron—is so thin that it will sit below the surface of the wall tile if you tile against it. That doesn't look good, so tile setter George Taterosian suggests removing the apron altogether (above) and tiling right up against the sill—a solution that also eliminates tricky tile notching later.

Preparing the Room

Whether or not your wall required any significant repairs, there are a few basic steps you may need to take to prepare for the tile job.

1 **REMOVE THE VANITY.** You can tile around a bathroom vanity, but you might regret it later. If you ever decide to replace the vanity, you'll be limited to one that is precisely the same size. So it's always best to take it out. See page 83 for removing a vanity and page 122 for reinstalling it.

2 **REMOVE THE TOILET.** To tile behind a toilet, you'll probably need to remove it in order to gain easy access to the wall. Before you remove the toilet, though, measure the space between the back of the tank and the wall. Any less than an inch or so could mean that your toilet won't go back in place after you add the thickness of the tile to the wall. In that case, you may need to tile around the tank, purchase a new toilet, or select a thinner tile. See page 82 for toilet-removal instructions and page 124 for reinstallation instructions.

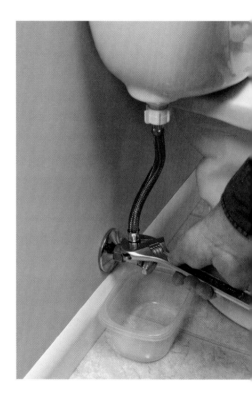

3 **TRIM WINDOWSILLS.** Rather than notching your tiles around the ends of windowsills where they jut past the rest of the trim, cut the sills before you lay the tiles so that the tiles can slide behind them. Place a tile on the wall as a guide and lay an undercut saw on the tile. Then cut the sill back flush with the rest of the trim. If necessary, use a small flathead screwdriver like a chisel to carve away the cut material.

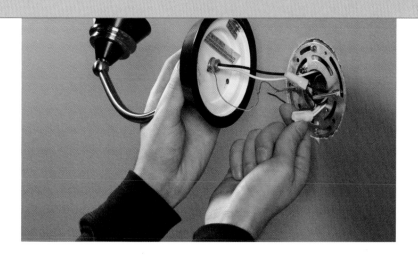

4 **REMOVE WALL SCONCES.** With the power turned off at the main electrical panel, remove any light fixtures that hang where you'll be tiling. Do this either by removing screws from the base of the fixture or by removing a decorative nut on a spindle in the center of the fixture. There's likely a bracket underneath the cover of the unit, which also should be removed. Unscrew the wire nuts and untwist the wires to completely remove the fixture. Then reattach the nuts over the exposed wires dangling from the wall. After the project is complete, re-attach the fixture by reversing this process, or hire an electrician.

5 **REMOVE RECEPTACLE AND SWITCH COVERS.** With the power turned off at the main panel, back out the screws that hold the covers on the receptacles and switches. Next, remove the screws holding each receptacle and switch in its box. If the connections where the wires are attached are exposed, wrap them in electrical tape, as shown, before turning the power back on. To reattach the switches and receptacles later, you'll need to buy longer screws at an electrical supply because the flange will sit on top of the tile.

TRICKS OF THE TRADE

Don't Dangle Receptacles and Switches

You could let the receptacles and switches hang on their wires during the tile job, but you're better off buying 2-inch screws and using them to reinsert the devices partway into their boxes now. "Just don't tighten them all the way down. Leave them a half-inch or so outside the box so you can run the tile behind them," says tile setter George Taterosian. This will ensure that the live wires aren't exposed, will keep the receptacles out of your way, and will require that you notch the tiles around those screws. This step is easy to miss otherwise, and if you don't do it, you'll have to drill through the tiles later to make way for the screws.

TILING A WALL

Turning Tiles

The smaller the tile, the more accommodating it will be to uneven surfaces, says tile setter John Bridge. That's why tiny mosaics are the best option for curved walls.

ONCE YOUR WALL IS PREPARED (see pages 134–141), you're ready to lay out the tile pattern. Before you start, read pages 52–53 for detailed instructions on laying out wall tiles and making layout lines. For a brick-lay pattern, as shown here, you don't need to snap additional vertical reference lines. Just set the first row on the reference lines and stagger the next row by half a tile. Then return to the reference lines for the third course, and so forth.

Installing Tiles

First select your adhesive. For walls, thinset isn't the only choice. There's also mastic, which is far easier to use. It comes ready-mixed, unlike thinset, and it's easier to apply because it's smooth and creamy. The biggest advantage to mastic is that it instantly grips the tiles and holds them in place, whereas thinset takes hours to bond the tile—a problem when you're working on a wall, because the tiles can sag out of place before they set. But mastic cannot be used behind stone tiles, as chemicals in the adhesive will bleed through the tiles. Also, mastic is not recommended for extremely wet applications, such as tub and shower surrounds. In dry locations, though, mastic will work for ceramic wall tiles. Just make sure you get a mastic that's appropriate for your tile by asking your tile supplier. The following steps show how to use mastic to hang wall tile. For instructions on using thinset, see the next page.

1 **APPLY MASTIC.** Using a trowel with notches of the size recommended by the mastic manufacturer for the size tile you're using, spread enough mastic on the wall to cover a 2-square-foot area. As long as you went over your reference lines with a dark marker, you can cover them with mastic, because they'll show through. As much as possible, apply the mastic with long, sweeping strokes. Hold the trowel at a consistent 45-degree angle all the time, to ensure a setting bed of even depth. The trowel's teeth should lightly scrape the wall surface.

2 **INSTALL TILES.** Press the first row of tiles into the adhesive, making sure to stay on the reference lines. Avoid sliding a tile more than ½ inch. Add spacers between the tiles as you go. For a brick-lay pattern like this, start every other row with a half tile. Every 15 minutes or so, check the entire installation to make sure no tiles have strayed out of alignment. Using a cloth dampened with water or mineral spirits (depending on the type of mastic), wipe away any mastic that squeezes onto the surface of a tile. *continued* ▶▶

Tiling with Thinset

If you're laying stone tiles or working on a wall that will get wet, you'll need to use thinset instead of mastic because mastic bleeds through stone and is susceptible to water. This complicates the job considerably. Mastic grabs and holds the tiles as you lay them, but thinset does not. And the tiles are likely large and heavy, since that's the typical style for stone wall tiles. This means they tend to sag down the wall before the mortar sets up. There are three ways to solve this problem:

LAY ONE OR TWO COURSES AT A TIME. The traditional way of laying large wall tiles was to lay the first row along the floor, let the mortar cure overnight, and then come back to add another row or two above it, wait another night, and so forth. Some tile setters still hang stone wall tiles this way because it gives the thinset a chance to grab onto the tiles before the weight of the course above gets added to the wall, but it is very slow.

USE WEDGES TO PROP THE TILES IN PLACE.
If you press wedge-style spacers between each course of tiles, as well as between the floor and the first course, they'll do a lot more than maintain the proper spacing. They'll support the weight of the tiles and keep them from moving while the thinset cures.

PURCHASE A NO-SAG THINSET. These quick-hold mortars grab and lock the tiles in position immediately, much like mastic, as long as you mix them precisely to the specifications listed on the bag. This means you can lay the whole wall of large heavy tiles at one time, though you'll still be wise to support the stones with wedge spacers.

3 **NOTCH TILES AS NECESSARY.** Most ceramic wall tiles are softer than floor tiles and can be cut easily with a snap cutter or a rod saw. If a ceramic tile is too hard for a rod saw, use a wet saw, nippers, or both (see pages 60–63). Stone tiles must always be cut with a wet saw. To make a cutout with a rod saw, hold the tile firmly in place, with the area to be cut overhanging the work surface. Saw with steady, moderate pressure. It's easy to turn corners with a rod saw.

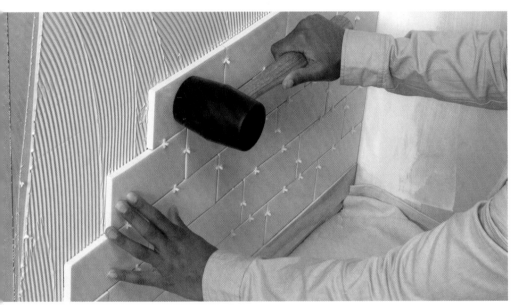

4 **BED THE TILES.** Tap each tile with a rubber mallet to make sure it's embedded in the mastic and flush with its neighbors. If a tile's surface is raised noticeably above the surface of its neighbor, give it an extra tap. If this doesn't do the trick, you may have to remove some tiles, reapply mastic, and start again.

Self-Spacing Tiles

If you're using standard 4-by-4-inch, 6-by-6-inch, or subway wall tiles, check them for nubs on their edges. These built-in spacers eliminate the need for plastic spacers and greatly simplify laying the tiles, as you can butt the nubs against each other. But don't force in a tile that's a tight fit, because it may crack. Instead, recut the tile or file the cut edge with a tile stone.

Installing Irregular Tiles

If the tiles aren't consistent in shape or size, use wedge-style spacers, which make grooves wider or narrower as you arrange them deeper or shallower. They allow you to account for varying sizes of grout lines. Also, use a straight-edge to check every other row or so to see that the tiles form a reasonably straight horizontal line.

Borders, Caps, Insets, and Accessories

In addition to the field tiles—that is, the main tiles you're using—you might want a number of other types of tile, such as decorative borders, caps that finish off the edges of tiles, insets that syncopate the field tiles, or accessories such as towel bars, soap dishes, and toilet paper holders. In many cases, these specialty tiles are sold as part of a kit with the field tiles. In other cases, you might mix and match tiles from different manufacturers (just make sure their sizes and thicknesses will work together). Decide where you want them as you're drawing your reference lines and mark their locations on the wall. Then place the specialty tiles as you tile the wall. You can also leave a space for them, as shown at right, but it's harder to do it this way.

At the top of a wainscot, for example, you might install a horizontal stripe of decorative tiles, such as a colorful mosaic or a line of pencil-thin tiles, as well as a row of trim tiles to finish off the top. And at an exposed edge or an outside corner (one that juts into the room), you'll need bullnose or cap tiles, which have one finished edge. There are also down-angle tiles, which have two finished edges. Tile stores have all sorts of suggested borders and edges mocked up on boards for you to see. For more information on trim tiles, see page 30.

Even if your trim tiles are supposed to be the same dimensions as the field tiles, don't be surprised if they are in fact slightly smaller. Just leave a bit more space between them in order to maintain the grout lines. But they're often a totally different size—such as 1-inch mosaics over a field of subway tiles—so not all of the grout lines will match up. Usually it looks better if you plan it so that none of them do. Lay out a dry run against a batten (see page 52) and transfer the marks to the wall, avoiding matching grout lines.

continued ▸▸

1 **APPLY THE MASTIC.** Spread the mastic over the area to be tiled, but no farther. The entire tile should be fully embedded in mastic, but you'll need to remove any mastic that you get on the wall beyond your tiles (see step 4).

2 **INSTALL THE BORDER.** Proceed with the next course of tiles, following the same reference lines but using the border tiles. For a corner that's jutting into the room or for an exposed edge where the tile ends, as seen on the left of this wainscot, use bullnose tiles to finish the edge. Tap the border tiles with a beater block to make sure they stick to the mastic.

3 **INSTALL THE TRIM.** Generally, border tiles are topped with one or two additional rows of field tiles before the trim is installed. Once the field tiles are done, proceed with laying the trim tiles, which provide a more detailed finish to the top edge of the tile than a bullnose tile would. To hold heavy trim tiles in place while the adhesive bonds, run masking tape over their faces and up onto the wall above.

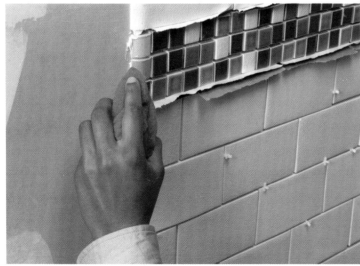

4 **WIPE THE SURFACE CLEAN.** Using a rag dampened with water or mineral spirits, depending on the type of mastic you're using, thoroughly wipe away all excess mastic from the surface of the tiles and the wall.

Grouting Wall Tiles

In the chapter on tiling floors, we sang the praises of tile joints that are wider than $\frac{1}{8}$ inch because they allow you to use sanded grout, which is easier to use on floors. But the opposite is true for walls, says tile setter George Taterosian. Unsanded grout is much lighter and stickier than sanded grout, and that makes it easier to work into the joints when gravity is working against you on a wall, instead of with you as it is on a floor.

Pour a few inches of room-temperature water into a clean 5-gallon bucket, then add some latex-enhanced grout and mix thoroughly with a margin trowel (or add latex additive to standard grout mix). Continue adding powder until the mix is about the consistency of toothpaste and free of lumps. Wait 10 minutes, then stir again.

1 **PUSH GROUT INTO PLACE.** Scoop grout out of the bucket with a laminated grout float and smear it onto the wall. Working with about 4 square feet of the tiles at a time, push the grout into the spaces between the tiles. Hold the float nearly flat and sweep it diagonally across the tile surface so it does not dig in. Press the grout in by moving the float systematically in at least two directions over each area.

2 **SCRAPE THE EXCESS.** Tilt the float up and use it like a squeegee to wipe away most of the grout from the face of the tiles. Again, scrape diagonally so the edge of the float cannot dig into the grout lines.

3 **WIPE THE SURFACE.** Dampen a sponge and wipe the tiles gently. Rinse the sponge every few minutes with clean water. If you see a gap in a grout line, push additional grout into the gap using your finger, then wipe away the excess. Wipe the surface two or three times.

4 **MAKE EVEN JOINTS.** Run the sponge gently along all vertical lines, then run it along all horizontal lines, to achieve grout lines of consistent width and depth. If you're having trouble making consistent lines, try tooling the joints by running a rounded handle like this one along each line. Allow the grout to dry, then buff the surface of the tiles with a dry, lint-free cloth.

Caulking

Wherever two sections of tile meet—such as at a corner where two walls join—you need more flexibility than grout will provide. So skip the grout for those joints and, after the grouting is done and dry, fill those joints with caulk. It's also best to caulk the area between the first row of wall tiles and the floor, countertop, or tub. Tile centers sell silicone-reinforced latex caulk in a range of colors, sometimes even designed to match standard grout colors precisely.

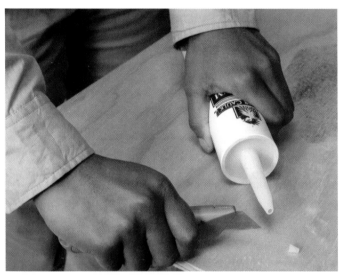

1 CUT THE TIP. With a utility knife, cut off the tip of the caulking tube's nozzle. The closer to the tip you cut, the thinner the bead of caulk will be. Some people like to cut at a steep angle, while others cut the tip almost straight across. With some caulking tubes, you also need to poke a long nail or a wire down through the nozzle to break a seal at the end of the cartridge.

2 APPLY THE CAULK. Squeeze the caulking gun's trigger until caulk starts to come out. Push down on the release button to stop the flow. Place the nozzle tip on the joint to be caulked, squeeze the trigger again, and move the nozzle along the joint as you continue to squeeze. Then release it again at the end of the joint to prevent the caulk from continuing to spill out of the tube.

3 TOOL THE JOINT. Smooth the caulk by first dampening a rag with water. Then place the rag over your finger and run it along the caulk line to press it into the joint and smooth the surface. As the rag gets filled with caulk, move your finger to a clean spot.

TILING A TUB SURROUND

WHETHER OR NOT YOU'RE TILING THE WALLS in the rest of the bathroom, tiling the walls around a tub enclosure or a walk-in shower is a separate process because you'll need to follow different procedures for this extremely wet location. You can tile all the way up to the ceiling, or just run the tile about 4 feet above the tub. On the sides, you can either stop the tile at the edge of the tub or extend the tile surface past the tub, blending it with the wall tile or ending it with a row of trim tiles that reaches to the floor (see page 30).

Choose Tough Materials

Because tub and shower surrounds get so wet so often, their tiles require tougher installation methods than tiles for other walls.

The substrate. You could use greenboard or fiberglass-coated board and get a long-lasting job, but tiles and grout are not completely waterproof. Water migrates through them, and over time it will begin to decay greenboard and possibly even fiberglass-coated board. So cement backerboard is the best choice for these surfaces.

The adhesive. For most walls, unless you're installing stone tiles or very large ceramic tiles, easy-to-use mastic is an excellent choice. But in damp locations, mastic will weaken over time as moisture migrates behind the tile. So it's best to use thinset.

White subway tiles in this tub surround are broken up by a three-row band of blue glass tiles. Two niches—one high and one low—hold shampoo and soap.

Protecting the Tub

It's easy to scratch a tub while doing demolition and tiling work. So cut a piece of rosin paper (a tough red paper that comes in a roll at any hardware store) to fit tightly over the bottom of the basin and another for the top edge of the tub. Fasten the pieces with masking tape and then lay a fabric drop cloth over the tub. If you're demolishing old plaster walls, cut a sheet of ¹⁄₂-inch plywood or thick cardboard to cover the entire tub from wall to wall to catch falling debris. After demolition, remove the board but keep the paper and drop cloth over the tub. Also be vigilant about picking up any dropped screws or nails, which can damage the tub's finish—even through a drop cloth and paper—if stepped on.

Prepare the Walls

If you're working in a new room or one that has been gutted, skip ahead to "Installing Cement Backerboard" on the next page. If not, you'll first have some demolition to do.

Removing plumbing. Faucet handles attach in different ways. In most cases, you'll first need to pry off a decorative cover in the center of the handle using a small screwdriver or a butter knife. Loosen and remove the screw underneath and pull off the handle. If there is an escutcheon (flange) behind the handle, it may simply lift off, or you may have to loosen a small setscrew first.

To remove a spout without damaging its finish, stick a wooden dowel (a hammer handle made of wood will also work) into the opening and turn counterclockwise. Or wrap the faucet with tape or a rag and use slip-joint pliers or a pipe wrench. Use the latter technique to remove a shower arm.

Removing tiles and substrate. Depending on how they were installed, it may be easy or very difficult to take out the old tiles and substrate. See pages 84–86 for instructions. If the plaster or drywall remains after the tiles are gone, measure and mark the dimensions of your new tile surround. Then use a drywall saw to cut along that line and remove the old wall material on the inside of those marks by prying it off the studs with a flat bar. If the wall also gets removed beyond where you're tiling, install new drywall over the studs in that area (see pages 137–139 for drywall installation instructions).

Installing Cement Backerboard

Remove all nails or screws from the exposed edges of the studs. Then staple roofing felt (tar paper) to the studs. This lends an added layer of moisture protection for the framing. Because it is saturated with tar, the paper will self-seal when you drive screws through it while installing the cement backerboard. Measure to find out how thick the backerboard must be in order to match the surrounding wall surface. See page 47 for instructions on cutting cement backerboard.

1 **INSTALL THE BACKERBOARD.** Place small strips of ¼-inch plywood on the rim of the tub as spacers. This creates a crucial gap between the tub and the cement backerboard. Without it, if the caulking ever failed, moisture could wick up into the backerboard, damaging the studs. Then, starting with the back wall, cut backerboard to fit, allowing a ⅛-inch gap between pieces. Make sure the boards overlap the flange on the top edge of the tub or the vinyl shower pan. Drive backerboard screws every 6 inches through the backerboard and into the studs. Make sure the heads of the screws are sunk just below the surface of the backerboard.

2 **CUT FOR PIPES.** Measure and mark the cement backerboard for the center of each pipe penetration you need. Drill each hole using a carbide-tipped hole saw about ¼ inch wider than the pipe. Alternatively, drill a small hole in the center using a masonry bit, then score the outline of the hole using a backerboard knife. Repeat on the other side and punch the hole out with a hammer.

3 **TAPE THE JOINTS.** Press fiberglass mesh tape along each joint. Mix a little thinset mortar (see page 54) and trowel a thin coat over the mesh tape. Feather the edges and scrape away any high spots. Use a silicone caulk to seal the gap between the tub and the cement backerboard. There's no need to tool the caulk, as it will be covered by tiles and more caulk later.

TRICKS OF THE TRADE

Sealing the Joints

Instead of taping the cement backerboard joints with thinset, which is water permeable, professional tile setters often use a waterproof sealant for tub and shower surrounds. "You can get waterproofing membrane at any tile shop," says tile setter George Taterosian. "Then paint it over the seams and corners and you've created one solid, waterproof substrate." Some waterproofing membranes require three steps: Brush on the product, apply a fabric over the joint, and then apply another coat. Others you simply brush on and you're done.

Setting Tiles

Establish your vertical and horizontal reference lines and lay out the
tile placement on them (see pages 52–53). Because tubs are often out
of level, it's a good idea to temporarily install a batten—a straight board
used for holding a row of tiles—along the level where your second
course will sit. See pages 52–53 for detailed instructions on how to
determine that location.

You'll tile from the batten up and come back to install the first row
once the rest of the tiles have set. Remember, tiles set in mastic typically
can be adjusted up to 15 minutes after you've set them (check the label),
but tiles set in thinset mortar should not be moved after 5 minutes. Use
a straightedge to check the tiles for alignment every few minutes.

To install irregularly shaped tiles, use wedge-style spacers, which vary
the spacing based on how far you push them into the joints. Also be
vigilant about checking every row of tiles for level. If you are installing
regularly shaped tiles that are not self-spacing, as shown here, place
a standard plastic spacer at every corner. Self-spacing tiles have spacer
nubs that simply butt against each other. Don't worry if the tiles go
slightly awry from the layout line; it's more important that the tile corners align with each other.

1 **START ON THE BACK WALL.**
Using a $1/4$-inch square-
notched trowel, spread thinset over
about 5 to 10 square feet of the
wall—or whatever area you're
comfortable working with in about
15 minutes. To make sure the tiles
will stick, back-butter each piece
with a thin coat of mortar. Starting
on the batten, press the tiles firmly
into the mortar and work your way
up the wall.

2 **CUT END TILES IN BUNCHES.**
Since the end tiles on the back wall will be covered by the sidewall tiles, they can be as much as ¼ inch short. So you can generally set the guide on your snap cutter or a wet saw only once and cut enough end tiles for a few rows or more at a time (see pages 60–63 for tile cutting instructions).

3 **COMPLETE THE BACK WALL.**
Install all the tiles above the batten for the back wall, including the cut pieces at the corners, any accent tiles, the border (if there is one), and the bullnose tiles at the top. Then move on to the sidewalls.

4 **TILE THE SIDEWALLS.** Tile the wall with no plumbing penetrations next, working over a batten and starting at the outside edge of the tub (you may need a bullnose tile for a finished edge). Work inward toward the back wall so that the cut tile will be against the back wall. Again, you may be able to set up your wet saw or snap cutter once for multiple cuts, or you may need to adjust it slightly. Repeat the process for the sidewall with plumbing, leaving out any tiles that need cutting. Use tape or scraps of wood to temporarily support the tiles right above the cutouts so they stay in alignment.

continued ▶▶

5 **MAKE THE PIPE CUTOUTS.** If a pipe falls in the middle of a tile, measure to the center of the pipe and bore a hole using a drill equipped with a carbide-tipped hole saw. But more often than not, the penetrations will cross two or more tiles and require notches:

Measure around a pipe. Hold a tile in alignment with the next course and place it against the pipe, then mark the cut you need with a pencil.

Cut the tile. Most ceramic wall tiles can be cut with a rod saw. A grinder, wet saw, or nibbling tool also works. Make the cut about $\frac{1}{4}$ inch larger than your mark to give yourself some wiggle room, as the plumbing flange will cover the gap.

Install the tile. Dry-fit the tile to ensure that it will sit properly against its neighbors, with no part less than $\frac{1}{8}$ inch from the pipe. If the mortar on the substrate began to harden while you were cutting the tile, scrape it off the wall and back-butter the tile.

6 **INSTALL THE BOTTOM ROW.** If you're using standard thinset, wait a day before installing the bottom row. But if you're using a sag-free thinset mixed to the exact specifications on the bag, you can do it immediately upon completing the rest of the job. Back out the screws holding the batten on the wall and remove it, then scrape away any dried thinset. You may be able to use whole tiles for the bottom row, but if the tub is out of level, you'll have to cut the bottoms off some tiles. Make sure to maintain a $\frac{1}{8}$-inch gap between the tub and the tiles. (You can use $\frac{1}{8}$-inch shims or scrap pieces of cardboard to maintain that spacing.) If possible, spread thinset on the wall; otherwise, back-butter the tiles and press them into place.

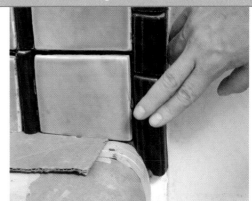

7 **INSTALL THE CAP TILES.** Unless you're continuing the tiles beyond the tub surround or you used a bullnose tile around the perimeter of the surround, you'll need to finish the job with trim tile. Where the trim tiles meet the tub, cut them to match the curved profile of the tub by making a cardboard template of the cut, transferring it to the tile, and then cutting with a rod saw or nibblers.

8 **GROUT THE TILES.** Wait overnight, then remove the spacers. Wherever the mortar in the joints is less than $1/4$ inch below the tile surface, dig it out with a grout saw, a small screwdriver, or a utility knife. (If you don't, the mortar may show through the grout.) Clean all mortar off the surface of the tiles using a damp cloth or a pot-scrubbing pad. Mix up a batch of latex-reinforced grout following the instructions on pages 64–66 (use sanded grout for joints $1/8$ inch or wider and unsanded grout for narrower ones). Scoop some grout out of the bucket with a laminated grout float and push the grout into the lines between the tiles with the float held nearly flat. Move the float in at least two directions at every point to ensure that the grout is

really pushed in. Once grout has been pushed into an area about 10 feet square, tilt the float on edge so you can use it as a squeegee. Scrape away most of the excess grout, moving the float at an angle so it won't dig into the grout lines. After you have grouted a wall, lightly clean the surface with a large, damp sponge. Turn the sponge over when it gets caked with grout, and rinse it often in clean water. Once all the walls have been grouted, rub the surface lightly with the sponge to achieve grout lines that are uniform in depth and width. If any gaps appear, push in a little grout with your finger and rub with the sponge again. Sponge the surface one more time, then allow the grout to dry for a day. After the grout is dry, buff the tile surface with a clean, dry cloth until it shines.

Tiling Down to the Floor

On the sidewalls, you may choose to extend the tiles past the tub by the width of a tile or two, in which case the outermost tiles will extend down to the floor. In that case, remove and save any baseboard trim (following the instructions on pages 80–81), install the tiles, and, once the grout is dry, cut the baseboard to meet the new tiles and reinstall it.

Caulking the Tub Joint

The line where the tile meets the tub must be caulked instead of grouted, because it needs to flex with the tub, which will move every time it's filled with water and emptied. Before caulking, remove the protective covering from the tub, clean the tile and the tub where the caulk will go, and dry the area thoroughly. Purchase a "tub and tile" caulk that matches the color of your grout.

1 MASK OFF THE JOINT. Apply a piece of masking tape along each side of the joint, leaving only a sliver of tile and tub exposed on either side of the gap.

2 APPLY THE CAULK. Cut the tip off the tapered caulk tube where it's roughly the width of your joint. Then apply the caulk in the joint starting at one front corner of the tub and working around the entire tub. Make sure to fill the joint, but try not to leave much excess caulk beyond the joint.

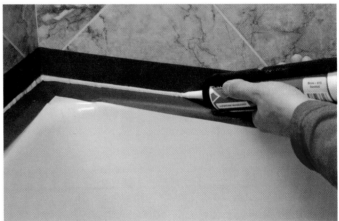

3 TOOL THE JOINT. Using a damp rag placed over your finger, start at the same spot where you began the caulk. Wipe your finger over the caulk to press it into the joint, then remove excess material and smooth out the surface. When the rag becomes filled with caulk, move your finger to a clean spot. Repeat as necessary.

4 PULL THE TAPE AWAY. Before the caulk has a chance to dry, but after you're satisfied with the tooling job, pry up one end of a piece of tape and pull it away, taking care not to smear caulk on the tub. Do the same for the other piece of tape. Then let caulk dry the amount of time specified on the tube.

INSTALLING A SHOWER NICHE

AS LONG AS YOU'RE TEARING THE WALLS DOWN to the studs in order to tile your shower enclosure, it's fairly easy to add a storage niche that will make an attractive and handy spot for keeping soaps, shampoos, and other bathing supplies. A good rule of thumb is to place the niche's shelf about 4 feet above the floor of the shower and to set the top of the niche about 12 inches above that. Try to align its top and bottom with your tile courses by dry-laying a row of tiles and spacers along a battenboard (or story pole), marking the tile locations, and then positioning the batten on the wall (see pages 52–53 for more details). If you locate the niche between existing studs, the framing process is minimal. If you want it to be wider than that—or if you want it where a stud happens to fall—you'll need to cut out the stud and do some more significant framing (see page 158).

1 **FRAME THE OPEN-ING.** To build a niche between two studs, use a circular saw to cut two 2 × 4s to fit the space. Then install the boards between the studs by inserting two nails or screws through the studs into each end of the 2 × 4s. Remember that cement backerboard, thinset, and tiles will raise the bottom by about an inch over the bottom 2 × 4 and lower the top by the same amount.

continued ▶▶

2 **TAR-PAPER THE WALL.** Starting at the bottom of the wall, staple a strip of tar paper over the back wall of the enclosure. Use a utility knife to cut it as necessary to fold it into the niche. Add another strip of paper, overlapping the first by about 6 inches, and continue until the whole wall is covered.

Making a Larger Niche

To frame a larger niche, you'll need to cut the studs, and before you do that, you should consult a contractor or engineer about whether the wall is structural and whether you'll need a building permit. If you're cleared to proceed, use a carpenter's square to mark the required cut on any studs that are in the way. Then use a reciprocating saw to cut the studs, working carefully so that the stud is cut neatly. Then, instead of using a single 2 × 4 to frame the top of the opening, make a sandwich of two 2 × 4s with ¼-inch plywood in the middle. In addition to fastening it in place through the studs at each end, cut two 2 × 4s to fit vertically between the sandwich and the 2 × 4 you install across the bottom and two more to ride directly under those (between the bottom 2 × 4 and the base of the wall). This arrangement will transfer the weight that was held by the stud you cut. Fasten the new 2 × 4s to the cut studs as well.

3 **INSTALL CEMENT BACKERBOARD.** Following the detailed cement backerboard instructions on page 151, start by cutting a sheet to fit the back wall of the niche opening. Apply construction adhesive to the back of the drywall on the other side of the opening and then insert the backerboard. Next cut strips to fit around the four inner edges of the niche

and use screws to fasten them to the framing. They will help to hold the rear panel in place. Then install the backerboard for the rest of the shower, cutting an opening for the niche.

4 **SEAL THE JOINTS.** Use waterproofing membrane to seal all of the cement backerboard joints in your niche.

5 **INSTALL A STONE SILL.** While you could tile the bottom of the niche, professional tile setters often prefer to use a piece of marble or other stone that's been cut to fit the opening so it extends slightly past the finished wall. Use thinset to adhere the stone to the cement backerboard, and make sure to pitch it slightly toward the tub. If you set a 6-inch level on the stone, when the bubble just slightly touches the line on the niche side of the level, the pitch is right. *continued* ▶▶

Installing Bullnose Tiles

When a bullnose tile meets a regular tile at a corner—as it will around the perimeter of a shower niche—install the field tile first. "That way you can ensure that the bullnose tile overlaps the field tile just right," says tile setter Jane Aeon.

6 **TILE THE SURROUND.** Next, tile the shower surround as normal and continue each course into the niche. Depending on the tile you're using, you may need to use bullnose tiles for the corners where the wall tiles meet the edge tiles of the niche. The bullnose tiles can be on the wall or on the niche's edge, whichever works best in your scenario.

7 **TILE THE TOP EDGE.** If you're using lightweight tiles and no-sag thinset (see page 143), you may be able to tile right across the top edge of the niche without difficulty. But if the tiles are heavy or the thinset won't lock them into place before gravity starts to pull them out of position, there are two ways to hold them while the thinset cures:

- APPLY VERTICAL STRIPS of masking tape across the face of the tiles and up onto the tiles on the wall above (shown at far right).

- OR ALLOW THE THINSET holding the stone sill to set up overnight before tiling the top edge, and then prop scraps of wood between the top edge tiles and the stone to hold them in place while the thinset cures (shown at right).

8 **GROUT THE TILES.** Grout the enclosure and the niche all at once, following the instructions on page 147.

TILING A WINDOW ALCOVE

A WINDOW ALCOVE IS A RECESS IN THE WALL that surrounds a window, which is common in apartment buildings, finished basements, and other masonry-walled structures. Tiling an alcove is much like tiling a shower niche. If it's in a shower, you'll need to install cement backerboard and waterproof membrane. If it's not, you can tile right over the existing drywall or plaster as long as the paint is in good shape. If it's never been painted, apply a coat of primer. For full instructions on wall preparation, see pages 134–141.

1 **TILE THE SIDES.** As you lay each course of tile along the wall, include the window alcove, maintaining consistent course lines throughout. You can install the bullnose tiles needed to finish the corners on either the wall or the alcove surface, whichever looks better in your situation.

2 **TILE THE TOP EDGE.** If you're using lightweight tiles and no-sag thinset (or mastic), you may be able to tile the top edge of the window alcove without difficulty. But if the tiles are heavy or if the thinset won't lock them into place before gravity starts to pull them out of position, there are two ways to hold them while the thinset cures: Use masking tape or scraps of wood to hold them in place while the thinset cures. See step 7 on the opposite page for instructions on both options.

3 **GROUT AND CAULK THE JOINTS.** See page 147 for instructions on grouting walls. Once you've cleaned the excess grout from the tiles the next day, caulk the joint between the tiles and the window or window trim, as this joint needs the flexibility of caulk. See page 156 for instructions on applying caulk.

Tile Casings

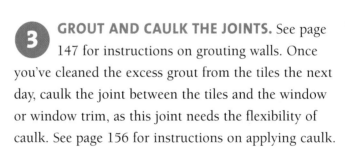

If you're looking for an easy weekend tiling project, try replacing wood casings around windows or doors with tiles. First remove the wood moldings. For a window, do not remove the sill, but trim it off the wall following the instructions on page 140 to allow a tile to slide behind it at each end. Then use mastic to install a band of tile in place of the old molding. Run a bead of caulk along the inner edge to seal the tile to the window frame.

TILING A FIREPLACE SURROUND

BECAUSE IT IS SPARK RESISTANT and easy to clean, tile is an ideal material for fireplace surrounds (the masonry area directly around the firebox) and for hearths (the masonry floor just in front of the firebox). And since you won't need much tile for these small areas, it's easy to splurge on expensive ones, such as Moroccan mosaics, translucent glass, or colorful stone like the slate shown here. Just check with your local building department before beginning this job, because there may be fire codes that you need to follow.

Prepare the Surface

The existing stone or brick that you see on your old hearth and surround are most likely veneers, which can be removed much like you'd remove old tile (see pages 84–86). But they're typically set in a thick mortar bed, making removal a back-breaking chore. If using a cold chisel, pry bar, and hammer doesn't work, you might need to rent a hammer drill or even an electric jackhammer. In this case, you might also seek the assistance of a professional tile setter, mason, or chimney maintenance company.

Or you can tile over the old surfaces, as long as the layers won't be so thick that the tiles won't tuck under the wood mantel or that the hearth gets raised high above the floor and becomes a tripping hazard. To tile over a rough surface like stone or brick, check with a straightedge for high spots and level them with a grinder. Then clean the surface with a mild solution of muriatic acid. For glazed tiles, go over the entire surface with a grinder to remove the glossy finish. In either case, mix a small batch of heat-proof thinset and use the flat side of a trowel to apply a thin "bond coat" of mortar to the surface. This fills in any grout lines and other irregularities.

If there's a wooden mantel, it likely covers the surround, so you need to temporarily remove it by carefully prying it off the wall in one piece (use the same techniques shown on pages 80–81 for removing wood moldings). Or you can simply butt the new tiles against its edges.

Ask your tile supplier for heat-resistant thinset and grout that are appropriate for your tile and the substrate you're covering. You will also need a recommendation for a sealer if you're using porous stone tiles (which must be sealed before they are installed, or the mortar will stain them permanently). Lay out the stones on a drop cloth and apply sealer with a brush or a rag to the top and sides of every tile. Plan to seal the tiles again after they have been installed (see pages 70–71).

Install Hearth Tiles and a Temporary Support

Refer to pages 54–55 for instructions on mixing and using thinset, pages 60–63 for cutting tiles, pages 52–53 for laying tiles, and pages 64–66 for grouting tiles. After the bond coat dries, mix up a batch of thinset and apply it to the hearth with a notched trowel recommended by your tile supplier for the tiles you're using. Set the hearth tiles, using spacers to maintain consistent grout lines. Allow the mortar to set overnight.

Next, construct a frame from 2-by-4s (left) as a temporary support for the first row of tiles above the firebox. Check that the tiles resting on it will be at exactly the correct height, and check that the support is level.

Setting the Surround Tiles

If you are installing glazed tiles, you may want to use bullnose tiles around the edges of the firebox, depending on how finished a look you want to achieve. Some installations also include a row or two inside the firebox, running vertically along the sides and sometimes along the underside of the top as well.

Use no-sag latex-reinforced thinset mortar for the wall tiles around a fireplace. Use a large-notch trowel to apply the mortar, to ensure that the tiles are fully bedded. Also use spacers so you can ensure consistent grout lines.

1 **PLACE THE TILE.** When installing large tiles like these, spread enough adhesive for only two or three tiles at a time. Back-butter each tile with a thin coat of mortar to ensure a firm bond. Place the tile on spacers for consistency and to support the weight of the tiles.

continued ▶▶

2 **BED THE TILE.** Press the tile firmly into place. Use a beater block to embed the tile firmly and to bring its surface flush with the surrounding tiles.

3 **CHECK FOR LEVEL.** Place a level on top of each row of tiles to make sure they are staying level. Adjust them by shifting the spacers if necessary. Wipe away any mortar from the surface of each tile before moving on to the next one.

4 **LAY TRIM PIECES.** This surround, like many, requires some trim tile pieces, which get installed last. Cut bullnose trim tiles to fit. Lay out a dry run, so you know that all the tiles are cut correctly and ready to install. Where a trim piece rests on top of another tile, spread a thick layer of thinset, taking care not to drip it on the face of the new tile. Gently set the trim piece in place, and use spacers to position it precisely. Wipe away any excess mortar. Set the adjacent trim tiles quickly so you can make any adjustments in all the pieces before the mortar starts to set.

5 **SEAL STONE TILES.**
Once the mortar has set overnight, apply sealer to stone or unglazed ceramic tiles. Pay attention to the rate of absorption. Some areas may be more porous than others and will need an extra coat. Allow the sealer to dry for the recommended amount of time, and then grout the tiles.

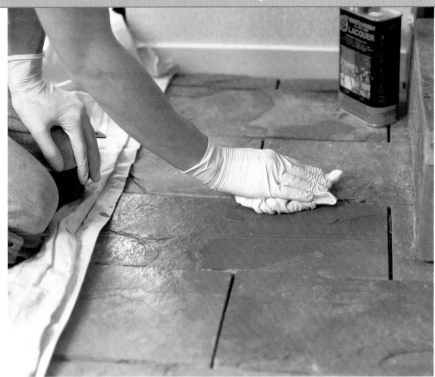

Grinding Bullnose Edges

Wherever a tile edge is exposed, it should be finished with a bullnose edge. For stone tiles that do not come with a bullnose edge, you can edge them yourself using a grinder. Consult your tile dealer to choose the grinding disks that will work best with your tile.

Place the tile on a stable surface; you may want to clamp it in place. Equip the grinder with the roughest recommended disk. (For these hard slate tiles, a diamond cutting blade was used.) Turn the grinder on and hold the disk at a 45-degree angle to the tile corner. Using gentle pressure, set the blade on the far side of the tile and pull it toward you. It will take four passes or so to create a slightly rounded edge.

Switch to a slightly less coarse disk (in this case, an extra-coarse marble-polishing disk) and repeat the process. Switch again to the smoothest disk (here, coarse marble) and repeat.

TILING A CEILING

RARELY DOES A CEILING NEED TO BE TILED for practical reasons. A coat of paint and a good exhaust fan will protect the ceiling from rising steam over a shower. Still, continuing the wall tile right across the ceiling creates a sense of enclosure, provides an easy-to-clean surface, and gives a bathroom a stunning look.

The only catch is that tiling a ceiling is difficult. You'll be working overhead, which means tired, sore arms and lots of adhesive and grout dripping all over you. But as long as you use mastic, which grabs and holds the tiles instantly, it's a project you can tackle yourself. If you're using stone tiles, however, mastic isn't an option, so use no-sag thinset (see page 143) or think about hiring a pro.

You'll want to tile the ceiling before tiling the walls, because that gives you $\frac{1}{4}$ inch or so of fudge factor around the outer edge of the ceiling, where the wall tiles will cover any gaps. The trickiest part of the job is aligning the ceiling tiles with the wall tiles so the grout lines will match up on all four walls. To see how difficult that will be, use a 4- or 6-foot level to check how true (level) the walls are, and a tape measure to compare the dimensions of the floor with those of the ceiling. If everything lines up perfectly, you'll be fine.

Stone Ceilings

If you're installing stone tiles on a ceiling, you can't use mastic, which will bleed through the stone. You have to use thinset. And because it won't hold the tiles until it begins to harden, you'll need to support the weight of the tiles while the mortar cures. That's probably best left to a professional, who will use a little jig to hold the tiles in place. Tile setter George Taterosian does it with 2 × 4s. One 2 × 4 gets laid directly under each row of tiles, held in place by a series of other 2 × 4s standing on end beneath it. "I cut the vertical 2 × 4s a tiny bit short and use shims to gently nudge them into position without jostling the tiles," he says.

If it doesn't, think about using a different size tile on the ceiling or running the tiles diagonally there so that the grout lines don't need to align.

1 **SNAP REFERENCE LINES.** Follow the instructions for preparing a wall surface, starting on page 134. Then follow the steps for snapping reference lines on floors, starting on page 49 (tiling a ceiling is much like tiling a floor, only with gravity working against you). If you'll be installing the tiles on a diagonal, see page 50.

2 **SNAP BATTEN LINES.** Next, make a mark a few inches from one corner of the ceiling and measure from it to one reference line. Then make a mark at the opposite end of the ceiling that's an equal distance from the reference line. Snap a chalk line on the ceiling between those points. Repeat on the opposite wall, and then for the other two walls, by measuring against the other reference line.

3 **MAKE BATTENS.** Cut a piece of 1 × 4 to match the length of each reference line. Lay the boards on the floor and arrange a row of tiles along each one, using spacers to get them aligned properly. Adjust the tiles so that the cuts required on each end are roughly equal and you're left with end pieces larger than half a tile. Mark the tile locations on the battens.

continued ▶▶

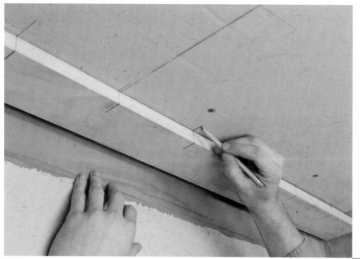

4 **TRANSFER THE MARKS.** Raise one of the battens to the ceiling and use drywall screws to fasten it temporarily along one side of the lines. Transfer the marks you made on the batten onto the ceiling. Repeat along the other lines, using the appropriate batten for each line. Snap chalk lines between corresponding marks every 2 feet or so in each direction, and then use a straightedge to go over the lines with a marker.

5 **TILE THE CEILING.** Apply mastic between a set of grid lines. Don't worry if the mastic crosses the lines, as they'll show through. Stick up tiles using plastic wedges to space them. Mastic grabs the tiles immediately, so as long as you get them fully bedded in the adhesive, you don't need to worry about them dropping or shifting. Then, if you're using the same tiles on the walls, base your wall layout on the tile rows on the ceiling.

6 **GROUT THE CEILING.** "Grouting a ceiling is just like grouting a floor," says tile setter George Taterosian, "except that the grout doesn't stay in the joints; it falls on your head." Follow the instructions starting on page 64 for mixing and applying grout. But tackle an area of 1 or 2 square feet at a time, work slowly, and expect much of the grout to fall out of the joints. You just have to keep doing it until you get the right consistency of grout (fairly dry) and figure out the right way to press it into the joints with the grout float to make it stay.

HANGING SHELVES AND HOOKS FROM TILE WALLS

MANY TOWEL RACKS, SOAP DISPENSERS, SHOWER BENCHES, shelves, lighting sconces, mirrors, and other wall-hung accessories have mounting hardware that attaches with screws. For a heavy object, the best way to anchor those screws is into studs, by using an electronic stud finder to locate the stud, and a masonry bit to drill through the tile (see steps 1 and 2 below). This should be done long after the mortar or mastic and the grout have hardened. The drill bit must be larger than the shank of the screws so that the tile doesn't crack when you install the screws. Then drive a screw into a stud or other framing member behind the tile. If you cannot screw into a stud because there isn't one where you need to install the accessory, use a plastic anchor or a molly bolt.

1 **NICK THE TILE SURFACE.** Mark the location for the hole you need using a fine-tipped marker. Then hold the tip of a screw right on that spot and tap the screw with a hammer to chip the tile surface. Starting the hole like this will prevent the drill bit from wandering across the slick surface of the tile.

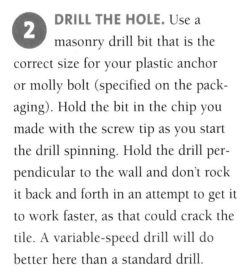

2 **DRILL THE HOLE.** Use a masonry drill bit that is the correct size for your plastic anchor or molly bolt (specified on the packaging). Hold the bit in the chip you made with the screw tip as you start the drill spinning. Hold the drill perpendicular to the wall and don't rock it back and forth in an attempt to get it to work faster, as that could crack the tile. A variable-speed drill will do better here than a standard drill.

3 **TAP IN THE ANCHOR.** Push the plastic anchor into the hole, then tap it lightly with a hammer until it's flush with the surface of the tile. You can now hand-drive a hook or a screw into the anchor.

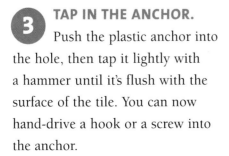

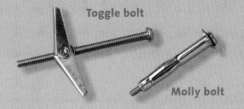

countertops
and
backsplashes

CHOOSING TILES FOR COUNTERTOPS AND BACKSPLASHES

YOU CAN USE ALMOST any tile for a backsplash. Despite being adjacent to sinks and countertops, the tiles face very little physical wear and few damaging splashes (see pages 128–133 for advice on selecting tiles for any wall application). Countertop tiles, on the other hand, need to be chosen carefully. Though countertops don't take as much weight as floors, they do face attack from knife blades, sweating drinks, and the corrosive acids in everyday foods. So only tough tiles should be used on them.

This eye-catching mosaic of red, orange, and antique gold glass tiles came pre-assembled from the factory on 12-by-12-inch squares of mesh backing.

A stripe of tiny pearlescent glass tiles lies flush in a concrete countertop and continues up a small backsplash next to the cooktop.

This full-wall backsplash
was created using tiles
painted in a design that
fits together to form a
continuous pattern.

Glazed ceramic tiles offer a shiny surface that's
easy to wipe clean, but many glazes are so fragile
that they'll scratch quickly if used for a countertop. Make sure to select a tile that's rated 5 or 6
on the Mohs scale or Group 3 or higher on the
Porcelain Enamel Institute scale (see page 74). Higher ratings than those will provide a more wear-resistant counter. You might opt for a porcelain floor tile, which
you can be sure is sturdy enough for the job. But be wary of limestone and marble,
as they can be damaged by food acids. If you choose one of these stones—or any tile
that your supplier says is acid sensitive—be sure to regularly apply a sealant to protect
it from stains (see pages 70–71).

If you choose tile that's relatively bumpy, such as a handmade terra-cotta or one
that's embossed or has steep bevels around the edges, consider adding another surface for doing most of your chopping, kneading, and mixing. Use your chosen tile
for the rest of the countertop, and keep some large cutting boards handy for big holi-
day cooking projects when every inch of the countertop becomes a food-prep area.
Or you can avoid bumpy-tile syndrome by choosing a machine-made tile that's relatively flat and smooth.

A diagonal layout and a white color scheme are classic choices for a
farmhouse-style kitchen, as is the wood-topped island work surface.

Stone tiles can mimic stone slabs when you choose polished, gauged, or honed tiles that are "rectified," meaning the edges are square so the tiles can be pushed close together. Carefully select stone tiles that are uniform in appearance and have a fairly solid color, both of which help to down-play the seams. Then limit the grout lines to only $\frac{1}{8}$ or even $\frac{1}{16}$ of an inch wide and match the grout to the tile color. This may require mixing a couple of standard grout colors together.

Another thing to consider is how you'll edge the countertop. Many clay tiles have matching V-cap trim tiles that you can use to wrap the edges. For stone, you can cut tiles to fit the edges and then, if necessary, use a bullnose tile around the perimeter of the countertop's surface. If the grout blends well with the stone, that can help maintain the illusion of a solid countertop material. If it doesn't, the grout lines between the edge tiles can actually high-light the fact that it's a tiled countertop. Other edging options include wood or metal trim pieces designed for the task. See page 30 for more about edging.

The top edge of this subway-tile wainscot is finished with a simple bullnose edge rather than a chair rail or other ornate trim tile.

A square of premounted glass mosaic tiles offers an abstract, almost pixilated pattern.

The traditional look of handmade subway tile is modernized with a colorful glaze, unusual embossed designs, and a vertical installation pattern.

PREPARING THE COUNTERTOP SUBSTRATE

IF THERE'S AN EXISTING COUNTERTOP on the cabinets, the cabinet layout isn't changing, and the surface is solid and strong, you could just tile over it. But this works only if the old surface has square corners (without any curves or bevels) and doesn't have an integral 4-inch backsplash. Scuff up plastic laminate first with a rotary sander fitted with 100-grit sandpaper to give the tiles something to grab onto. Also use a thinset that's sold for the specific surface you're tiling. You'll get a stronger, longer-lasting result, however, if you remove the old countertop and start from scratch.

Removing the Old Countertop

Don't bother peeling the old plastic laminate or tiles off the substrate, because it's very labor intensive. Plus, the remaining adhesive or thinset will be problematic, and it will likely leave you with a fiberboard surface, which is not a good one for tile to bond with. You'll get the best results by removing the old countertop entirely and building a new one.

1 **DISCONNECT THE PLUMBING.** Turn the hot and cold shutoff valves all the way clockwise and then try turning on the faucet to ensure that the water is off. If the valves let water through and tightening them a bit more doesn't solve the problem, you'll need to install new valves before moving forward, or hire a plumber to do it. Then, with a bucket placed underneath to catch water escaping from the pipes, and with some old towels handy for mopping up spills, use an adjustable wrench to disconnect the water lines from the valves. Use your hands to unscrew the P-trap from the sink. If there's a garbage disposer under the sink, disconnect it next using the key that came with it. If that's not available, insert a screwdriver into one of the keyholes and turn the locking ring (usually to the left as you're facing the disposer).

2 **DISCONNECT THE SINK.** If you're replacing the sink, you can proceed to step 3. If you're saving it, you'll want to detach it from the old countertop. Put your head and arms inside the cabinet and find the screws or bolts holding the sink to the countertop. Unscrew those fasteners. Then, standing in front of the sink, lift it off the countertop. You may need to have someone else push from below to disengage the putty or caulk that's sealing the sink's rim to the counter. And if it just won't let go, remove the countertop with the sink still attached, to make it easier to work the sink free.

3 **REMOVE THE COUNTERTOP.** Look inside each base cabinet and find the screws or bolts holding the countertop to the cabinets. Unscrew those and do the same with the screws fastening the dishwasher and any other under-counter appliances to the countertop. Next, use a sharp utility knife to break the caulk seal where the countertop meets the backsplash. For an integral backsplash, break the seal where it meets the wall. Then, with a few helpers stationed along a large countertop, lift it off the cabinets. If it's stuck, don't use force. Look for screws you might have missed or grout or caulk that's still locking it in place.

Building a New Countertop Substrate

Construct the new countertop substrate using ¾-inch CDX plywood and ½-inch cement backerboard.

1 **MAKE A MEASURED SKETCH.** Draw a quick pencil sketch of the countertop's footprint and use a tape measure to determine the length you'll need for each dimension, marking the results on the sketch. Make the countertop overhang the front of the cabinets—as well as their ends and backs where they aren't against a wall, appliance, doorway, or other obstacle—by one inch.

continued ▶▶

2 **CUT OUT THE PLYWOOD.** Transfer those measurements to ¾-inch CDX plywood at each edge of the board and snap chalk lines between the marks. Then cut your plywood using a circular saw or a table saw. If you'll be installing a new sink, use the template provided by the manufacturer to mark the sink cutout. If you're reusing the old sink, check the marks on the old countertop to see how much the rim of the sink overlapped the counter's surface and then use a tape measure and a framing square to adjust the traced lines

accordingly. Use a drill to start a hole in the plywood and then cut out the sink hole with a jigsaw. Test-fit the cut plywood over the cabinets and make any necessary adjustments by trimming sheets if they're too large or cutting new ones if they're too small. Insert the sink to check its cutout. Use a marker to write "TOP" in large letters on each plywood sheet.

3 **MARK THE CEMENT BACKERBOARD.** Once the plywood fits over the countertops, use it as a template for the cement backerboard. Lay out sheets of backerboard with the tile side (the rougher side, which should be marked with a label) facedown and arrange the plywood over it facedown as well. Keep the joints in the plywood as far away from the joints in the backerboard as possible. Trace around the plywood with a pencil, making sure to keep the lead tight against it. Alternatively, you can use the old countertop as a template (see tip at left).

TRICKS OF THE TRADE

Use the Old Top as a Template

Unless you're changing the configuration of your kitchen, the old countertop makes a perfect template for the new one, says tile setter George Taterosian. Simply lay sheets of ¾-inch CDX plywood down on the floor, butting them end to end as necessary, and then place the old countertop facedown over the plywood. Trace around it with a pencil. If you're reusing the sink, trace its old cutout as well.

4 **CUT THE BACKERBOARD.** To cut the cement backerboard, hold a straight 2 × 4 against a line and score the sheet with a carbide-tipped cement-board knife. Press hard and make a dozen or so passes so that you wind up with a $\frac{1}{16}$-inch-deep grove. Then, following the detailed instructions on page 47, snap the board, cut the back, and smooth the edges with a tile stone. Place the plywood on the cabinets and test-fit the backerboard over it, adjusting or recutting as necessary. Place the sink in its cutout and use a speed square to ensure that the edges of the plywood and backerboard align. Adjust as necessary.

5 **ASSEMBLE THE SHEETS.** Remove the cement backerboard, mix a batch of thinset, and use a $\frac{1}{4}$-by-$\frac{1}{4}$-inch notched trowel to spread it over the entire surface of the plywood. Then replace the backerboard and, while using the square to check alignment around the edges, fasten the sheets together using 1-inch backerboard screws every 6 inches or so across the entire top. (Any longer and your screws will penetrate the cabinets, potentially screwing the drawers shut, warns tile setter Jane Aeon.)

6 **INSTALL THE NEW SUBSTRATE.** Adjust the plywood, thinset, and cement backerboard sandwich so it's positioned exactly where you want it over the cabinets, with the overhangs even. Use a level to make sure that it's level, both side to side and front to back. If necessary, raise low spots using shims with a dab of wood glue on each side by inserting them between the cabinet and plywood. Then, with wood screws, fasten the countertop to the cabinets, using the cabinets' attachment hardware that held the original countertop in place. Reuse the original screws or use new screws of the same length.

TILING A COUNTERTOP

IF YOU'RE TILING BOTH the countertop and the back-splash, start with the countertop. But prepare the wall for the new backsplash (see pages 134–141) before you start tiling the countertop. If you're tiling the counter-top but keeping an existing backsplash, you'll need to make extra nice cuts in the tiles along the back of the countertop, though the joint will be caulked, which will help to hide minor imperfections.

1 **PLAN THE EDGE.** Dry-fit a sample of your edging tile or mold-ing, along with a field tile, placing spacers between them. That will tell you whether your field tile should sit flush with the front edge of the substrate or be set back the appropriate depth for the edging that you're using. Make a mark at the location where the field tile begins (unless it is right at the substrate's edge) and then repeat this process around the countertop (left). Snap a chalk line along each front edge of the countertop to repre-sent the start of the first row of field tiles. Check that line with a trim tile, spacer, and field tile again (below left).

2 **INSTALL A BATTEN.** To ensure that your tiles stay straight, install a batten along the chalk line, says tile setter Jane Aeon. Use drywall screws to temporarily fasten a strip of straight 1 × 2 on the chalk line so you can quickly and easily lay your tiles against it. If you're using wood trim for the countertop edge, then install the batten on the edge of the counter-top substrate, so it extends about 1 inch above the surface.

continued on page 184 ▶▶

Edging the Countertop

There are a few ways you can create an edge for your tiled countertop:

TILE EDGING. Some manufacturers sell ceramic tiles designed to cap the countertop edge. Most are shaped like a V. They cover the front edge and extend an inch or two onto the countertop surface (previous page, top). The V-caps may have corner blocks (right) or you will need to miter the V-caps at corners—that is, cut the mating tiles at 45 degrees.

WOOD EDGING. The easiest way to finish the countertop edge is with wood molding (left). To do that, simply lay field tiles flush against the front edge of the countertop substrate. After you've grouted the counter-top and given it a chance to cure, install the molding on the edge so that it's flush with the top of the tile. If you're staining, painting, or coating the molding with polyurethane, do so before installation and touch up the finish as necessary afterward. Miter the corners by cutting matching 45-degree angles on each side. Install the moldings with 6d finish nails countersunk with a nailset. Then caulk the joint between the tiles and the wood edging using a caulk that matches the grout color.

BULLNOSE TILES. Another solution is a bullnose tile (below), which is just like a standard field tile but with a finished edge along one side (and on two sides for the corners of the countertop). Begin the installation by cutting tiles to fit the width of your countertop edge, then install those tiles first, starting with a full piece at the inside corner of the countertop—that is, an L that juts away from the cook. Keep the edge tiles flush with the top of the cement backboard on the countertop's surface. Then tile the top, starting with a row of bullnose tiles overlapping the exposed top edge of the edge tiles.

3 **BEGIN AT AN INSIDE CORNER.** Following the instructions beginning on page 54, mix a batch of latex-fortified thinset that's approved for your tiles. Starting on one side, trowel thinset over the full depth of the counter and a few feet across it. Press the first full tile into the thinset, making sure it's against the batten and on the chalk line. Then, using plastic spacers between all tiles, set a few more tiles. Cut the tiles to fit the back row as necessary, using a snap cutter or a wet saw, as explained on pages 60–63.

4 **SET THE TILES WITH A BEATER BOARD.** Press the tiles into the thinset by placing a beater board over them and striking it with a rubber mallet. Apply more thinset to the cement backerboard (mixing fresh batches every 30 minutes or so) and continue laying tiles down that leg. Then come back to where you started and proceed in the other direction.

5 **TILE AROUND THE SINK CUTOUT.** You'll need to cut the tiles around the edges of the sink opening (see tip on opposite page). One at a time, dry-fit each tile with plastic spacers to keep them in alignment, and then mark the cuts you need. Use a rod saw to make rough cuts around the edges of the sink. The cuts don't need to be perfect, as they will be covered up by a drop-in sink that overlaps the tile edges, which is the recommended sink installation for any tiled countertops. Once you have all the tiles cut and dry-laid, spread thinset and lay the tiles.

6 **INSTALL THE EDGING.** With all of the field tiles installed, let them cure for a few hours and then carefully remove the battens by removing the screws. Go back to the interior corner to begin installing the V-cap tiles, mitering the joint by cutting the corner tiles at 45 degrees. To install the edging, apply thinset to the top and edge of the substrate—and also back-butter the edge tiles themselves. Don't rely solely on the spacers to align the edge tiles, as they may be slightly different sizes than the field tiles. Adjust them as needed as you proceed. If necessary, use tape to hold the trim tiles in place while the thinset cures.

TRICKS OF THE TRADE

Quick Sink Cuts

Here's a shortcut for trimming tiles around the sink opening: Don't cut them until after you lay them. Just set full tiles around the edges, letting them overhang the opening. "Then, once the thinset has cured overnight, use a rotary cutter with a tile-cutting bit to trace the perimeter of the sink and cut all the tiles at once," says tile setter George Taterosian.

7 **GROUT THE TILES.** Grouting countertop tiles is much the same as grouting any other tiled surface (see pages 64–66), but consider using epoxy grout. It's costly and a little stiffer to work with than standard grout, but it has a big advantage: It's nonporous, so kitchen spills and drips won't absorb into the grout on your countertop, where they could cause stains and, more important, could harbor unhealthful bacteria. It's crucial that you wear a respirator when mixing epoxy grout, because the airborne dust is harmful to breathe.

TILING A BACKSPLASH

TILING THE BACKSPLASH—the section of wall between the countertops and overhead cabinets—is just like tiling any other wall. But a kitchen backsplash typically extends only 18 inches high and 12 to 20 feet long, making it an ideal weekend project for a do-it-yourselfer. Start by pulling the refrigerator and range away from the wall (if they're freestanding as opposed to built in). Then remove any old backsplash tiles as described on page 134, extend the receptacle and switch screws as described on page 141, and remove the window aprons, as described on page 140. You'll also need to remove old wallpaper or flaking paint following the instructions on page 135.

1 **START AT AN OPEN END.** You'll want to begin with a whole tile at an open end of the cabinets—in other words, where the cabinets end but the wall continues. It's possible that your kitchen has two such open ends, in which case you should start at the more visually prominent end. But pantry cabinets or the refrigerator will usually cover one end of the backsplash. If there happens to be a door at an open end and the upper cabinets butt against the door's molding, you can butt the tiles against the molding as well. Otherwise, use bullnose tiles for the first vertical row and align them with the upper cabinet rather than the countertop, which likely extends farther along the wall. Use a pencil and a level to draw a line from the outer edge of the upper cabinets to the countertop.

Dealing with a Plastic Laminate Backsplash

Some old kitchens have plastic laminate backsplashes. Removing them is difficult because, rather than cutting them to fit, installers often glued them to the wall before installing the upper cabinets and so they're wedged behind the cabinets. "You probably won't be able to wiggle the material free," says tile setter George Taterosian, "but you can cut it along the bottom of the cabinets using a wood-cutting keyhole saw." Then make sure to scrape away all remaining adhesive and patch the plaster or drywall with spackle as necessary.

2 **WORK ACROSS THE WALL.**
Spread mastic (for ceramic tiles) or thinset (for stone tiles) on a 2- to 3-foot section of the wall from the open-end line. Then begin installing tiles, starting with a bullnose tile at the point where the end line and the countertop meet (if you need bullnose edges for the tiles you're using). Put plastic spacers between all tiles (unless they're self-spacing tiles) as well as between the tiles and the upper cabinets. Also place a ⅛-inch spacer between the tiles and countertop; that joint will get caulked later.

Lay about 2 feet of tile across the countertop, then add a course over that, stopping one tile short of the end. Move up the wall in this way, so that you're creating diagonal lines of tile. If you're installing subway tiles, simply start with a half tile (bullnosed half tiles sold by the manufacturer, if necessary) for the second row, the fourth row, the sixth row, and so forth. Cut the tiles along the top edge as necessary following the instructions beginning on page 60. When you've covered the first batch of mastic or thinset, use a beater board to set the tiles (as described on page 57) and then apply another batch. You don't have to tile very far behind ranges and refrigerators to give the illusion that the wall is entirely covered behind them. Ranges are taller than countertops, so you can simply continue the tiles along the level of the countertop, by snapping a line or drawing one with a pencil and a level. For refrigerators, extend the tile about 1 foot beyond the edge of the fridge.

3 **NOTCH AROUND OBSTACLES.** When you come to switches and receptacles, use a tape measure and a pencil or wax pencil to mark the tiles with the cuts you need. The tile should extend to the edge of the metal or plastic electrical box, with room for the attachment screws at the center of the top and bottom of the box. If you followed the Tricks of the Trade on page 141 and loosely installed the receptacles with long screws, the receptacles won't be dangling in your way and you won't accidentally cover any screw holes. *continued* ▶▶

Turning the Corner

Step 4 shows how to use matching cuts of tile on a corner so that it appears the tile has turned the corner. Tile setter George Taterosian makes the cuts $1/8$ inch short for those first-side tiles, creating a space between those tiles and the adjoining wall. Then, when he installs the mating tile on the adjoining wall, he skips the spacer and butts the tiles together. That way, the $1/8$-inch gap that's hidden behind the tiles serves as a hidden grout joint and the tiles look like they turn the corner. "You just have to really push the grout behind those tiles to get it into the gap, working from the top once you've set all the corner tiles," he says. Alternatively, you can fill the hidden joint with caulk that matches the grout color (and let it dry) before installing tiles on the second wall.

4 **MATCH UP THE CORNER CUTS.** When you reach a corner, chances are you'll need to cut the last vertical row of tiles to fit. As you do this, save the scrap tiles from each cut and use them as the first vertical row coming out of the corner on the next wall. "That way, you create the illusion that the tiles have turned the corner," says tile setter George Taterosian, who takes this concept even further in his installations (see Tricks of the Trade at left).

5 **GROUT THE TILES.** After the mastic or thinset has cured overnight, grout the tiles following the instructions starting on page 64. You can grout the joint where the backsplash and countertop meet, but because the countertop tends to move around, that grout may crack and chip. "You are much better off leaving that joint open and, after the grout dries, filling it with a silicone caulk that matches the grout color," says tile setter Jane Aeon. See page 156 for caulking instructions.

Dressing Up the Backsplash

Because the backsplash is a small area, it's a relatively affordable place to use pricy tiles—and an easy place to get a little fancy with your installation pattern. Here are some simple ways to do that.

DECORATIVE ACCENTS. Purchase a handful of dressy tiles—perhaps painted with culinary images, embossed with a sea-life motif (right) or glazed in bright colors—and sprinkle them throughout the backsplash. Don't attempt a random pattern. You need to plan a regular interval for the accent tile by dry-laying the backsplash on the countertop or floor.

COLORFUL STRIPES. Another great design involves using one or more rows of decorative tiles, such as pencil-thin tiles, embossed tiles, or regular tiles that contrast the color of the main tile. Do this by laying a row of the main tile along the countertop, then a row or two of decorative tile, and then another row of the main tile against the upper cabinet. Frame the decorative row with a main tile at any open ends of the backsplash.

DIAGONAL LAYOUTS. Just turning the tiles 45 degrees lends drama to the backsplash. To do this, snap grid lines for every row of tile. Rather than laying the tiles' sides against the lines, you'll place their tips against them. You'll also need to cut tiles to fill the triangular gaps created by the diagonal installation.

MAKING A TILE MURAL

THE STANDARD KITCHEN BACKSPLASH is 18 inches high everywhere except over the cooktop or range, where the hood or microwave is installed higher up the wall than the surrounding cabinets. You can simply lay additional courses of backsplash tiles in this area, or you can make it a focal point by installing a tile mural. The mural sets the placement of the entire backsplash, so install it first.

The typical over-the-range mural consists of a decorative panel, which could be any array of decorative tiles, or even just the standard backsplash tile turned on the diagonal (as shown here). This example is surrounded by a picture frame, which is a band of narrow decorative tiles that box in the mural.

1 **BEGIN LAYING OUT THE MURAL.** If you can, move the range completely out of the way. Otherwise, cover it with a drop cloth. Create a work surface on the floor with a sheet of plywood or sturdy cardboard. Then begin dry-laying your mural on the surface. It should be a few inches smaller than the space between the upper cabinets so you can surround it with regular backsplash tiles. Plan the same gap over the mural, and a full backsplash tile's width below it. Start your dry layout at the center of the bottom of the mural with picture frame tiles. Complete that bottom line in both directions, cutting the ends of the last tiles at 45-degree angles. Next lay the first vertical picture frame tile on each side of the mural, again cutting the ends to 45 degrees.

2 **COMPLETE THE MURAL.** Still working with the dry layout on the floor, lay the first course of mural tiles, which in this case are the regular backsplash tiles turned 45 degrees for a diagonal installation. To fill the triangular spaces created by the diagonal installation, you'll simply slice full tiles in half diagonally. You can set up the guide on a wet saw or snap cutter to mass-produce these cuts. Proceed up the mural in this manner, adding picture frame and mural tiles one course at a time and topping the mural with more picture frame tiles.

3 **MAKE REFERENCE LINES.** Find the midpoint between the two upper cabinets on each side of the range and use a level to draw a vertical reference line at that point. Use a tape measure and a level to mark off the perimeter of your mural so that it's centered. Then, following the instructions on page 50, snap diagonal chalk lines representing the tile grid.

4 **SET THE FIRST ROW OF FIELD TILES.**

Normally you can install backsplash tiles straight up from the countertop, as the first row of tiles is supported by that surface. But over a range, there is no countertop to hold that first row, so you'll need to install a horizontal batten on the wall (see pages 52–53) for this purpose. Install the batten so that the top is level with the surrounding countertop. Dry-

lay tiles on the batten starting with one on each side of the vertical center line you drew on the wall. Extend the tiles all the way to the ends of the wall, placing spacers between each one. Check the cuts you'll need to make at the ends. If they will result in less than half a tile, remove the dry-laid tiles and start over by placing the midpoint of the first tile on the centerline. Remove the batten and then apply mastic (for ceramic tiles) or thinset (for stone) in the area over the range and install the first course of wall tiles there. You'll complete the full course after the mural is done. *continued* ▶▶

5 **LAY THE MURAL.** Once you have the first row of field tiles installed, you're ready to lay the mural. The mural tiles go up just like any other wall tiles, from the bottom upward. Working from the centerline outward, transfer the dry-laid tiles from the floor to the wall. Then move up to the next course, all the way up the wall.

6 **COMPLETE THE FIELD TILES.** Once the mural is done, complete the first course of field tiles that you began. Work your way up the backsplash and then, while maintaining the grout lines, cut and lay tiles around the perimeter of the mural. Once the mastic or thinset has cured overnight, grout the backsplash and mural following the instructions starting on page 64.

INSTALLING A METAL BACKSPLASH

METAL TILE BACKSPLASHES ARE EASY TO CLEAN and look great adjacent to stone countertops. The basic installation procedure is similar to that for any backsplash tile, with a few idiosyncracies. Note that manufacturers of metal tiles often provide special installation instructions for their products, so ask your supplier for the manufacturer's instructions and follow them if they differ from these.

1 START AT AN OPEN END. Begin with a whole tile (or whole sheet of mosaics) at an open end of the cabinets, where the cabinets end but the wall continues. Spread mastic or thinset (depending on what the manufacturer recommends) on a 2- to 3-foot section of the wall from the open-end line. Then install the sheets of metal mosaic tiles. Start at the point where the end line and the countertop meet. Use plastic spacers between the tiles and adjacent surfaces. Lay about 2 feet of tile across the countertop, then add a course over that. Press the tiles in place with your hands, but do not use a beater board to set metal tiles, as it could damage them.

2 CUT THE TILES. Solid metal tiles cannot be cut on site. In some cases, you can factory-order cut tiles to the exact dimensions you need. In other cases, you'll need to use the metal as accent tiles only, to avoid any cuts. However, many metal tiles aren't solid metal; they're ceramic or resin tiles coated with metal, and they can be cut with a diamond-tipped wet saw, hole saw, or rotary cutter (though not with a snap cutter or nibbling tool). Always cut them metal side up, to avoid scratching the finish, and wear a respirator. If you're using a small enough mosaic tile, you may be able to make the "cuts" you need simply by peeling tiles off the 12-by-12 sheets and then cutting the backing with a sharp utility knife. Otherwise, use mosaic tape and a wet saw, as shown on page 67.

3 GROUT THE TILES. After the mastic or thinset has cured overnight, grout the tiles. Generally, standard latex-fortified grout can be used for metal tiles. But because the metal surface is so easily scratched, you'll need a soft-rubber grout float. Some manufacturers recommend only unsanded grout because the sand itself can scratch the tiles.

TRICKS OF THE TRADE

Protecting Metal Tiles

When you are grouting extremely scratch-prone metal tiles, even unsanded grout and a soft-rubber float can mar the surface. So tile setter Jane Aeon covers each tile with blue painter's tape before grouting them.

tiling
outdoors

CHOOSING OUTDOOR TILE

IF YOU LIVE WHERE TEMPERATURES remain above freezing most of the year, you can use a wide range of tiles for your outdoor projects. Even a rare cold snap that brings frost or snow won't hurt the tile, because it takes persistent subfreezing temperatures to cause cracking and other damage.

But you don't need to be in a warm-weather climate to use tile outside. Any portable items, such as tables, sculptures, and some freestanding fountains, can be taken indoors in winter, much as you might move a sensitive potted plant. And thanks to modern tile-making technologies, there are also far more choices for fixed-in-place exterior tiling projects than were available just a couple of decades ago. In addition to stone tiles and thick ceramic tiles, many of which have always been safe outdoors, you can now choose from a wide array of thin porcelain tiles that are tough enough to withstand winter.

What you don't want to use for a permanent outside installation in a cold climate is any tile that will absorb much moisture. A waterlogged tile that freezes will crack or shatter, because water expands as it turns to ice. So nonporous tiles are the most cold friendly. Depending on where you live, that means one of two tile types. A tile labeled as frost-resistant (also known as vitreous) will absorb less than 3 percent of its weight in water. A frost-proof (or impervious)

This pebbled porch was tiled with preassembled mosaic sheets of river rock, one of the easiest tiles to install. See pages 120–121 for instructions.

Clay tiles set on the diagonal give this dining terrace a traditional feel.

A once mundane concrete porch becomes a colorful welcome mat with a patchwork of bright Arts and Crafts–style tiles.

Stone tiles in random sizes create a patchwork effect on this covered porch.

Imagine that the blue-glazed tiles are water and the white hearth and benches are cliffside dwellings, and you'll find yourself transported from this backyard sitting area to the Greek isles.

tile can absorb only half of a percent of its weight, so it's even more durable. A good tile seller in your area can tell you which type you need for your project.

A frost-proof or frost-resistant tile is by definition hard and strong, so you won't need to worry about scratching and staining if you are using it for an outdoor floor. If, on the other hand, you're in a hot climate and not using a frost-safe tile, keep hardness in mind for patios and porch floors. For a tough-wearing floor, follow the same requirements as for indoor flooring, using tile that's classified as at least a 7 on the Mohs scale or at least Group 4 by the Porcelain Enamel Institute's system (see page 74). And watch out for glossy glazes, which can get quite slippery in the rain or around a pool. That's why the most common tile choices

Yellow ceramic terrace tiles pick up the color of the building, while black inset tiles lend visual interest to the floor.

Painted tiles brighten the walls of a fish pond, with tiny tile pieces adorning the beveled edges of the concrete substrate.

A concrete birdbath makes an ideal canvas for creative and colorful tiling—and offers something beautiful to admire even when the birds are vacationing in the South.

Planter boxes tiled with slate are a fresh, simple, and affordable alternative to traditional stacked stone walls.

for walks, patios, pools, and exposed porches are unglazed ceramics, textured porcelain tiles, and stone, all of which have a naturalistic look.

For other outdoor surfaces, such as walls, fountains, garden edging, planters, and fireplaces, neither scratch resistance nor slipperiness is a concern. Just make sure to choose something that is rated for your climate and that will look great nestled in with its natural surroundings.

Flagstones make a naturalistic and nonslippery poolside patio. See pages 206–208 for instructions on laying randomly shaped stones.

PREPARING A CONCRETE SUBSTRATE

YOU CAN TILE OVER CONCRETE PORCH FLOORS and concrete slab patios, as well as concrete walls and objects like planters, but pouring a concrete slab from scratch is usually not a do-it-yourself job. You'll need to bring in a masonry contractor who specializes in excavating the earth, pouring the footings, spreading layers of gravel and sand, and then pouring a flat, smooth concrete surface. Footings must extend below the depth that soil freezes in your climate, in order to prevent the slab from being pushed out of position as the water in the ground freezes and expands. Be sure to wait three weeks—or for however long the contractor recommends—for the concrete to cure completely before you lay tile.

If you have an existing concrete slab to work with, getting it ready for tile is likely a job you can handle yourself. The following steps apply to any concrete surface, including indoor floors in basements, garages, or living spaces. Use a hammer and a cold chisel to remove any old tile. If you can, also knock old mortar off the concrete. Remove any loose paint or concrete with a stiff wire brush or a power washer. Next, use a powerful vacuum to remove all debris, dust, and dirt.

TRICKS OF THE TRADE

Bonding Agents

A concrete slab is just about the best possible substrate you can tile. After all, it's strong, flat, and coarsely textured. However, some concrete slabs that were never intended to be tiled may have such a smooth finish on top that the tiles need a little help bonding to them. You could etch the surface to roughen it up, but that requires harsh chemicals. A better choice is to apply liquid concrete bonding agent over the slab. Follow the manufacturer's directions. Usually, you need to wait for the bonding agent to dry partially and then apply mortar within a few hours.

1 **KNOCK DOWN HIGH SPOTS.** Use a 6- or 8-foot level to check the slab for high and low spots, circling them with a marker. If you find a few imperfections where bumps in the slab are less than $1/4$ inch high, you can just tile over them by using a smaller tile (6 by 6 inches or less) to ride the

contour of the floor and by back-buttering the tiles with extra mortar to help smooth out the finished surface. But for spots that are $1/4$ inch high or more, you'll need to flatten them. Otherwise, you'll have a noticeable high spot in your finished tile floor. You can use an angle grinder (right) with a masonry-cutting blade to shave down the concrete, but it's easy to cause damage with that tool, so tile setter George Taterosian recommends that amateurs use a small sledgehammer and a cold chisel instead. Don't worry if the finish isn't completely flat when you're done. You can use mortar to fill in any low spots you create (see step 2). Once you've lowered the high spot, use a wire brush to remove all loose material.

2 **FILL LOW SPOTS.** If you've knocked down high spots in the concrete, vacuum the surface again before proceeding. Next, fill any depressions in the substrate. For interior slabs, you can simply pour on some self-leveling compound, as described starting on page 92. Outside, however, the compound isn't tough enough to survive the elements. For depressions that are $\frac{1}{4}$ inch or less, you can simply be extra generous when back-buttering the tiles in that area and use a level to set the tiles in a nice, flat plane. Fill deeper depressions with fast-curing concrete patching compound, which needs only a couple of hours to harden before it's ready for tile. Use a straight piece of 2 × 4 to scrape the patch flush with its surroundings and then a flat trowel to smooth it. Err on the side of less material rather than more. Small depressions can be filled with thinset when you lay the tiles, but high points will become high points in the finished tile.

3 **SEAL CRACKS.** The problem with tiling over a cracked concrete substrate is that the tiles eventually crack along the same lines as the concrete when each side moves and shifts independently of the other, much like two tectonic plates along an earthquake fault line. But you can protect the tiles by "floating" them over the area, so they're not actually adhered to the substrate in the area of the crack, only to each other. Start by making sure all loose chunks of concrete are removed from the crack. Then use a taping knife to spread quick-curing concrete-patching compound into it, scraping it flat against the surface. Once that has cured overnight, apply a crack-suppression membrane. Paint the latex adhesive supplied with the product over the crack and 4 inches on each side of it. Then apply the membrane, which is a strip of thick fabric that prevents the thinset from adhering to the substrate in that area. Finally, paint all untreated surfaces with a latex binding agent.

Fixing a Chipped Edge

If the edge of the slab has deep chips or gouges in it, the edge tiles won't have enough substance to bond with, so you'll need to repair that edge. Stake a 2 × 6 against the edge of the slab so that the board is 1 inch higher than the concrete's surface. Then mix a batch of fast-curing patching compound and trowel it into the depression, pressing it against the 2 × 6 and smoothing it flush with the surrounding surface using a margin trowel.

TILING A PORCH FLOOR OR PATIO

INSTALLING TILES OUTDOORS is much like installing them indoors, so you can refer to the instructions in chapter 2 for information about planning the layout, working with thinset, cutting tiles, and grouting. The tiles used here, Mexican pieces called saltillos, are approved for outdoor use only where winters are warm, because they're too soft to survive a freezing winter. They are also handmade, so they vary in size and shape. The bottoms are often severely curved and will need to be back-buttered with lots of mortar. Note that saltillo tiles will be stained by mortar and grout if they aren't sealed first or bought presealed.

1 **SNAP REFERENCE LINES.** For a patio or porch with an exposed outer edge, plan for a whole tile along that edge and tile back toward the house, where the cuts will be made. On a patio, begin at the most prominent outer corner of the slab. Use a framing square to check that the corner is a 90-degree angle. If it's not, check the next most prominent outer corner. If that one isn't square either, use the strategy for interior floor layouts on pages 49–53. Dry-lay enough tiles to cover roughly 9 square feet of floor using plastic spacers. For irregular tiles like saltillos, space them with adjustable wedges, with straightedges, or by eye. Measure the space that the dry-laid tiles require, add another grout line, and you've got your working grid size. Measure and mark that increment in both directions from the most prominent corner so that the cuts will be against the house. Then snap chalk lines.

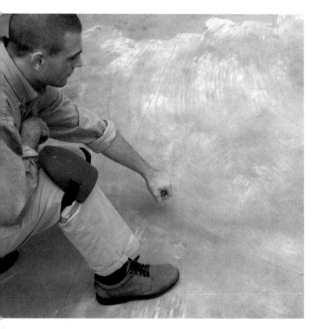

2 **APPLY THE MORTAR.** Purchase medium-bed thinset mortar, which holds its shape when laid on thick. For a small job, mix the mortar in a bucket using a mixing paddle. If the patio is more than 100 square feet, you may want to mix larger amounts in a wheelbarrow (see page 207). The mortar should be just stiff enough to cling to a trowel held vertically for a second or two. Apply the mortar to one grid section using a flat trowel. Then comb it with a trowel that has notches that are at least $3/8$ by $1/4$ inch (consult your tile dealer to choose the best notch size for the tile).

3 **SET THE TILES.** Starting with the tile at the prominent corner of the patio, or somewhere else along the prominent outer edge of the slab, begin setting tiles. Use a margin trowel to back-butter the tiles as you proceed. Work from the outer edge back toward the wall of the house. Unless you're working with uneven tiles like these, use spacers, wedges, and the chalk lines to ensure that they're spaced equally. Also use a straight-edge to ensure proper alignment and an even surface. When you are completely satisfied with the first square, bed the tiles by placing a beater board over them and hitting it with a rubber mallet. When you reach an obstacle that you need to notch a tile around, or a row that needs to be cut down to size, cut the tiles following the instructions starting on page 60.

4 **GROUT THE TILES.** Because you laid down such a thick bed of mortar, you'll need to let it cure for two days before walking on the tiles. Then insert a flathead screwdriver between two tiles to test whether the mortar is rock hard. If you feel any movement, give it another day. Once it's fully hardened, grout the tiles using a latex-reinforced sanded grout following the instructions beginning on page 64. For large, uneven joints, as shown here, mix the grout just to the point where it does not pour readily. Work in the grout by pushing with a grout float in two directions at all points. Squeegee away as much of the excess grout as you can. Drag a wet towel over the area, then wipe lightly with a damp sponge. Once the grout starts to stiffen, use the sponge to create grout lines that are consistent in depth. Allow the grout to harden, then buff the surface with a dry cloth.

TRICKS OF THE TRADE

Cleaning Grout off Stones

Grout tends to stick to textured stones and unglazed ceramic tiles. You can help prevent problems by sealing the tiles before installing them, but even that isn't a surefire solution. Always take care to wipe grout away promptly. Then, if you still wind up with grout haze on your finish, head to the tile shop for assistance. Tile setters use a variety of products, such as muriatic and sulfamic acids (at varying concentrations), to remove grout haze. There are also spray cleaners that work. Ask your tile supplier what approach will be safe for your tile (because acids can damage some tiles), and always test the product on a spare tile before applying it to your finished work. Follow the package instructions for use and for the safety equipment required for working with these harsh chemicals.

LAYING A FLAGSTONE WALK OR PATIO

THE TERM "FLAGSTONE" is occasionally used to refer to a specific type of bluestone that's mined in Pennsylvania. More commonly, the term refers to pieces that were cut to size not with a saw but with a splitter along the stone's natural fault lines, as seen in this project. The resulting stones are randomly sized; have rough, semiflat surfaces; and make wonderfully naturalistic pathways. Large flagstones can be set in sand or directly on top of tamped soil, but for the firmest installation, lay them in a bed of mortar over a concrete slab.

Flagstones vary from 1 to 3 inches in thickness. Save money and lessen back strain by choosing the thinnest possible stones. Even with thinner stones, though, it's a good idea to enlist some helpers.

At a stone or landscaping supply yard, you can purchase for delivery a pallet of stones weighing from 1 to 2 tons. Some suppliers allow you to choose individual stones. The supplier should be able to give you a general idea of how many square feet you can cover with a ton of each type of stone, and add about 20 percent to that order to allow for breakage. Consult your stone dealer to choose the best mortar for your type of stone.

TRICKS OF THE TRADE

Mix Up the Stone Sizes

One common mistake that beginners make is to leave the arrangement of the stones to chance, but if you do that, you may wind up with the largest stones in the area where you start and/or the smallest ones at the other end of the walk. That's why tile setter John Bridge recommends beginning by making three or four piles of stones arranged according to size. As you dry-lay the area, choose stones from each pile so you end up with an even distribution of large, medium, and small stones.

1 **DRY-LAY THE WALK OR PATIO.** Begin placing stones onto the concrete substrate, with each piece's best side up. Unlike tiles, which get arranged in even, orderly rows, flagstones must be pieced together like a puzzle. Take your time and expect to spend hours on a large area. Allow the stones to overhang the slab by as much as 2 inches for a natural appearance. Aim for grout lines that are roughly uniform in width. As you work, you will find yourself shuffling, rearranging, and reorienting stones. Rest often to avoid hurting your back. From time to time, you will need to cut a stone in order to make the jigsaw puzzle fit. Hold the stone in place, draw a cut line, and then proceed to step 2.

2 **CUT THE STONES.** Cutting flagstones with a wet saw, a circular saw loaded with a diamond-tipped blade, or any other saw would give you a straight, even edge that doesn't match the rough-hewn look of the stones. Instead, you need to split the stones. Wear protective eye gear, because shards of stone will fly. Move the stone to an area where flying debris won't be a problem. Using a cold chisel and a small sledgehammer, tap along the cut line to produce a series of small indentations. Then, with the tip of the chisel on one of the score marks, strike the chisel with a sharp blow. If the stone does not break, move the chisel to another part of the cut and try again. The stone will break the way you want it to about 60 percent of the time. The rest of the time, it will choose its own course. When that happens, grab another stone and try again.

3 **MIX THE MORTAR.** Once your entire walk is dry-laid, it's time to start setting the stones. Pour a bag of latex-fortified thick-bed mortar mix into a wheelbarrow and gradually add water, mixing with a shovel or garden hoe and making sure to scrape the bottom of the wheelbarrow to get up all the dry ingredients. The mortar must be stiff enough to hold up a stone yet wet enough to stick. It should cling for a second or two to a shovel held vertically.

4 **BED THE STONES.** Rather than spreading a layer of mortar over the slab as you would for tiles, you're going to apply mortar one stone at a time. Start with the thickest stone of the walk, as it will establish the surface height for the rest. Carefully pick it up, trowel a 1-inch-thick bed of mortar under it, smooth the mortar slightly with a mason's trowel, and then set the stone in place, being careful to keep it oriented the same way it was in the dry lay. Repeat for the surrounding stones. continued ▶▶

5 **LEVEL THE STONES.** Set a short piece of 2 × 4 on the stones and place a 2-foot level on that. Then press the stones into the mortar, making sure their surfaces wind up being relatively level in both directions, or pitched slightly with the underlying slab. Repeat the mortaring process for the stones adjacent to the first one, using a proportionally thicker bed of mortar the thinner the stone is. Use a straight 2 × 4 that is long enough to span the walk from one side to the other to check the surface alignment of the stones. If a stone is low, remove it, apply more mortar, and reset it. If a stone is too high, tap it down and, if necessary, scrape away the excess mortar that oozes out. Continue laying stones along the path, gradually setting the entire field. Every 10 minutes or so, use a shovel or hoe to remix the mortar in the wheelbarrow. If it starts to stiffen, add a little more liquid. If it stays stiff, throw it out and make a new batch.

6 **FILL THE SPACES.** Once the mortar has cured for two or three days, you can fill the gaps between the stones with additional mortar, but the job is different from grouting tile. Don't spread the material over the entire surface. Just trowel it into the gaps, tamp it down, and smooth it with a wet sponge. Work carefully to get as little mortar on the surface of the stones as possible. Allow an hour or two for the mortar to begin to harden, then sweep the surface lightly with a broom. Once the mortar is hard, spray the entire walk with water and clean the stones with a brush.

For a more natural look, as shown here, fill the joints with fine, crushed stone. This will become fairly hard, but it will permit a small amount of water to seep in. Consult your dealer to determine whether crushed stone is safe to use in your area. After the mortar underneath has set, pour some crushed stone onto the surface. Sweep the stones in several directions to work it in deeply between the flagstones. Using a garden hose with the nozzle set to mist, spray the entire surface so the finer particles settle downward. Allow the surface to dry, sweep more crushed stone into the cracks, and spray again.

TILING STAIRS

CONCRETE STAIRS AND STOOPS are also fair game for tiling, as long as the steps don't have an overhang that juts past the riser. Where the ends of the stairs aren't bordered by walls, use bullnose tiles. Also, it looks best if you choose tiles that cover each tread and riser with a single row.

1 **PREPARE THE SUBSTRATE.** Get the concrete ready for tile by following the instructions starting on page 202. If you need to repair a chipped edge, hold the form in place with bricks, since you cannot stake it. Then apply bonding agent to the concrete substrate and, after waiting the appropriate time stated in the package instructions, move to step 2.

continued ▶▶

Tiling Just the Risers

A much easier way to bring decorative tile to a staircase is to tile only the risers. Choose a colorful ceramic tile, a stone tile, or anything that complements the setting—and preferably that's sized to fit the height of the riser with a single row of tiles. You can do this for concrete stairs, or for wooden stairs on the interior or exterior of the house. It works best for stairs that have two closed stringers—in other words, with walls on both sides as opposed to exposed edges. Otherwise, the edges of the riser tiles will show. If that's the case, use bullnose tiles at the edges. For exterior wooden stairs, apply cement backerboard over the risers, then apply the tiles with thinset. For interior stairs, you can simply thinset the tiles to the wooden risers, unless the risers are severely cracked or deteriorated, in which case cement backerboard is a good idea.

2 **SNAP REFERENCE LINES ON THE STOOP.** If there's a stoop at the top of the stairs, start by tiling it. If you're using tiles that are all the same size and shape, measure each of the stoop's four sides and mark their midpoints on the concrete. Snap chalk lines between the opposing marks to create two reference lines for your tile layout. Using a framing square, check that they're at a 90-degree angle to each other and adjust them as needed. Then dry-lay tiles along each reference line, making a grout line where the opposing reference line crosses the row. Check the cuts you'll need at the ends of the rows (accounting for the thickness of the tiled risers at the front edge if necessary). If the tiles will be smaller than half size, start over with a new dry-laid row, but this time make the opposing reference line the midpoint of your first tile. If you're using random-sized stones, you don't need reference lines. Just dry-lay the stone, using spacers as needed, planning full stones along the front edge and making the cuts as you go. Make sure to orient factory edges along all sides of the stoop, with your cuts facing inward along grout lines.

3 **TILE THE RISERS AND STOOP.** For random-sized stones, transfer your dry-lay to a nearby surface, then apply thinset to the stoop and begin laying the stones, with spacers. For stone or ceramic tiles that are all the same size and shape, apply thinset to a rear quadrant of the stoop, then lay the tiles, beginning at the center and working outward and cutting tiles as necessary to complete the quadrant. For instructions on working with thinset, see page 54; for cutting tiles, see page 60. Repeat the process for the remaining rear quadrant, then for the front quadrants, but wait to tile the front edge of the stoop, as you'll need to work on the riser first. If you're using a V-cap trim tile, a specially designed stair tread tile, or a tile that's different from the riser tile, you'll need to tile the riser before installing those tiles, in order to get the front edge of the stair tiles flush with the face of the riser tiles. If you're using the same tiles for the treads and risers—a trickier job—you'll need to miter their front edges and the top edges of the riser tiles at 45 degrees and install the mated pairs at the same time in order to get a finished edge on the tiles.

4 **GROUT THE TILES.** Continue down the stairs one step at a time. Make sure to maintain alignment with the grout lines on the stoop (if appropriate) and to tile the risers first if you are using different tread and riser tiles, or to miter the joints if you're using the same tiles for both surfaces. Allow the thinset to cure overnight and then grout the tiles as described on pages 64–66.

TILING A PLANTER

SIMPLE PLANTERS also make ideal tiling projects. You can use mosaic tiles to cover a planter of almost any shape. Here we're covering a rectangular terra-cotta planter with colorful glazed ceramic tiles.

1 **PREPARE THE SURFACE.** Clean the planter well with dish soap and water, then rinse it with a garden hose and allow it to dry thoroughly. Because terra-cotta is porous, we applied a coat of primer to the surface before tiling. If you are using a concrete planter, apply a concrete bonding agent following the instructions provided with that product.

2 **LAY OUT THE PATTERN.** Dry-lay the pattern, making sure there won't be any awkward cuts needed. We didn't use spacers in this project so the end result would have more of a handmade look, but you can use spacers, or butt-joint the tiles by pressing them tightly together (to do that with stone, you would need "rectified" tiles, which have been given a tiny bevel at their edges to provide for a $1/16$-inch grout line). Cut the tiles as necessary using a wet saw.

3 **CREATE A CLEAN EDGE.** If you're using stone tiles, you can miter the corners by cutting 45-degree angles on each adjoining tile edge to create a seamless look. To get that look with ceramic tiles, you can sand down the edge of a tile, as shown, which creates a similar mitered edge without requiring a wet saw, or you can use bullnose tiles and lap them over the edges of the adjacent tiles.

4 **TILE THE SIDES.** Apply thinset (see pages 54–55) to one end of the planter and then press the tiles into place, keeping the first one flush with one corner and with the top edge. Next, tile the sides, using bullnose tiles or trim tiles (if necessary, depending on the tiles you're using) to cover the exposed edges of the tiles on the ends of the planter. Or, if you mitered the edges, hold a mating tile against the adjacent edge to help align the edge tile you're installing.

5 **GROUT THE TILES.** Once the thinset has cured overnight, fill the joints with an unsanded grout, assuming the lines are narrower than $1/8$ inch (see pages 64–66). For wider lines, use sanded grout.

TILING A BIRDBATH

YOU CAN PURCHASE an inexpensive concrete bird-bath at a home center, plant nursery, or landscape supply yard and transform it into something colorful and beautiful with tiles. Whether you tile just the bowl or the entire birdbath, create abstract designs or floral patterns, or use contrasting colors or like colors, your only limit is your own imagination. If you choose a design approach different from ours, simply adjust the process accordingly.

1 **DRY-LAY THE TILES.** Position your tiles in the basin in whatever pattern you choose. Your design will dictate how you do this, but in general it's best to use small tiles. The tinier the tiles, the easier it will be to create a round pattern without awkward grout lines. Place a single tile at the center point of the basin, a larger one if you're using a range of different tile sizes. You can build your pattern from the center outward in circles, or in wide strips. If you're also tiling the exterior of the basin, sketch your design on the concrete using colored permanent markers.

2 **RELOCATE THE TILES.** Lay a sheet of transparent mosaic tape over the dry-laid tiles, press it down against their surfaces, and gently lift the edges of the tape to pick up the entire dry-laid mosaic. Set the mosaic on an adjacent work surface. The tape, which is a super-strong contact paper, comes in 6- and 12-inch widths, so you may need to overlap two pieces if you're doing a larger surface, says tile setter Jane Aeon.

3 **LAY THE TILES.** Apply bonding agent to the concrete surface, let it dry for the time specified on the package, and spread latex-fortified thinset over the entire bowl using a small-notched spreader, available at tile shops. Then place the taped mosaic into the basin and press each tile down into the mortar.

4 **GROUT THE TILES.** Once the mosaic has cured overnight, peel off the tape and grout the tiles using a latex-fortified grout. If you tiled the entire birdbath, use any grout color you want. If you tiled only the basin, as shown here, choose a grout that roughly matches the color of the concrete planter. A standard grout float is too large, so try using a plastic spatula instead. Mix, apply, sponge, and buff the grout following the instructions on pages 64–66.

TILING A TABLETOP

TILE CAN MAKE THE MOST MUNDANE TABLE a beautiful centerpiece of a patio, screened porch, or living room. It can make a wooden tabletop weatherproof and is a great weekend project for a beginning tiler. For an indoor table or one used on a covered porch, you can tile directly over the tabletop, as we've done here. For an out-

door table, or an indoor table whose surface you want to last for decades, cut a matching sheet of cement backerboard (see pages 46–48) and fasten it to the wooden top using construction adhesive and backerboard screws spaced every 6 inches or so. You can also build your own tabletop from scratch using ³/₄-inch CDX plywood and ¹/₂-inch cement backerboard, following the instructions for building a countertop substrate beginning on page 178. You can tile the top with butt-jointed stone tiles, sheets of pre-laid mosaic tiles (see page 67), or just about any tile you like, following the instructions for tiling countertops beginning on page 182. Just avoid tiles that are porous or bumpy, as they will make a poor tabletop. Here we've used loose mosaic tiles to make a one-of-a-kind decorative tabletop.

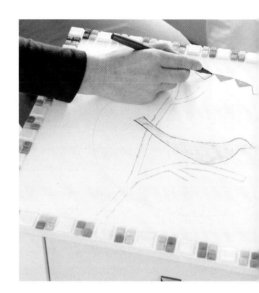

TRICKS OF THE TRADE

Umbrella Holes

If you want an umbrella hole in the center of your table, you could drill one in the plywood and the cement backerboard and then carefully cut your tiles around the opening. Or you can complete the entire tile job, then find the center of the table by finding the midpoint of each side, placing a straightedge between opposing marks, and then making a light pencil mark along the straightedge from each direction. Where the lines intersect is your center point. Drill the hole using a diamond-tipped hole saw. While the most common size for patio umbrella poles is 1¹/₂ inches, poles can be as large as 2¹/₄ inches, so check your umbrella. To determine the size of the hole to cut, add ¹/₄ inch to the pole's diameter.

1 **SKETCH A PATTERN.** Dry-lay a ring of tiles around the perimeter of the table. Use a pencil to trace the interior edge of those tiles onto the substrate. Next, use the pencil to draw a pattern onto the surface.

2 **DRY-LAY TILES.** Fill in the pattern you drew with mosaic pieces, cutting them as needed with a tile nibbler.

3 **PICK UP THE DESIGN.** Once you're happy with the design, lay a sheet of transparent mosaic tape over the dry-laid tiles, press it down against their surfaces, and gently lift the edges of the tape to pick up the entire dry-laid mosaic. Set the mosaic on an adjacent work surface.

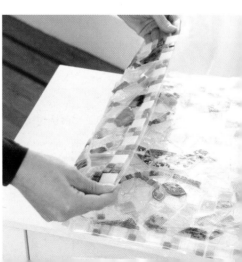

4 **SET THE TILE.** Following the directions beginning on page 54, mix and spread a batch of latex-fortified thinset over the tabletop using a ¼-by-¼-inch notched trowel. Lift the sheet of dry-laid mosaics into position and gently press each tile down into the thinset.

5 **GROUT THE TOP.** Once the thinset has cured overnight, gently pull off the mosaic tape. If you'll be serving food or beverages on the table, consider an epoxy grout. Because it's non-porous, it is less susceptible to staining and less likely to harbor food-borne bacteria. For a table that's tiled in one color or in a series of like colors, you might choose a colorful grout that matches or contrasts with the tile color. But for a multihued tabletop like this, white or gray grout is the best option.

Designing Your Tabletop

Here are some alternative ways to design your tiled tabletop.

• You can make concentric rings by first partially inserting a nail into the center of the table, tying a string to the nail, and tying the other end of the string to a pencil. Wrap the string around the pencil until the pencil is the distance you want it from the center. Then pull the string taught and draw a circle around the nail. Adjust the radius of the circle by wrapping more or less string around the pencil, then draw another circle.

• Make a star by cutting out 6 to 10 matching cardboard triangles and arranging them in a circular pattern around the center of the table. Make sure they're evenly spaced and then trace them with pencil.

• Purchase stencils of foliage, animals, geometric shapes, or anything else you want from a crafts supplier, arrange them on the table substrate, and trace them with a pencil.

• Draw a freehand spiral that begins in the center of the table and grows larger as it spins out to the perimeter.

Once you have a basic pattern sketched on the table, dry-fit some mosaic tiles into it to make sure you like the way it looks. Then use felt-tipped markers to quickly color each portion of the table in the color you intend to tile it.

MAKING MOSAIC PAVERS

YOU CAN PURCHASE concrete steppingstones or make your own from concrete mix and a simple wooden frame. In either case, here's how to tile the surface.

1 **MAKE YOUR OWN SHARDS.** Shard mosaics consist of broken pieces of ceramic tile, stone tile, other types of pottery, or even tumbled sea glass. For pavers, however, it's a good idea to use a non-glossy ceramic material so you wind up with nonslippery steppingstones. To make the shards, simply wrap the tile or other material in an old towel, place the bundle on a sturdy work surface, put on safety goggles, and hit the wrapped tiles hard with a hammer. Do one color at a time, so you don't have to sort the shards later, and check the shards as you go to ensure that you wind up with pieces in the size you want. You might even break certain colors into smaller chunks than others for textural variety.

2 **DRY-LAY THE MOSAIC.** If you are doing multiple pavers, dry-lay them all at once so you can mix up your various colors and textures across all of the pavers. Here we're using cookie cutters to create a geometric design in the center of the paver. If you're going to set the pavers flush with the grass, or mulch around them, don't worry about using bullnose tiles on the perimeter of each paver. If, however, the pavers will be set on top of the grass or mulch, consider laying a line of whole bullnose tiles around the perimeter of each paver. Or, better yet, break up some bullnose tiles and use their shards around the edge. The edges will look better this way, but it does complicate the job, so you may decide to live with unfinished edges. Once your design is set, transfer the pieces to a nearby surface.

3 **APPLY THE THINSET.** Use a $\frac{1}{4}$-by-$\frac{1}{4}$-inch notched trowel to spread a layer of thinset over the tile surface. Then use the cookie cutters to create lines in the thinset that you can fill in with different colored shards.

4 **SET THE TILES.** Place the bullnose shards around the perimeter of the paver first. With the other shards, fill in the geometric shapes created by the cookie cutters. Then cover the remaining surface with shards of different colors. Cut pieces as needed with a nibbling tool.

5 **GROUT THE TOP.** Once the thinset has cured overnight, fill the joints with an unsanded grout using a spatula, assuming the lines are narrower than $\frac{1}{8}$ inch (see pages 64–66). For wider lines, use sanded grout.

tile care
and
repair

CLEANING TILES

TILES ARE EXTREMELY DURABLE and easy to clean if properly installed and, in the case of stone and unglazed ceramics, regularly sealed. The key to keeping your tiles looking their best is to use a cleaning product that's designed specifically for the surface. Don't use all-purpose cleaners. Go to a local retailer that sells the type of tile you have and ask for a recommendation. Obviously, the best cleaner for laminate tiles isn't the best cleaner for carpet or parquet tiles. But even among traditional tiles, there are a wide range of products. Some are better for porcelain tiles, some for marble, others for granite and fieldstone. And keep in mind that no matter how fastidious you are about sealing stone tiles, unglazed ceramic tiles, and grout, you need to quickly wipe up spills that get on those surfaces, especially if the liquid is acidic, such as juice, wine, soda, coffee, salad dressing, and marinade. In just seconds, the acids in common foods can etch some stones, even if the tiles are sealed.

Glazed Ceramic Tiles

Avoid multisurface cleaners, which may contain waxes, oils, acids, or other ingredients that discolor or disintegrate grout. To clean a tile floor, use dishwashing soap and warm water. If you need something a little stronger, use undiluted white vinegar instead. For bathroom walls and especially showers, where soap scum and lime deposits can build up, use a cleaning product labeled specifically for bathroom tiles and preferably one sold by a tile store (or in the tile aisle of a home center) rather than one found among the general cleaning products, suggests tile setter George Taterosian.

Stone and Unglazed Ceramic Tiles

"A lot of people think that as long as they're sealed, stone and unglazed ceramics are impervious to stains and heavy-duty cleaners," Taterosian says. "But all that sealer does is buy you some time." Rather than soaking right into the porous stone or ceramic tile and grout, spilled liquids will pool briefly on the surface of the tile, giving you a chance to wipe them away. The quicker you get them off, the less chance you'll wind up with a stain. Similarly, only the gentlest cleaners are appropriate for these surfaces. "Your best bet is to ask your tile supplier what cleaner to use when you buy the tiles—and pick up a few bottles," Taterosian says. Some specialty manufacturers offer dozens of different cleaning formulas for different surfaces, such as one for limestone and another for granite.

Resilient, Laminate, and Cork Tiles

Purchase a product formulated specifically for the tiles you're cleaning, one either made by the manufacturer of your flooring or recommended by the store that sold it to you. When using that cleaner, make sure to use a mop that's damp, not soaked, because applying too much moisture to the surface can shorten the life of the adhesive underneath. In the case of laminate, the fiberboard backing can be compromised as well. More important than mopping, however, is routine vacuuming, because tracked-in grit can permanently scratch the surface when it's trampled on by feet and sliding chair legs. Use a canister vacuum—without a beater brush —to pick up dirt. Welcome mats and entryway carpets can help prevent dirt from getting tracked inside.

Parquet Tiles

Ask about cleaning when you're choosing parquet tiles. Some products require waxing, while others don't. When you order the parquet tiles, make sure to buy some of the recommended cleaner as well. For routine cleaning, use a damp mop, not a wet one, because water can otherwise seep between the wood pieces, causing damage to the adhesive and the wood fibers. More important than mopping, however, is routine vacuuming, as tracked-in grit can permanently scratch the surface when it's trampled on by feet and sliding chair legs. Use a canister vacuum—without a beater brush—to pick up dirt, and put down welcome mats and entryway carpets to help prevent dirt from getting tracked inside.

Carpet Tiles

Routine vacuuming with a beater brush is the best way to keep carpet tiles clean. But like any carpet, your tiles may eventually become so soiled that they need deep cleaning, with either steam or dry-cleaning methods. Check with your carpet tile manufacturer or retailer to see what method is safe for your floor. You can even pick up a soiled or stained tile or two (see page 233 for removal and replacement instructions) and take them to your favorite dry cleaner for spot cleaning. They may not perfectly match the color of the rest of the tiles when they come back, but you can swap them into an out-of-the-way spot, such as under a cabinet or desk.

RESEALING TILES AND GROUT

MANY TYPES OF TILES, especially unglazed ceramics and natural stones, as well as almost all grouts, are extremely porous. So unless you seal them after installation and reseal them every few years, they're going to become stained. You can test a tile yourself by simply dripping a little water onto it. If the tile darkens, it's porous and needs sealing. If water beads up on the surface, no sealer is needed. Unless you use a high-tech epoxy grout, the grout should always be sealed too. See pages 70–71 for more information about applying an initial coat of sealant over a newly tiled surface.

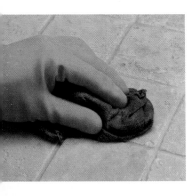

1 **CHECK THE OLD SEALER.** Some sealers work by creating a surface layer on top of the tile rather than absorbing into the pores. If a surface sealer has been used on your tile, it should be removed before you reseal the surface. Otherwise, new sealer won't bond properly and the built-up sealant might yellow the grout. Test the sealer by placing masking tape over a tile and then ripping the tape up. If you see sealer on the tape, you need to strip the tile. Purchase a sealer stripper from a tile seller after explaining what kind of tile you have. Then mop the stripper onto the floor and remove it using rags, sponges, or a wet-dry vacuum, following the package instructions.

2 **CLEAN THE SURFACE.** Whether or not you stripped the old sealer, you next need to get the floor or counter perfectly clean. Vacuum it thoroughly with a high-quality vacuum to pick up dust and debris, damp-mop it, and then go over every square inch of the surface looking for dirt and stains. As shown on this countertop, use a pot-scrubbing brush to remove any caked-on debris, and follow the stain-removal and spot-cleaning techniques outlined on page 225 to eliminate discoloration.

3 **APPLY THE SEALER.** The application process for an impregnating sealer depends on whether you're treating the entire surface or just the grout. If you're sealing both the grout and the tiles, you can simply mop the sealant onto the surface. A new, clean sponge mop works well for floors, while a tiling sponge works well for other surfaces. Be sure to wear rubber gloves. Apply a generous amount of sealant, mop it

over the surface, and then remove excess material by repeatedly wringing out the sponge or mop. If the sealant soaks into the tile or grout quickly, wait for it to dry and then apply another coat. Porcelain tiles, glazed ceramics, and other tiles that don't need to be sealed actually make the sealing job a bit more complicated, because you still need to seal the grout while keeping the sealant off the tiles. You can apply the sealer with a small art paintbrush, or you can use a grout-sealing bottle, which has a wheeled applicator at the end that makes quick work of the job. In either case, keep a supply of clean white terry-cloth towels on hand to quickly wipe away any sealant that gets on a tile.

REFURBISHING GROUP

A TILED SURFACE THAT LOOKS OLD AND DINGY can be made attractive and new-looking with refurbished grout. If there are a few holes or gaps in a newly grouted tile job, you can simply patch in new grout. Do it as soon as possible, before moisture has a chance to work its way behind the tiles. Mix a small batch of latex-reinforced grout (see page 229 for information about matching the grout color). Use sanded grout for lines $1/8$ inch and wider, and unsanded grout for narrower lines. Press it into place with your finger. Wipe away the excess, allow it to dry, and clean the area with a wet sponge. If the grout is stained in spots or is a dirty color, try cleaning it.

If old grout is coming loose over wide areas of the tile job, or if it's stained beyond repair, the grout should be removed and the whole surface regrouted. The fastest way to remove the old grout is with a rotary cutter loaded with a masonry-cutting bit (left). Use a grout bit, which is specially designed to remove grout without damaging ceramic or porcelain tile. You still have to be careful not to touch the tile with the bit, but if you graze a tile slightly, you won't damage it. You can also get an attachment for the tool that helps to center it in the grout lines. Or you can use a grout saw, a hand tool that's cheaper to buy but takes a lot longer to do the job. For the tiny grout lines of self-spacing tiles or butt-jointed stone, use a utility knife. Once the grout is gone, vacuum away all dust and wipe the area with a wet sponge. Then you can regrout the tiles following the instructions beginning on page 64.

TRICKS OF THE TRADE

Dust Control

Sawing out grout is a messy, dusty job. Before you do it, remove all of your belongings from the room and seal the doorways with plastic. Then use tile setter George Taterosian's trick for reducing the clouds of dust that kick up: Have a helper hold the hose of a high-filtration wet-dry vacuum near the grout saw or rotary cutter to grab the dust as it flies off the blade.

Chemical Grout Removal

Sawing and drilling aren't the only ways to remove old grout. There are acid-based products that will dissolve it. They can't be used on tiles that are susceptible to acids—such as limestone, marble, and unglazed ceramic—but for porcelain and glazed ceramics, ask your tile seller to recommend the right product. Then test it on a tile in an inconspicuous spot to make sure it won't cause any damage. If it passes the test, spray the product over the tiled surface, wait the allotted time specified on the label, and then apply the neutralizer. The acid will eat away the top surface of the grout (the longer you leave it on, the more it will remove), creating a groove to hold a new grout layer. "Etching is easy," says tile setter George Taterosian, "but the chemicals are extremely harsh, so you need to be very careful not to get it on your skin and to use proper ventilation."

REPLACING CAULK

IT'S THE BANE of many a tub or shower surround: The caulk in the joint where the tub or shower base meets the tiled wall is black with mold. You try to kill the mold with a cleanser sold for the job, but it won't go away. You try to put new caulk over the blackened caulk, but the black gunk just reappears in the new caulk. The problem is that the mold is growing inside the bead of caulk, so you can't kill it by spraying the surface with any cleaner you can buy. The mold also quickly attacks any new caulk you apply. The only way to get rid of it is to remove the old caulk and install fresh, mold-resistant caulk.

1 **REMOVE THE OLD CAULK.** Use a straight razorblade—the kind used for cleaning paint drips from windows—to scrape the caulk away from the surface of the tile along its top edge and from the surface of the tub along its bottom edge. Be very careful to avoid scratching the tub, especially if it's not made from cast iron. Change the razorblade frequently to ensure a sharp edge. Then use a flathead screwdriver or a can punch (a can opener that creates a triangular puncture in a can's lid) to dig the caulk out of the groove. Again, take care not to mar the surface of the tile or tub. Once all of the caulk is removed, clean the empty joint with denatured alcohol or acetone to prepare it for fresh caulk.

2 **RE-CAULK THE GROOVE.** Allow the tub to dry for 24 hours after the most recent time the shower or bath water was on. Then apply a strip of painter's tape on each side of the joint to protect the surfaces from excess caulk. Next squeeze into the joint a bead of high-quality tub and tile caulk that contains silicone and mildewcides. (Ask your tile seller for the best product available, because low-grade caulk is what causes mold problems.) Smooth the caulk into the joint using your finger wrapped in a wet rag. Once you're satisfied with the way it looks, peel away the tape before the caulk has a chance to harden. Allow the fresh caulk to cure for 24 hours before using the shower or bath.

TRICKS OF THE TRADE

Drying the Joint

If you cannot wait 24 hours to let the joint dry, or if the weather is so humid that even that much time doesn't do the job, try doing what tile setter Jane Aeon does and dry it with a heat gun, a tool sold for paint removal. A blow dryer will work too, she says, though not as quickly.

REMOVING STAINS FROM TILES

IF A TILE GETS STAINED, head to a tile supplier for a cleaner designed to remove stains from that particular type of tile, because different materials require different products. If that doesn't get rid of the stain, try a poultice, which is another tile-specific product you can pick up from a good supplier. A poultice is a powder that you mix with water to create a paste and then spread over the stain. Next cover the poultice with plastic kitchen wrap secured to the surrounding tile surface with masking tape. This will prevent the poultice from drying out. "The paste literally sucks the red wine or other stain out of the tile," says tile setter George Taterosian. Let the poultice work overnight and then remove the plastic and wash away the poultice with a tiling sponge, soap, and water. Repeat the process as necessary until the stain is gone.

REPLACING TILES

THE TRICKIEST PART OF THIS JOB is finding a replacement tile that matches the existing ones. Hopefully, the original installer had a few extra tiles left over and the foresight to stash them away in the basement, garage, or attic. If you can't find any, check the back of the broken tile for any manufacturer's markings and show them to a tile retailer to find out whether the product is still available. There are even a number of historic tile-making factories that have been reopened and are once again making tiles that are identical to the ones made generations ago. There are also companies that specialize in helping customers find replacement tiles. For more information, see "Preserving Historic Ceramic Tile Floors," a publication by the National Park Service that is available online (just do a search for its title). For nontraditional tiles, the good news is that most of these products are fairly new and more easily accessible than ceramic tiles, plus there's a resurgence in "retro" designs, from linoleum to cork. If you can't find replacements from local suppliers, head to the Internet.

Ceramic and Stone

If more than one or two tiles are loose or broken, there is probably an underlying problem that will cause the same thing to happen to the replacement tiles. Jump on a floor or push on a wall with the heel of your hand. If you feel any flex, you may need to remove all of the tiles in the area (see page 134 for removing wall tiles and page 84 for removing floor tiles), shore up the substrate (as shown beginning on page 88), and re-install the tiles (pages 54–66). Also check the substrate for damage. If you find wet or loose plywood, cement backerboard, or drywall, remove as many tiles as necessary to cut out the damaged substrate and perhaps even the framing. Install a patch of new cement backerboard (see pages 46–48) before reinstalling the tiles.

Repairing Scratched or Etched Stone

For some stone tile countertops, all it takes is an unnoticed puddle of orange juice or red wine to etch the surface. You could replace the damaged tiles, of course, but you may not have to. A stone countertop contractor may be able to repair the problem by applying a filler or sanding the surface of the countertop down slightly. These are not do-it-yourself jobs, but they're worth considering before you embark on a tricky tile replacement.

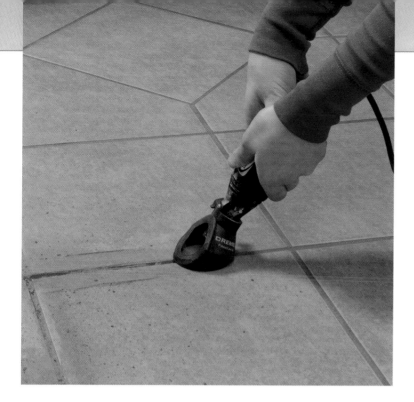

1 **REMOVE THE GROUT.** To help loosen the tile and prevent damage to neighboring tiles, begin by removing the grout around the perimeter of the damaged tile. The easiest tool for this is a rotary cutter loaded with a grout bit and attachment, both of which reduce your chances of damaging surrounding tiles. You can also use a grout saw. In a pinch, you can use a utility knife turned sideways. Make sure to cut through the full depth of the grout. If you can slice through the thinset underneath, that's all the better.

TRICKS OF THE TRADE

Removing Porcelain Tiles

A drill won't cut through the hard surface of porcelain tiles, so you'll need to use an angle grinder. "The problem is that it can easily damage adjacent tiles," says tile setter Jane Aeon. So protect them by using duct tape to adhere pieces of fiberboard over their surfaces. Then, with a masonry-cutting blade, use the angle grinder to cut an X through the center of the tile before smashing it with a hammer and a cold chisel, as described in step 3 on page 228.

2 **BREAK UP THE TILE.** Load a masonry-cutting bit into a drill and, starting in the center of the tile and working outward, drill holes in the damaged tile. These help to weaken the tile, making it easier for you to remove without causing damage to the surrounding tiles.

continued ▶▶

3 **REMOVE THE TILE.** Use a cold chisel and a hammer to chip away the tile. On a wall where the tile was installed with mastic, this will be easy. However, if the tile was installed with thinset or, even worse, in an old-fashioned mortar bed, this will take time and lots of elbow grease. The key to tackling a tough removal job, according to tile setter George Taterosian, is not trying to pry up the tile, because that will damage the neighboring tiles. "You just want to break up the tile," he says. "Keep smashing at it until the fragments let go of the mortar." Then smash out the old mortar using the same technique, or use a putty knife to remove the mastic from the substrate.

4 **PATCH THE SUBSTRATE.** Getting all of the adhesive out, which is essential for setting the replacement tile properly, usually means damaging the substrate. The surface of drywall will come away with mastic, and chunks of plywood or cement backerboard may get removed along with mortar. So the next step is smoothing out the substrate. Do so with a two-part epoxy filler recommended for the job by your tile supplier.

5 **INSTALL THE NEW TILE.** Use the same adhesive that was used originally—mastic or thinset—but don't spread it onto the substrate. Otherwise, you'll get it all over the neighboring tiles. Instead, liberally back-butter it onto the replacement tile. Then place the tile into position. Since you don't have spacers, just center it into position visually and, using a level as a gauge, press down on the tile until it's flush with the neighboring tiles. If excess mortar or mastic oozes from the grout lines, remove it with a flathead screwdriver or a pencil tip. If you're tiling a wall and using a slow-curing thinset, use plastic wedges between the new tile and the old to prevent the replacement from sagging. Or secure it to the existing tiles with masking tape.

6 **GROUT THE NEW TILE.** Once the adhesive has hardened overnight, you're ready for grout. Rather than float it over the whole surface, just trowel it over your newly cleared grout lines and press it into place with a wet sponge. As you smooth it into the joints, carry it past the new tile and overlap it onto the old grout slightly. This will help to blend it in with the old tile.

Matching Old Grout

Even if you find a bag of the original grout in the basement, don't use it for the repair job, as grout goes bad over time. But it's still handy because it will give you the brand and color information. Otherwise, you'll have to look for grout that matches the old as

closely as possible. And even if you have the exact same grout, of course, it won't look the same as the existing grout, which has darkened over time, as all grouts do. So it's a good idea to use a grout-cleaning product to refresh all of the grout before replacing a tile. That way you can match the new grout to the true color of the old grout and both will darken together. (Otherwise, if your new grout matches the time-darkened color of the existing grout, then the new grout will eventually darken and no longer match the old.)

Go to your tile supplier and pick up a grout chart, which is simply a plastic card showing all of the various grout colors the seller offers. Take it home and hold it against the freshened old grout. Select the best match, or go to a different tile supplier and try the color chart for its brand of grout. Over time, the new and old grouts will darken and the contrast between them will become less obvious.

Resilient Tiles

If you cannot find an exact replacement for a damaged resilient tile, remove an existing tile from under the refrigerator or from some other inconspicuous place.

If the damaged tile has started to curl up, or if there is a crack in it, slip in a putty knife and pry the tile up. If there is no easy point of entry, or if the tile is difficult to remove, heat it with a clothes iron (set on high) to soften the mastic. Keep a cloth between the iron and the tile to avoid dirtying the face of the iron. Keep the iron moving, and stop if you smell burning. Once the tile is loosened, pry it up with a putty knife. If you're removing a tile from under the fridge to use as a replacement, work slowly and make sure you get it up in one unharmed piece.

Scrape the repair area absolutely clean and vacuum away all dust. Even a small particle will show through most resilient tiles. Test to make sure the new tile will fit. Apply mastic to the floor, allow it to become tacky, and then set the tile. Use a kitchen rolling pin to press the tile firmly into the mastic. Place a heavy weight, such as a stack of books, on the tile and leave it there for a day or so.

Laminate Tiles

Laminate tiles interlock with tongues and grooves (see pages 112–115 to understand how they are installed), but you need to cut out the tile and install its replacement with glue instead.

1 **MAKE THE CUTOUT.** Use a pencil and a straightedge to draw a rectangle that's about 1 inch smaller on all sides than the full size of the damaged tile. Set a circular-saw blade to the exact thickness of the laminate by setting it at $1/8$ inch and gradually cutting a hair deeper until you fully penetrate the laminate. Cut along the inner edge of those lines, but keep the blade an inch from each corner. Then complete the cuts with a sharp chisel. Use a thin, flat pry bar to remove the cut-out section of laminate. Then use the chisel to make angled cuts from each corner of the cutout to the nearest corner of the laminate tile. Pry out those end scraps and remove any remaining tongues and grooves from the surrounding tiles.

2 **INSTALL THE REPLACEMENT PIECE.** Before you can install your replacement tile, you'll need to remove the lower lip of its grooves (there are usually two sides with grooves and two with tongues). Turn the tile upside down and measure the thickness of each lower lip, as they may be different. Set the blade of your circular saw to that dimension and, with the back side of the tile up, cut off those lower lips. Dry-fit the tile in the opening, remove it, and make any adjustments that are necessary. Then apply a bead of a laminate adhesive that's recommended by the manufacturer to the four exposed edges of the surrounding tiles. Pop the replacement tile into place, press it into position, and use a damp rag to wipe off any excess glue that squeezes up onto the surface. Place a heavy stack of books over the tile and let the glue cure for 24 hours before removing the books.

Repairing Laminate

It's easy to repair gouges, dings, and dents in laminate flooring. Manufacturers sell putty in colors that match all of their various ceramic, wood, and stone lookalike flooring tiles, and you can use it to fill a hole and make it disappear. You can purchase a few different products, take them home to see which one is the best match, and then return the unused ones. Alternatively, you can take an extra unused tile with you to the store, or you may be able to take home a putty color chart from the flooring store or home center. In any case, it's usually best to use a putty from the company that manufactured your laminate tiles, if possible.

If the problem area is just a dent that doesn't break the finish, use a sharp utility knife (below, right) to cut out and remove the material from the bottom of the indentation so the putty has something to grab onto.

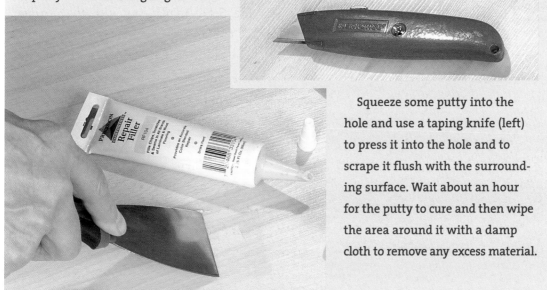

Squeeze some putty into the hole and use a taping knife (left) to press it into the hole and to scrape it flush with the surrounding surface. Wait about an hour for the putty to cure and then wipe the area around it with a damp cloth to remove any excess material.

Parquet Tiles

Even if only part of a parquet tile is damaged, it's easier to replace the whole tile rather than some of its component strips. See pages 108–111 for instructions on installing parquet tiles. The parquet may have changed color over the years. To find a correct replacement, try to match a tile that has been hidden under the refrigerator or a cabinet.

Set the blade of a circular saw to cut just through the thickness of the parquet. Make several cuts across the tile, taking care not to cut any adjacent ones. Now you can pry the tile out piece by piece. Scrape away all of the adhesive from the floor.

Before installing a replacement tile, you must cut away the bottom portion of its groove on two sides, as well as one of the tongues. Set the circular saw appropriately for each of these very shallow cuts, then remove the sections with the tile upside down. Lay the new tile in place without adhesive to make sure it will fit. Then remove it and apply parquet tile adhesive to the floor using a notched trowel, or use a caulking gun to apply construction adhesive that is labeled for floors. Slip the tile into place, press down until its top is flush with the adjacent tiles, and wipe away any excess adhesive that oozes out. Place a heavy weight, such as a stack of books, on the tile and leave it there for a day or so.

Cork Tiles

Don't try to pry the problem tile up at its edge, because you'll damage the neighboring tile. Instead, use a sharp utility knife to slice a line through the middle of the tile. Run the blade along a straightedge, stop short of the edges of the tile to avoid cutting the next tiles, and make repeated passes until your knife cuts completely through the tile. Work a taping knife into the cut and pry the tile up, working from the center outward and being careful not to damage the neighboring cork. Once you have removed the entire tile, use the taping knife to scrape up any remaining adhesive. Then apply new adhesive, taking care not to get it on the adjacent tiles. Press the replacement tile into position and set a heavy stack of books on it overnight or for however long the adhesive packaging says it requires to cure.

Carpet Tiles

One advantage of carpet tiles versus standard wall-to-wall carpeting is how easy it is to replace a tile. If the tile has been installed with sticky dots (as shown beginning on page 118) or with self-stick backing, you can simply pull the tile up. Start at a corner, grasp the fibers in your hands, and pull. If you can't get it to come up, work a taping knife into the joint and pry the tile up. Then simply pop a replacement tile onto the sticky dots or peel off its paper backing and apply its self-sticking adhesive to the subfloor. For carpet tiles that were applied with mastic or another adhesive, you'll need to gradually pry up the tile with the taping knife, then scrape up the adhesive and spread new adhesive onto the floor, taking care not to get any on the adjacent tiles. Press the replacement tile into place, then set a heavy stack of books on it overnight or for however long the adhesive packaging says it requires to cure.

Comparing Tiles

Tile	Characteristics	Installation
Concrete	Strong but porous. Many types are easily stained and scratched. Available in almost any imaginable color.	Make all cuts with a wet saw. Set in latex-reinforced thinset mortar. Depending on the type, you may need to seal it both before and after installation.
Cork	Soft underfoot, with a natural appearance. Can be very long-lasting.	Cut with a utility knife. Set in special cork tile adhesive and seal the tile immediately after installation.
Glass	Impervious to stains and moisture. Some glass tiles are strong enough for floors, but most are used on walls. Expensive, so they are often used for accents only. Available in a wide variety of textures and colors.	Cut with a snap cutter. Consult the tile dealer to determine whether to use white mastic, white latex-reinforced thinset mortar, or epoxy mortar. Epoxy grout may be needed.
Glazed ceramic (floor)	Glazed surface is usually very water, stain, and frost resistant. Comes in almost any color and texture.	Make straight cuts with a snap cutter or wet saw. Make cutouts with a wet saw or nibbling tool. Set in latex-reinforced thinset mortar.
Glazed ceramic (wall)	Typically soft and covered with a glaze that resists water but may be easily scratched. Available in virtually all colors. You can install floor tile on a wall, but never install wall tile on a floor.	Make straight cuts with a snap cutter or wet saw, cutouts with a wet saw or nibbling tool. Set in mastic, or in latex-fortified thinset if the wall will often get wet. Caulk inside corners. All grout lines should be completely filled.
Hardwood	Durable and resistant to water but more easily scratched than ceramic tile. Made of wood infused with resin. Woody and pastel colors with streaks and mottles.	Cut with a circular saw or table saw. Set in latex-reinforced thinset mortar and fill joints with latex-reinforced grout.
Laminate	Surface is strong and easy to keep clean with little or no maintenance.	Cut with a circular saw or jigsaw. Lay foam backing, then the tiles simply snap together.
Limestone	Very soft and easily stained. Like the limestone found on building facades, limestone tiles and slabs are rough and pitted. Some are cut precisely, and some are not.	Make all cuts with a wet saw. Set in latex-reinforced thinset mortar. When installing large pieces on a wall, support the pieces with plastic wedges while the mortar sets. Seal before and after installation.

TILE	CHARACTERISTICS	INSTALLATION
Metal	Strong enough to be used on floors. Colors depend on the type of metal—typically copper, brass, stainless steel, or iron. Expensive, so they are often used as accents.	Some tiles cannot be cut, which is another reason to use them as accents only. Consult the tile dealer to find out whether to set them in latex-reinforced or epoxy mortar.
Mexican saltillos	Very soft and almost sponge-like in their ability to soak up water. May come with a glaze, which can also be prone to staining. Reds, browns, and dark yellows.	Make all cuts with a wet saw. Set in a thick bed of thinset or medium-bed mortar. Because tiles are irregular, you'll need to set them using grid lines rather than spacers. Seal before and after installation.
Mosaic	Individual tiles range from 3/4 inch to 3 inches square. Tiles may be glazed ceramic, marble, stone, glass, or metal. Decorative patterns, already assembled on 12-inch-square sheets, are available.	Cut the backing of mosaic sheets with a knife as needed for fit. Set in latex-fortified thinset mortar. Use white mortar if the tiles are marble. For walls, use mastic. Take extra care to make sure all tiles are embedded in the mortar.
Onyx	Soft and porous and subject to stains and scratches. Natural stone with distinctive tan and brown swirls.	Make all cuts with a wet saw. Set in white latex-fortified thinset mortar. For stain resistance, apply sealer before and after grouting.
Polished granite	Very hard, strong, and scratch resistant. Well suited for countertops and floors. Speckled, with colors ranging from very light to very dark.	Make all cuts with a wet saw. Set in latex-reinforced thinset mortar.
Polished marble	Usually very soft. Scratches easily and soaks up water and stains. Distinctive veined patterns with a wide range of colors.	Make all cuts with a wet saw. Exposed edges should be polished or sanded smooth and painted with clear lacquer. Set in white latex-reinforced thinset mortar. Usually, these tiles are set with the narrowest of grout lines.
Porcelain	Extremely resistant to stains and abrasion. Can mimic the look and texture of glazed ceramic, polished marble, and even rough stone.	Usually, cut with a wet saw, though a nibbling tool may work for cutouts. Set in latex-reinforced thinset mortar.
Quarry	Prone to staining unless protected by a sealer. Earth tones, gray, or pastel colors.	Cut with a wet saw or make straight cuts with a snap cutter and cutouts with a nibbling tool. Set in latex-reinforced thinset mortar. For stain resistance, apply sealer before grouting.

continued ▶▶

COMPARING TILES

TILE	CHARACTERISTICS	INSTALLATION
Resilient	Soft and flexible, requiring very smooth floor substrate. The surface is "no-wax" but needs to be renewed if traffic is heavy.	Cut with a utility knife. Some are self-sticking, but it's better to use vinyl adhesive to ensure a strong bond.
Slate	Hard and resistant to scratches and staining. Gray, green, black, and ruddy brown colors. Most slate tiles are made via splitting rather than cutting, so the surface is textured. Some types are polished or honed, while others are left rough.	Make all cuts with a wet saw. Set in latex-reinforced thinset mortar. Seal it before and after installation to protect against stains.
Terra-cotta	Soaks up water and stains readily unless sealed. A range of earth tones reflecting the color of the clay.	Make all cuts with a wet saw. Set in latex-reinforced thinset mortar. For irregularly shaped types, back-butter each tile as you install it and use a grid rather than spacers.
Travertine	Almost as easily scratched and stained as marble. Small and large pits in the surface may or may not be filled with a light-colored grout. Shades of tan.	Make all cuts with a wet saw. Set in white latex-reinforced thinset mortar, and avoid grouts that can stain. For protection against stains, seal after installation.
Tumbled or honed marble and granite	More prone to staining than polished marble or granite, but it's a less slippery surface and is easier to keep clean and free of fingerprints. Comes in all the same colors as polished stone.	Make all cuts with a wet saw. Set in white latex-reinforced thinset mortar, and avoid grouts that can stain. Seal the tiles before and after installation.
Vinyl, vinyl composition	Soft enough to show underlying irregularities. Floor substrate can be flexible but must be smooth. Resilient, covered with flecks of color to hide dirt. Often called commercial tile, but by combining colors you can achieve an attractive floor. Many types are prewaxed.	Cut with a knife. Spread vinyl composition adhesive, allow it to dry, then set the tiles.
Wood parquet	Needs to be protected with wax or polyurethane finish but will still buckle if the floor gets very wet. Easily scratched. Made of strips of natural wood, usually oak or birch. Stains range from dark mahogany to a light maple color.	Cut with a circular saw or other wood-cutting saw. Set in special wood-parquet adhesive.

CREDITS

PHOTOGRAPHY
All photography by Image Studios, unless otherwise credited

Dave Adams: 77L, 79; Jean Allsopp: 7R, 13L, 17BL; Courtesy of Ann Sacks: 4T, 132T; Courtesy of Artistic Tile: 75; Rob Blackburn/Jupiterimages: 212; Marion Brenner: 163 all, 164–165 all; Rob D. Brodman: 176B; Courtesy of Bruce Hardwood: 18TR 19BR; Wayne Cable: 64–65, 66T, 66M, 36TL, 36TR, 36BL, 37 all, 38 all, 39TR, 40TR, 40 left, 41 all, 43 all, 44R, 45M, 45R, 54–55 all, 60 all, 61T, 61B, 62 all, 73M, 73R, 88B, 104T, 104T, 105 all, 106–107 all, 108–109 all, 110TR, 110BR, 111 all, 122B, 123T, 126R, 127 left, 127M, 142R, 143T, 144 all, 146–147 all, 148 all, 150–151 all, 152–153 all, 154–155 all, 169TL, 169ML, 169BL, 194R, 195L, 195M, 204–205 all, 206–207 all, 208 all; James Carrier: 14TR, 15TL, 19BL, 33BL, 220T, 229B; Van Chaplin: 10BL, 198T; Bieke Claessens/Red Cover: 189M; Comstock/Jupiterimages: 44–45T; Crane Plumbing: 103B; davidduncanlivingston.com: 170–171T, 175; Courtesy of De Walt: 39BL; Directfrommexico.com: 15BR; Andrew Drake: 200B; Courtesy of Fireclay Tile: 14BR; Courtesy of Fired Earth (photography by Emma Lee): 2T, 6L, 6M, 8L, 11B, 16BL, 24T, 31L, 31R, 74R, 132B, 189 top; Courtesy of Forbo Marmoleum: 7M, 18TL, 18BR, 76; Turner Forte Photography/Jupiter images: 209B; Frank Gaglione: 35TR, 194M, 203T, 203B; Tria Giovan: 78L, 78R; Laurey W. Glenn: 8R; Steven Gunther: 201; Margot Hartford: 99B, 183B; Phil Harvey: 197; Tom Haynes: 9TR, 9BL, 10BR, 11TR, 12TR, 13BR, 16BR, 17TM, 17BR, 18BL, 112; Douglas Hill/Beateworks/Corbis: 194–195T; InsideOutPix/Jupiterimages: 218–219T; Island Stone: 196T; Look Photography/Beateworks/Corbis: 183T; E. Andrew McKinney: 10TR, 27BL, 77R, 183M; Stephen O'Hara: 35B, 36ML; Rik Olsen: 86T; Norman A. Plate: 218L, 220B; Lisa Romerein: 1, 6R, 9BR, 131R, 142L, 173, 174; Eric Roth: 25, 72–73T, 74L, 126–127 top; David Schiff: 34 all; Courtesy of Sicis: 7L, 26, 28T, 28B; Michael Skott: 131L; Thomas J. Story:

9TL, 12TL, 13T, 14L, 15TR, 15B, 16TL, 16M, 19M, 20, 21L, 21R, 22L, 22R, 23, 24B, 27TL, 27BR, 29, 33TR, 99T, 99M, 128T, 129, 133, 172, 176T, 177, 200M; Tim Street-Porter: 2B, 128B, 130, 198B, 200T; Tim Street-Porter/Beateworks/Corbis: 90; Dan Stultz: 34T, 35MR, 35L, 36MR, 36BM, 36BR, 39TL, 61M, 85M, 86B, 194L, 202, 230B, 231T, 231B; Don Vandervort: 35BL; Christopher Vendetta: 124T, 124B, 178T, 178B; Michal Venera: 189B; Courtesy of Walker Zanger: 17TR, 30, 32; Courtesy Wicanders Cork Flooring: 19T; Michele Lee Willson (styling by Laura Del Fava): 6–7T, 17TL, 35BR, 58L, 136 all, 149, 195R, 209T, 210 all, 211 all, 213 all, 214–215 all, 216–217 all; Karen Witynski: 196B, 199; Courtesy of Zinsser: 135 all

DESIGN
1: Kevin Stephenson, architect, Semple Brown Design, kitchen design by Donna McMahon, The Open Cupboard; 4T: Ann Sacks; 6–7T: Kathryn A Rogers, Architect; 6R: Interior Design by Artistic Environments, Architecture by David George & Associates, Architopia, Construction by HyMax Building Corp.; 7R: Interior Design by Lovelace Interiors, Architecture by Folck West + Savage, Construction by J.M. Sykes, Inc.; 8R: Brooks Interior Design, Looney Ricks Kiss Architects, Construction by The St. Joe Company; 9TL: Jeff Shelton, Architect; 9BR: Interior Design by Artistic Environments, Architecture by David George & Associates, Architopia, Construction by HyMax Building Corp.; 10TR: Heidi M. Emmett; 10BL: Interior Design by Woodvale Interiors, Architecture by Ben Patterson, Construction by Frank Stone & Son Construction Co.; 12TL: Francesca Quagliata, 4th Street Design; 13L: Interior Design by Lovelace Interiors, Architecture by Folck West + Savage, Construction by J.M. Sykes, Inc.; 13T: Dirk Stennick Design; Jacqueline Bucelli Designs, Patty Glikbarg, Pannagan Designs; 15TR: Flesher + Foster Architecture; 15B: Flesher + Foster Architecture; 16TL: Mark De Mattei Construction, Dahlin Group Architecture, Nuvis Ladnscape

Architecture and Planning; 16M: Lara Dutto, D-Cubed; 17TL: Anne Laird-Blanton, architect; 17BL: Interior Design by Lovelace Interiors, Architecture by Folck West + Savage, Construction by J.M. Sykes, Inc.; 20: David Feix Landscape Design; Construction by Trejo's Design; 21L: Mosaic Tile Market; 21R: Charles de Lisle, Your Space Interiors, Heidi Richardson, Richardson Architects; 22R: Jeff Shelton, Architect; 23: Jeff Shelton, Architect; 25: Heidi Pribell Interior Design; 27TL: Kenneth Brown Design, Los Angeles; 27BL: City Studios; 29: Huettl-Thuilot Associates; 33TR: Michelle Kaufman Designs; XtremeHomes construction; 77L: Annette M. Starkey, CKD, CBD, Living Environment Design; 77R: D. Kimberly Smith/Deer Creek Design; 78L: Architecture and Interior Design by Bill Ingram Marie Blackwell, and Darla Davis, Construction by Francis A. Bryant & Sons; 78R: Interior Design by Steven Gambrel, Architecture by Historical Concepts, Construction by Windward Builders LLC; 79: Reynolds Gualco Architecture-Interior Design, interior design by Robin Hardy Design, Construction by Thomas Irvin; 99M: Tiles by Oceanside Glasstile, Design by Janice Stone Thomas, Sacramento; 99B: David S. Gast & Associates, Architects, interior design by Kathy Geissler Best, KGB Associates, construction by Plath & Co. Inc., Lighting by Anna Victoria Koldoff; 128T: Thomas B Hood; 129: Jensen & Macy Architects, San Francisco; 131R: Architects Dave George and Martin Rincon of Architopia; 149: Anne Laird-Blanton, architect; 172: Pamela Pennington Studios Interior Design; 173: Architecture by Kevin Stephenson, Semple Brown Design, Kitchen design by Donna McMahon, the Open Cupboard; 174: Architects Dave George and Martin Rincon of Architopia, HyMax Building Corp.; 176T: Anna Labbee, J.A.S. Design-Build; 183B: Michael Connell Architect; 189B: Karin Payson architecture + design, Suzanne Myers/Elite Interior Design; 198T: Frank Stone & Son Construction Co.; 200M: Julie Chai; 200B: Claire Donha; 201: Michael Buccino

INDEX

Boldface type denotes photograph captions.

A

Accent tile, **31**, **33**, **78**, 145. *See also* Decorative tile
Accessories. *See* Bathroom accessories
Acids, 162, 205, 223
Adhesive. *See also* Mastic; Thinset mortar
  about, 43, **43**
  checking, 59
  for membrane, 101
  removal of excess, 106, 143, 146
  for tile, 105, 108, 116, 117, 232, 233
Anchors and bolts, 169, **169**
Arrangement of tile. *See* Pattern

B

Back-butter technique, 56, **56**
Backerboard
  about, 42, **42**, 87, 88
  countertop, 180–181
  installation, 42, 46–48, 102, 151
  tub or shower, 120, 149, 159
Backing, mesh, 14, **14**
Backsplash
  to bathroom sink, **189**
  behind stovetop, 31, **189**, 190–192, **192**
  installation, 186–188, 190–193
  to kitchen countertop, 25, **28**, **131**, **173**
  metal, 193, **193**
  tile selection, 172–177, **172–177**, 189
Bars, 35, **35**
Baseboards, 80–81, 120, 122
Bathroom. *See also* Countertops; Plumbing; Showers; Tub surround
  demolition, 150
  examples, 74, 78, **90**, **129**, **132–133**, **142**, **176**, **189**
Bathroom accessories, 15, **15**, 31, 145, 169. *See also* Walls, niches in
Bathtub. *See* Tub surround
Batten board, 52–53, **52–53**, 58, 152, 167–168, 182
Beater board, 41, **41**, 57, 68–69, 97, 184
Birdbaths, **200**, 212, **212**
Bit, grout, 223, **223**
Blueboard, 42
Bonding agents, 202, 213
Borders and trim pieces. *See also* Bullnose tile; V-caps
  about, 15, **15**, 30–31, **30–31**

examples, **99**, **190**, **192**
installation, 99, 145–146, 164
planter, 211, **211**
Bullnose tile
  about, 15, 30
  countertop, 15, 176, 183, **183**
  creation by grinding, 165
  fireplace surround, 164
  installation, 145, 146, 155, 159, 161, 164
  paver, 216
  tub surround, 155

C

Cabinets and islands, 83
Caps. *See* Bullnose tile; V-caps
Carpet, removal, 85
Carpet tile, 19, **19**, 118–119, 221, 233
Caulk gun, 41, **41**
Caulking, 66, 107, 148, 156, 161, 188, 224
Ceiling tile, 17, 166–168
Cement backerboard. *See* Backerboard
Ceramic tile
  about, **8**, 8–9, **9**
  cleaning, 220
  examples, 78, **132**, **199**
  installation, 55–59
  replacement, 226–229
  unglazed, 201, 205, 220
Chalk line, 37, **37**
Chisel, 34, **34**
Clay tile, **196**
Cleaning, 29, 78, 108, 162, 205, 220–221, 225
Color, 26–27, **27**, 32–33, **33**
Concrete, 86, 88, 202–203, 209
Concrete tile, 16, **16**, 234
Cork tile, 19, **19**, 116–117, 221, 233, 234
Cost estimate, 20–21
Countertops
  installation, 182–185
  kitchen, **28**, **173**, **174**
  preparation of substrate, 179–181
  removal of old, 178–179
  repair, 226
  tile selection, 11, 172–177, **172–177**
Cushioning, 113
Cutters
  rotary, 39, **39**, 63, **63**, 185, **185**, 227
  snap, 38, **38**, 60, 69, 153, 190
Cutting
  backerboard, 47, 181
  for backsplash corner, 188, **188**
  drywall, 138
  45-degree, 183, 190, 210, 211
  notches, 62, 107, 110, 111, 114, 138, 144, 187
  for sink opening, 184, 185

tile, 60–63, 67, 106–107, 110–111, 114, 117, 119, 193, 207
tools (*See* Tools, cutting)
for tub surround, 153, 154, 155

D–F

Decorative tile. *See also* Accent tile
  about, **14**, 14–15
  backsplash, 31, **189**
  kitchen wall, **174**, **177**
  outdoor use, **22–23**, 197, 200
  planter, **211**
  stair riser, **131**, 209
  stripes, 78, **128**, **131**, 145, **189**
Doors and doorways, 82, 91, 104, 125. *See also* Thresholds
Drills, 36, **36**
Drywall, 42, **42**, 136–139
Electrical connections, 138, 141, 187
Entryways, 74, 78
Fiberglass board, 42, **42**, 137, 149
Fireplace surround, **131**, 162–165
Flagstone, **201**, 206–208
Floor
  concrete, preparation for tile, 86, 202–203
  finish work after tiling, 122–125
  heat mat under, 78, 90, 94–95
  height issues, 47, 81, 84, 88, 90, 125
  preparation for backerboard, 46, 47
  preparation for tile, 46, 48, 80–81, 84–93, 100, 104, 108, 112, 116
  removing obstacles, 80–83
  strength, 87, 90, 92
Floor tile
  examples, 74–79, **198**, **199**
  installation, 55–59, 96–121
  layout, 25, 49–51, 113, 204
  selection, 74–79
Foot pads for furniture, 221
Frost-resistant or frost-proof tile, 196, 198

G

Glass tile
  about, 16, **16**, 68, 74, 234
  backsplash, **28**, 32
  mosaic, 14, **21**, **28**, 69, **173**, **176**
  recycled, **22**
  thinset for, 54
Glazed tile
  about, **8**, 8, 74, 174, 234
  examples, 78, **198**, **211**
  installation, 162, 163, 234
Granite tile, 10, **11**, 235, 236
Greenboard, 42, 149
Grinder, 39, **39**, 162, 165, 202, **202**, 227
Grout
  colored, 32–33, **33**, 64, 176, 213
  epoxy, 33, 185

hardness, 33
latex-reinforced, 43, 64, 69, 155, 205
matching old, 229
refurbishing, 223
removal, 223, 227
removal of excess, 65, 70, 121, 147, 155, 205
resealing, 222
sanded, 64, 69, 205
sealer for, 33, 70, 71
tiles without, **32**
unsanded, 33, 64, 69, 147, 193
Grout float, 41, **41**
Grout lines
consistent, 58, 66, 147, 148, 155, 161, 205
as contrast, **33**
width, 33, 51, 145, 176
Grout sealer bottle, 41

H
Hallways, **18**, 74
Hammer, 34, **34**
Hardness and durability, 33, 74, 174, 198
Heat, 81, 91, 122
Heat gun, 224
Heat mat, 78, 90, **94**, 94–95

I, J
Irregularly-shaped tile, 14, 56, 145, 152
Joint compound, 136–137, 139
Joints
expansion, 66, 188
sealer for, 151, 159
tongue-and-groove, 18, 108, 109, 112, 230–231

K, L
Kitchen, **31**, 77, **131**, **173**–174, **177**, **189**. *See also* Backsplash; Countertops
Kits, 101, 103, 131, 145
Knives, 34, **34**, 36, **36**, 134, 136, 138, 233
Laminate tile, 18, **18**, 85, 112–115, 221, 230–231, 234
Layout process
backerboard, 46–47, 48
birdbath, 213
countertop, 180, 182
paver, 216
planter, 211
tabletop, 214
tile, 25, 49–53, 104, 108, 113, 145, 166–167, 190–191, 204, 206, 210
tools, 37, **37**
Leather tile, **16**, 16–17

Level, 37, **37**
Limestone tile, **10**, 10–11, 174, 234
Linoleum, 18, **18**, 77

M, N
Mallet, 41, **41**
Marble tile, 12, **12**, 174, 235, 236
Marking techniques, 53, 61
Mastic, 43, **43**, 149
Membranes, 43, **43**, 101, **101**, 102, 203
Mesh. *See* Backing, mesh; Tape, mesh; Wire mesh
Metal tile, 17, **17**, **28**, 193, **193**, 235
Miter box, 39, **39**, 110, 114, 123
Moisture, 17, 42, 43, 46, 70, 142, 196. *See also* Safety, avoiding slips
Mold and mildew, 224
Molding, 80–81, 91, 122–123, 161, 183, **183**
Mortar, 100–101, 103, 202, 207–208. *See also* Thinset mortar
Mosaic tile
about, 14, **14**, **176**, 235
bathroom, **90**, **103**, **128**, **132**, **142**
birdbath, 212–213
installation, 67–69, 99, 193, 213, 214–215, 235
kitchen, **173**, 193
pavers, 216–217
precut, 68, **68**
from shards, 24, **200**, 213, **216**, 216–217
tabletop, 214–215
Mudroom, **78**
Mural, 190–192, **192**
Nibbling tool, 38, **38**, 61, 69, 155, 217
Nontraditional tile, 16–19, **16–19**

O, P
Onyx tile, 12, 235
Outdoor tile, **29**, **196**–201, 204–210
Paddles, mixing, 40, **40**, 54
Paint, loose, 135
Paneling, removal, 134
Paper
rosin, 150
tar, 43, **43**, 100, 151, 158
Parquet. *See* Wood parquet tile
Patching compound, 104, 116, 203, 228
Patios. *See* Outdoor tile
Pattern
about, 24–25, **24–25**
all-over, **24**, 174
checkerboard, **99**, 99, 105, 118, **199**
diagonal, 50, 78, 99, **174**, **189**, **196**
staggered brick, **28**, 99, **99**
vertical, **32**, 177
Pavers, 216–217
Pipes. *See* Plumbing

Pitch sticks, 101, **101**
Planter boxes, **200**, 211
Plaster, repair, 136
Plumbing
connection, 90, 102, 124
cutouts, 48, **48**, 61, 107, 121, 151, 154
disconnection, 82–83, 91, 100, 150, 178
Plywood, 42, **42**, 87–89, 100, 104, 116, 180
Porcelain tile, 8, **9**, **75**, **132**, 174, 227, 235
Porches, **196**, **197**. *See also* Outdoor tile
Preparation of substrate
concrete floor, 202–203
for countertop, 179–181
for fireplace surround, 162
floor, 46, 48, 80–81, 84–93, 100, 104, 108, 112, 116
for outdoor tiling, 202–203
for sealer, 70
stairs, 209
threshold, 92, 96
wall, 134–141, 150
Professional, when to call, 87, 166, 202
Putty, for laminate repair, 231

Q, R
Quarry tile, 9, **9**, 235
Quartzite tile, 13, **13**, 21
Radiator, 91, 122
Reference lines, 49–50, 104, 116, 167, 191, 204, 210
Register, 81
Repairs, 136–139, 203, 222–225, 231
Resilient tile, 18, **18**, 104–107, 105, 221, 230, 236. *See also* Linoleum; Vinyl and vinyl tile
River rock, **74**, 120–121, **196**
Roller, flooring, 106

S
Safety
asbestos warning, 85
avoiding slips, 28, 77, 199, 201
health protection, 35, **35**
lead warning, 135
Saltillo tile, 204, 205, 235
Sanding process, 116, 125, 178
Saws
circular, 36, **36**
drywall, 136, 138, 150
grout, 223, 227
hole, 39, **39**
jigsaw, 36, **36**
keyhole, 186
offset, 36, **36**
radial-arm, 110
reciprocating, 35, **35**

rod, 38, **38**
table, 39, **39**
undercut, 91, **91**
wet, 38, **38**
Scrapers, 34, **34**
Sealer
about, 70
application, 70–71
for cork, 19, 117
for grout, 33, 41, 70, 72
importance of, 10, 11, 28, 74
for joints, 151, 159
removal and resealing, 71, 222
river rock, 120
for stone tile, 70, 96, 162, 165
for unglazed tile, 70
for wood parquet tiles, 111
Self-leveling compound, 86, 90, 92,
93, 203
Self-spacing tile, 52, 144, 152
Self-stick tile, 105, 118
Shower prefab pan, 100, 103
Showers, 29, **33**, 100–103, **100–103**, 128
Sinks, 178, 180, 184, 185
Size, 24, 25, **25**, 74, 77, 206
Slate tile, 13, **13**, 77, 200, 236
Spacers, 40, **40**, 51, 57, 64, 143, 145
Specialty tile, 14–15, **14–15**
Square (tool), 36, **36**, 37, **37**
Square, check for, 50
Stain removal, 225
Stairs, **131**, 196, 209, 209–210
Stone tile
about, 10–15, **10–15**, 176
for ceilings, 166
cleaning, 220
cutting, 60
faux, 8, 18
floor, **29**, 78, **198**
grinding bullnose edge on, 165
installation, 96–98, 143, 166, 206–208
"living finish" on, 12
outdoor use, **29**, 170–173, **196**, **198**,
200–201
"rectified" edges, 176
replacement, 226–229
sealer, 70, 96, 162, 165
for wall niche bottom, 159
Straightedge, 37, **37**, 56, 58, 98
Strip flooring. *See* Laminate tile
Style, 22–31, **22–31**
Substrate. *See* Preparation of substrate
Subway tile, **28**, 99, 149, 176, 177

T
Tabletop, 214–215
Tape
duct, 92, 227
masking, 92, 146, 150, 156, 160
mesh, **43**, 48, 137, 139, 151
mosaic, 40, 67, 213, 214
painter's, 92, 185, 193
Tape measure, 37, **37**
Terra-cotta tile, 9, **9**, 174, 236
Terrazzo tile, 17, **17**
Texture, **26**, **28**, 28–29, **29**
Thinset mortar
application basics, 55–56 (*See also*
Back-butter technique)
for backerboard joints, 151
for birdbath, 213
for heat mat, 95
heat-resistant, 162
latex-reinforced, 43, **43**, 54
mixing, 40, **40**, 54–55, 204
for mosaic tile, 29, 215, 217
no-sag, 143, 160, 161, 163, 166
removal of excess, 59, 64, 69, 98, 155
for river rock, 120
for tile, 143, 166, 187, 204
time to set, 56, 64, 95, 152, 205
Thresholds, 47, 81, 90, 92, 96, 98, 103,
115, 123
Tile
cleaning, 221
historic, 17, 226
innovations, 22, 196, 198
keep a few extra, 226
removal of old, 84–86, 134, 162, 186
replacement, 226–233
stain removal, 225
Tile comparison chart, 234–236
"Tin" tile, 17, **17**
Toilet, 82, 90, 94, 124, 140
Toilet paper holders. *See* Bathroom
accessories
Tools
backerboard smoothing, 47
baseboard removal, 80
caulk removal, 224
cutting, 38–39, **38–39** (*See also*
Cutters; Nibbling tool; Saws)
demolition, 34–35, **34–35**, 80–81,
84–85, 134
door removal, 80
drywall screw setter, 139, **139**

finishing, 41, **41**
grinding, 39, **39**, 165, 202, 227
grouting, 65
layout, 37, **37**
plumbing removal, 82
sanding, 116, 125, 178
setting tile, 40–41, **40–41**, 68
substrate preparation, 36, **36**,
80–81, 89
Towel racks. *See* Bathroom accessories
Travertine tile, 11, **11**, 236
Trim. *See* Borders and trim; Bullnose
tile; V-caps
Trowels, 40, **40**
Tub surround, 30, 90, **128**, **142**,
149–156

U–W
Underlayment, 42, **42**. *See also* Backer-
board; Greenboard; Plywood
Vanity, 83, 122, 140
V-caps, 176, 183, **183**, 185, 210
Vinyl and vinyl tile, 18, **18**, 42, 74,
85, 236
Wallpaper, removal, **35**, 135
Walls
curved, **21**, **128**
layout for tile, 25, 52–53
niches in, **128**, **149**, 157–160
preparation for tiles, 134–141, 150
repair, 136–137
shower, 102
Wall tile, 128–133, 142–148
Water. *See* Moisture
Water pipes. *See* Plumbing
Windows, 140, 161
Wire mesh, 100
Wood parquet tile, 19, **19**, 77, 108–111,
221, 232, 236